Britain in a Global World

Britain in a Global World

Options for a New Beginning

ed. Mark Baimbridge, Philip B. Whyman and Brian Burkitt

imprint-academic.com

Published in the UK by Imprint Academic
PO Box 200, Exeter EX5 5YX, UK

Published in the USA by Imprint Academic
Philosophy Documentation Center
PO Box 7147, Charlottesville, VA 22906-7147, USA

ISBN 9 781845 401917

A CIP catalogue record for this book is available from the
British Library and US Library of Congress

Contents

Part I: Options for Economic Renewal

Part II: Options for Political and Sovereignty Renewal

GLOBAL ISION

Global Vision was launched in 2007 to create a campaign which would offer a refreshing, forward and outward looking alternative to the existing polarised choices of going along with the full European project or pulling out and breaking all ties with our European neighbours. By advocating this middle way, Global Vision promotes a constructive new relationship between the UK and Europe based on free trade and mutually beneficial cooperation, whilst opting out of the process of political and economic integration.

Global Vision is a non-partisan campaign group that believes Britain needs to negotiate a looser, more modern relationship with the EU to reflect the rapidly changing world of the 21st century. The new relationship should be based on trade and cooperation, whilst opting out of political and economic union.

Britain is a great trading nation and its prosperity depends on trade. But Britain, as a full member of the EU, will increasingly be held back by the EU's inflexibilities which include costly and restrictive regulations and protectionism. This vision recognises the reality that increasing global economic integration is profoundly reshaping the world's economy. The rise of China and India is especially significant. Economic flexibility will be the increasingly important key to any country's economic prosperity in the 21st century global economy.

Preface

There are many people to think for their input into making of this book possible. Most obviously, we must thank Lord Blackwell and Ruth Lea from Global Vision for their immediate support for this project and Sara Rainwater for logistical assistance. Secondly, we would like to thank our colleagues at the universities of Bradford and Central Lancashire for their comradeship and general support for our research on European economic integration. Finally, we owe a deep sense of gratitude to our families and partners for their forbearance during the preparation of this book. It is to them that this book is dedicated: MB: Mary, Ken, Beibei and Douglas; PW: Barbara, Boyd and Claire; BB: Beryl, Ivan and Marvin.

Any remaining errors and omissions we gladly attribute to each other.

Haworth, Sheffield & Guiseley
July 2010

European Integration Timeline

From its beginnings, half a century ago, in the immediate aftermath of the Second World War, through the expansion of the seventies and eighties and the great debate surrounding the Maastricht Treaty, here we highlight some of the key events which have shaped the development of the EU towards closer integration.

1948	The Organisation for *European Economic Cooperation (OEEC)* is set up in Paris in April 1948, co-ordinating the distribution of the Marshall Plan financial aid which will amount to $12.5 billion from 1948 to 1951. The OEEC consists of one representative from each of the 17 Western European countries which join the organisation. In May 1948 in The Hague, the Congress of Europe (a meeting of delegates from 16 European countries) agree to form the *Council of Europe* with the aim of establishing closer economic and social ties.
1951	The *European Coal and Steel Community (ECSC)* is established by the signing of the Treaty of Paris in April 1951. Along with France and West Germany, Italy, Belgium, Luxembourg and The Netherlands have also chosen to join the organisation. Members of the ECSC pledge to remove all import duties and quota restrictions on the trade of coal, iron ore, and steel between the member states.
1952	The *European Defence Community (EDC)* Treaty is signed by France, West Germany, Italy, Belgium, Holland and Luxembourg in May 1952. It includes the provision for the formation of a parallel *European Political Community (EPC)*. However both initiatives are destined to founder since the French National Assembly never ratifies the EDC Treaty, finally rejecting it in August 1954.

1955	The process of further European integration is given fresh impetus by a conference of ECSC foreign ministers at Messina, Italy, in June 1955. The meeting agrees to develop the community by encouraging free trade between member states through the removal of tariffs and quotas. Agreement is also reached to form an Atomic Energy Community to encourage co-operation in the nuclear energy industry
1958	The two Treaties of Rome are signed, establishing the *European Economic Community (EEC)* and the *European Atomic Energy Community (Euratom)*. As well as stipulating the eventual removal of customs duties on trade between member countries (over a period of 12 years) the EEC Treaty sets out allow the free movement of workers, capital and services across borders and to harmonise policies on agriculture and transport
1960	At the Stockholm Convention in January 1960 Austria, Britain, Denmark, Norway, Portugal, Sweden and Switzerland form the *European Free Trade Association (EFTA)*. The objective of EFTA is to promote free trade but without the formal structures of the EEC
1961	UK applies to join the EEC.
1963	British application for EEC membership fails.
1967	UK submits second application to join EEC
1968	Customs union completed and *Common Agricultural Policy* enacted.
1972	In October, following the recommendations of the *Werner Report*, the EEC launches its first attempt at harmonising exchange rates. The mechanism adopted is the so called 'snake in the tunnel' whereby participating governments are required to confine the fluctuations of their currencies within a range of +/- 1% against each other. The value of the group of currencies (the snake) is also to be maintained within a range of +/-2.25% against the US Dollar (the tunnel). Countries requiring assistance to keep their currencies within the required band may receive help only in the form of loans
1973	Denmark, Ireland and the UK join the EEC.
1975	UK referendum supports staying in EEC.

1978	At a summit in Bremen in July, the French and West German governments announce their intention to create the *European Monetary System (EMS)*. At the centre of the EMS is the *European Currency Unit (ECU)*. The value of the ECU is to be derived from a weighted basket of all participating currencies with the greatest weighting against the West German mark
1981	Greece joins the EC.
1986	Portugal and Spain join the EC.
1986	In October, following the recommendations of the Werner Report, the EEC launches its first attempt at harmonising exchange rates. The mechanism adopted is the so called 'snake in the tunnel' whereby participating governments are required to confine the fluctuations of their currencies within a range of +/- 1% against each other. The value of the group of currencies (the snake) is also to be maintained within a range of +/-2.25% against the US Dollar (the tunnel). Countries requiring assistance to keep their currencies within the required band may receive help only in the form of loans
1990	UK joins EMS.
1992	At a summit of the European Council in Maastricht, Holland, the *Treaty on European Union (TEU)*, also known as the Maastricht Treaty, is signed. Originally intended to include a declaration of an intention to move towards federal union, at Britain's insistence this aspect is played down. Subsequent to the signing of the Maastricht Treaty, the European Community is referred to as the European Union (EU). UK leaves EMS.
1993	The Single European Market takes effect. Trade tariffs are scrapped, but Duty Free shopping remains until 1999.
1994	Stage 2 of EMU is initiated on January 1st with the establishment of the *European Monetary Institute (EMI)* to oversee the co-ordination of the monetary policies of the individual national central banks. The EMI will also work towards the introduction of stage 3 by organising the creation of the European Central Bank

1995	Austria, Finland and Sweden join the EU, bringing membership to 15. *The Schengen agreement* comes into force and scraps border controls. UK and Ireland stay out of the agreement.
1997	Heads of Government draft a new agreement in Amsterdam which updates the Maastricht Treaty and prepares the EU for its eastward expansion. Qualified majority voting is introduced into new areas, reducing individual countries' powers to veto new measures.
1998	At the beginning of May, at a summit of EU officials and heads of state in Brussels, the announcement is made as to which countries will participate in the launch of the euro the following January. In June the *European Central Bank (ECB)* is established in Frankfurt, Germany. The ECB together with the national central banks of the 15 EU member states form the *European System of Central Banks (ESCB)* which will be responsible for setting monetary policy for the euro countries and managing those countries' foreign reserves. The EU opens accession negotiations with Hungary, Poland, Estonia, the Czech Republic, Slovenia and Cyprus.
1999	Romania, Slovakia, Latvia, Lithuania, Bulgaria and Malta are invited to begin accession negotiations. Eleven countries adopt the euro as their official currency (although national currency notes and coins remain in circulation), but Sweden, Denmark and the UK stay out.
2000	The Nice summit agrees to limit the size of the Commission and increase the President's powers. Qualified majority voting is introduced in new areas, but members keep their vetoes on social security and tax. A timetable for taking forward accession negotiations is endorsed.
2001	The Laeken European Council establishes the *Convention on the Future of Europe.*
2002	Euro notes and coins are introduced in twelve EU countries. The European Commission announces that ten countries are on course to meet the criteria for accession to the EU in 2004.
2003	The UK has been a member of the EU for 30 years.

2004	EU enlargement to 25 member states with addition of Slovakia, Latvia, Lithuania, Malta, Hungary, Poland, Estonia, the Czech Republic, Slovenia and Cyprus.
2005	*EU Constitution* ratification ended by referendum defeats in France and the Netherlands.
	The UK holds EU Presidency, but fails to make progress on new 2007–13 budget.
	Accession negotiations are opened with Turkey and Croatia.
2006	Slovenia's entry into the euro on 1 January 2007 is confirmed.
	Accession negotiations with Turkey are suspended.
2007	EU enlargement to 27 member states with addition of Bulgaria and Romania.
2008	Slovenia becomes the first of the recent enlargement member to hold the Presidency of the Council of the EU.
	Treaty of Lisbon ratification ended by referendum defeat in Ireland.
2009	Final year of the *Barroso Commission*.
	Seventh series of elections to the *European Parliament*.
	Second Irish referendum approves the *Treaty of Lisbon*.
	Herman Van Rompuy is appointed first permanent *President of the EU Council*.
2010	Spain is the first country to hold the presidency under the Lisbon Treaty and the new *trio presidency system* working Belgium and Hungary.
	Heads of state and government agree to support the Greek government in its efforts to meet the Stability Programme targets for 2010.
	European Council adopts a 10-year strategy for smart, sustainable and inclusive growth: Europe 2020.
	The EU agrees to support the Irish economy to help safeguard the stability of the euro.

2011	Estonia adopts the euro, becoming the 17th member of the euro area.
	The first *European semester* of economic policy coordination between EU countries to help prevent economic crises like the one in 2008-10.
	A comprehensive package of measures to strengthen the European economy is finalised with the *Euro Plus Pact* to reinforce economic policy coordination in the EMU.

Notes on Contributors

Mark Baimbridge is a Senior Lecturer in Economics at the University of Bradford. His main research area is the political economy of European integration: monetary integration; UK-EU relationship; applied microeconomic aspects; political integration. He has published over 50 articles in learned journals including: *Journal of European Integration, New Political Economy, The Political Quarterly, Capital and Class, Politics, New Economy, Ethnic and Racial Studies.* He is the author/editor of: *The impact of the euro* (Macmillan, 2000), *Economic and monetary union in Europe* (Edward Elgar, 2003 & 2005), *Fiscal federalism and European economic integration* (Routledge, 2004), *Current economic issues in EU integration* (Palgrave, 2004), *Britain and the European Union: alternative futures*, (CIB, 2005), *Implications of the euro* (Routledge, 2006), *Analysing the 1975 referendum: lessons for the future?* (Imprint Academic, 2007), *Analysing the 1975 referendum: reflections on the 1975 referendum* (Imprint Academic, 2007) and *Britain, the euro and beyond* (Ashgate, 2008). His forthcoming texts include: *The political economy of the European Social Model* (Routledge) and *New Labour, new Europe? The Europeanisation of Britain and the anglicisation of Europe* (Manchester University Press).

Philip Booth is Professor of Insurance and Risk Management at Cass Business School, City University, London and the Editorial and Programme Director of the Institute of Economic Affairs. Prior to this he was Associate Dean of Cass Business School and Professor of Real Estate Finance. He began his career working in the Investment Department of Axa Equity and Law (1985-1988), with a period on secondment to the Bank of England (1998-1999) and working there as a special adviser from 1999-2002. Philip has published widely on numerous financial matters, ranging from social insurance, actuarial science, real estate finance and pension reform. He is also the editor of *Economic Affairs* and Associate

Editor of the *British Actuarial Journal* and the *Annals of Actuarial Science*. His publications for the IEA include: The way out of the pensions quagmire (2005), Towards a liberal utopia (2005), Issues in monetary policy (2006), The road to economic freedom (2006), Were 364 economists all wrong? (2006) and Investment mathematics (John Wiley & Sons, 2003).

Brian Burkitt was a Senior Lecturer in Economics at the University of Bradford. He wrote two widely quoted reports, *Britain and the European Economic Community: an economic re-appraisal*, and *Britain and the European Economic Community: a political re-appraisal at the time of the 1975 referendum on EEC membership*. He is also author/editor of: *Trade unions and wages* (Crosby Lockwood Staples, 1975 & 1980), *Trade unions and the economy* (Macmillan, 1979), *Radical political economy* (Harvester Wheatsheaf, 1984), *The political economy of social credit and guild socialism* (Routledge, 1997), *The impact of the euro* (Macmillan, 2000), *Britain and the European Union: alternative futures*, (CIB, 2005), and *Implications of the euro* (Routledge, 2006). He is a frequent contributor to, and commentator on economic issues to television and radio programmes, including Newsnight and A Week in Politics. In addition to the economics of European integration, his research interests include unemployment and crimes of racial violence, the relative cost of unemployment and inflation, and disequilibrium economics and time.

Brent Cameron is a Canadian writer and activist and a member of the Board of Directors of the Commonwealth Advantage. He is a graduate in Political Studies at Queen's University, Canada, and Municipal Administration at St. Lawrence College, Canada. Following a brief career in the Federal Civil Service, he worked as Research Associate at SES Canada Research, as an Assistant to a Member of the Ontario Legislature and Parliamentary Secretary to Ontario's Minister of Agriculture and Rural Affairs. In addition, he served as a member, and contributing writer, to the Community Editorial Board of the Kingston Whig-Standard newspaper. A long-time community activist, his activities have included serving as Chairman of Central Frontenac Community Services Corporation and as Conservative Party President in the federal riding of Lanark-Frontenac-Lennox and Addington (Ontario). He is the author of *The Case for Commonwealth Free Trade: Options for a new globalization* (Trafford Publishing, 2005).

Philip Davies has represented Shipley as Conservative Member of Parliament since 2005, whilst other involvement in the local community came through service as both a parish councillor and a school governor. Before being elected to Parliament he worked at Asda in Leeds as a Marketing Manager. He was elected to the Executive Committee of the 1922 Committee of backbench Conservative MPs in 2006 and is a member of the Culture, Media and Sport Select Committee. He became the first MP to publicly call for Britain to withdraw from the European Union and is a member of The Freedom Association's 'Better Off Out' campaign.

Matthew Elliott graduated with a First class BSc in Government from the London School of Economics where he was involved with the LSE Hayek Society and worked for the European Foundation, Britain's leading Eurorealist think-tank. After graduation, Matthew worked for a number of MPs and MEPs in the House of Commons and the European Parliament. In 2004, he co-founded the TaxPayers' Alliance (TPA). Outside of his work at the TPA, Matthew has visited Azerbaijan (2000), Ukraine (2001) and Serbia (2006) on behalf of the Westminster Foundation. In June 2007 he was elected a Fellow of the Royal Society for the encouragement of Arts, Manufacturers & Commerce. Matthew is on the Advisory Council of the European Foundation, Freedom Week and the Young Briton's Foundation and on the Advisory Committee of the New Culture Forum. His publications include: *The bumper book of government waste* (Harriman House, 2006) and *The bumper book of government waste 2008: Brown's squandered billions* (Harriman House, 2007).

Marc Glendening is director of the Democracy Movement, an all-party EU-critical campaign. He has worked for the BBC Political Affairs and Documentaries units. He attended Warwick University and was chairman of the Federation of Conservative Students in 1984. He taught public policy at City Polytechnic and is a founder of the Sohemian Society which is dedicated to the history of Soho.

Roger Helmer won a State Scholarship to Churchill College, Cambridge, where he read mathematics. He was first elected to the European Parliament in 1999 and has been a member of several committees: Unemployment, Petitions, Constitutional Affairs and the Parliament's Temporary Committee on Climate Change. During the course of his long business career before 1999, he spent a total of twelve years running businesses in East and South East Asia as a resident, so he brings a wealth of detailed knowledge of the region to his work on interparliamentary delegations. Roger has also recently been given new membership of the delegation to Croatia following its accession to the EU. He has developed close relationships with conservative political groups in the USA, and has been a regular speaker at American conferences. He was recently appointed 'Adam Smith Scholar' by the American Legislative Exchange Council. He has self-published two books on European issues: *Straight talking on Europe* (2000) and *A declaration of independence* (2002).

Brian Hindley is a Senior Fellow of the European Centre for International Political Economy (ECIPE) located in Belgium. He is an Emeritus Reader in Trade Policy Economics at the London School of Economics and has published widely on trade policy and the World Trade Organisation. He has a PhD in Economics from the University of Chicago and has lectured on international trade and trade policy at Sciences Po (Paris); LUISS (Rome); the University of Leuven; the University of Amsterdam; and KDI (Korea). He is active as an economic consultant, where as well as private businesses, he has advised a number of international organizations, including the World Bank and OECD, on matters relating to international trade.

Lord David Howell of Guilford studied Economics King's College, Cambridge. His first job was in HM Treasury from 1959-60, then he was a leader writer for the *Daily Telegraph* from 1960-64. In 1964 he contested his first seat in the general election, and in 1966, he was elected MP for Guildford. He was Minister of State in Northern Ireland (1972-74), Secretary of State for Energy and later for Transport in Margaret Thatcher's first Cabinet (1979-83). From 1987-97, he was Chairman of the House of Commons Foreign Affairs Committee, Shadow Spokesperson in the House of Lords on Foreign Affairs and adviser to the Conservative Opposition leadership on European Reform. He was made a life peer in 1997. He is the author of several books, including the best selling *The edge of now* (Macmillan, 2000) and writes columns for *The Japan Times*, the *International Herald Tribune* and the *Wall Street Journal*.

David Lascelles is co-founder and Senior Fellow of the Centre for the Study of Financial Innovation (CSFI), an independent City of London think-tank sponsored by leading banks and financial institutions to research the future of financial services. He has written papers for the CSFI on a wide range of subjects, including the impact of the euro, the EU's plans for a single market in financial services, and competition among financial centres. David was previously with the Financial Times, where he held several key positions including Banking Editor and New York bureau chief. He is now a non-executive Director of Arbuthnot

Banking Group, a diversified financial services company, and the author of several books: *The ethics of influence* (Institute of Business Ethics, 2002), *Other people's money* (Institute of Financial Services, 2005), *Ethical due diligence* (Institute of Business Ethics, 2007).

Vo Phuong Mai Le is a post-doctoral Research Fellow at Cardiff Business School, Cardiff University. Her research project is entitled 'Modelling nominal rigidities in general equilibrium framework' and it is funded by the Economic and Social Research Council. Her primary work is concentrated in the area of macroeconomics, monetary policy and economic growth. Also, she conducts research on international trade and is currently working on a project of comparing the EU countries' competitiveness against that of developing and emerging countries.

Ruth Lea is Director of Global Vision and Non-Executive Director and Economic Adviser to Arbuthnot Banking Group. She is the author of many papers on economic matters and writes regularly for the press. Ruth was Director of the Centre for Policy Studies from 2004–07. She was also Head of the Policy Unit at the Institute of Directors (IoD) between 1995 and 2003, before which she was the Economics Editor at ITN, Chief Economist at Mitsubishi Bank and Chief UK Economist at Lehman Brothers. She also spent 16 years in the Civil Service in the Treasury, the Department of Trade and Industry and the Central Statistical Office. She has served on the Council of the Royal Economic Society, the National Consumer Council, the Nurses' Pay Review Body, the ONS Statistics Advisory Committee, the ESRC Research Priorities Board and the Retail Prices Advisory Committee.

John Mills is an economist who has spent all his working life running companies involved in making and selling consumer products. He thus combines a theoretical background in economics with years of practical experience in international business, together with being responsible for the budget of a major London borough. He is Secretary of the Labour Euro Safeguards Campaign. His publications include: *Monetarism or prosperity?* (Macmillan, 1981), *Tackling Britain's false economy* (Palgrave, 1997), *Europe's economic dilemma* (Palgrave, 1998), *America's soluble problems* (Palgrave, 1999), *Managing the world economy* (Palgrave, 2000), *A critical history of economics* (Palgrave, 2003).

Ian Milne has been the Director of the cross-party think-tank Global Britain since 1999. He was the founder-editor in 1993 of *The European Journal,* and the co-founder in 1995 and first editor of *Eurofacts*. He is the translator of *Europe's Road to War*, by Paul-Marie Coûteaux, (The June Press, 1999), and the author of numerous pamphlets, articles and book reviews, mainly about the relationship between the UK and the European Union. His recent publications include: *A cost too far?* (Civitas, 2004), an analysis of the net economic costs and benefits for the UK of EU membership, *Backing the wrong horse* (Centre for Policy Studies, 2004), a review of the UK's trading arrangements and options for the future and *Lost illusions: British foreign policy* (The Bruges Group, 2007) in which he examines the history of British foreign policy since its participation in the European project. He is chairman of companies involved in publishing and book distribution. He has degrees in engineering and business administration, and a 40 year career in industry and merchant banking in the UK, France and Belgium.

Patrick Minford is Professor of Economics at the Cardiff Business School, Cardiff University. His previous position was as Edward Gonner Professor of Applied Economics at the University of Liverpool (1976-97). He served as Director of the Merseyside Development Corporation (1988-89), as member of the Monopolies and Mergers Commission (1990-96), together with being as member of the H.M. Treasury's Panel of Economic Forecasters (1993–96). His publications include: *Substitution effects, speculation and exchange rate stability* (North-Holland, 1978), *Unemployment: cause and cure* (Blackwell, 1985), *Rational expectations and the new macroeconomics* (Martin Robertson, 1983), *The supply side revolution in Britain* (Edward Elgar, 1991), *The cost of Europe* (Manchester University Press, 1992), *Markets not stakes* (Orion Books, 1998), *Britain and Europe: choices for change (Politeia, 1999), Advanced macroeconomics* (Edward Elgar, 2002), Money matters: essays in honour of Sir Alan Walters (Edward Elgar, 2004) and *Should Britain leave the EU?* (Elgar, 2005).

Andrew Mullen is a Senior Lecturer in Politics at the University of Northumbria. His research interests include: Geopolitical relations (European integration, Anglo-EU relations, Anglo-American relations and the emergence of the EU as a superpower); the British Left (history of the Labour Party, trade union movement and far left); International Relations / International Political Economy; Media and communication; Post-war United States and British foreign policy; State terrorism; Extremism; Geopolitics of hydrocarbons; Climate change. He is the co-author of 'European Integration and the Battle for Hearts and Minds: New Labour and the Euro' and 'Spinning the European Union: Pro-EU Propaganda Campaigns in Britain, 1962-1975' both published in the *Political Quarterly*.

Additionally, his books include: *The British left's great debate on Europe* (Continuum, 2007), *Analysing the 1975 referendum: lessons for the future?* (Imprint Academic, 2007) and *Anti- and pro-European propaganda in Britain* (Continuum, 2009). His forthcoming texts include: *The political economy of the European Social Model* (Routledge) and *New Labour, new Europe? The Europeanisation of Britain and the anglicisation of Europe* (Manchester University Press).

Eric Nowell is a Research Associate in Cardiff Business School, Cardiff University and is an Honorary Fellow of Liverpool University Management School, Liverpool University. His publications include; *Should Britain leave the EU?* (Elgar, 2005).

John Redwood has represented Wokingham as Conservative Member of Parliament since 1987. Having received a DPhil from Oxford University he became a Fellow at All Souls College (1972-87), before he became Head of the Prime Minister's Policy Unit (1987-89). Upon entering Parliament, he became Parliamentary Under Secretary of State at the Department of Trade and Industry (1989-90), before becoming Minister of State at the DTI (1990-92), the Department of the Environment (1992-93), together with Secretary of State for Wales (1993-95). He resigned in 1995 in order to set out the case against the euro and for lower taxes. In 1997 he joined the Shadow Cabinet handling the DTI brief, becoming Shadow Secretary of State for the Environment in 1999. In 2000, he was appointed Head of the Parliamentary Campaigns Unit and subsequently became Shadow Secretary of State for Deregulation in 2004. Since December 2005 he has been the Chairman of the Party's Economic Competitiveness Policy Group. He is a leading writer regarding economic and constitutional matters and a regular contributor to major newspapers and journals, his books include: *The single European currency* (Tecla Editions, 1995), *Our currency, our country* (Penguin, 1997), *The death of Britain?* (Palgrave, 1999), *Stars and strife* (Palgrave, 2001) and *Superpower struggles* (Palgrave, 2005).

Philip B. Whyman is Professor of Economics at the University of Central Lancashire. He is the author/editor of: *The impact of the euro* (Macmillan, 2000), *Economic and monetary union in Europe* (Elgar, 2003 & 2005), *Sweden and the Third Way* (Ashgate, 2003) and *Fiscal federalism and European economic integration* (Routledge, 2004), *An analysis of the economic democracy reforms in Sweden* (Mellen Press, 2004), *Britain and the European Union: alternative futures* (CIB, 2005), *Third way economics* (Palgrave Macmillan, 2006), *Implications of the euro* (Routledge, 2006), *Analysing the 1975 referen-*

dum: lessons for the future? (Imprint Academic, 2007) and *Britain, the euro and beyond* (Ashgate, 2008). His forthcoming texts include: *The political economy of the European Social Model* (Routledge) and *New Labour, new Europe? The Europeanisation of Britain and the anglicisation of Europe* (Manchester University Press). His research interests include the impact of European integration upon labour markets, fiscal federalism, international monetary developments and the UK's future relationship with the EU. In addition, he has written extensively on the development of progressive political economy, evaluation of the Third Way and evolution of the 'Swedish Model'.

Mark Baimbridge, Philip B. Whyman and Brian Burkitt

Britain Beyond the EU

Introduction

The relationship between Britain and the European Union (EU) has been a difficult one over many decades, beginning with disinterest upon its formation, increasing desperation to gain membership when this appeared to guarantee superior economic performance, and latterly disquiet about the net drain that membership has upon the vitality of the national economy. There is no doubt that an organisation that has recently expanded to twenty-seven (and counting) member states is a significant player in the world economy. It has a larger population size and gross purchasing power than the USA, whilst the introduction of Economic and Monetary Union (EMU) is without precedent in world economic history, since it has occurred without first attaining political integration intended to govern the single economy so created. Therefore, the EU is certainly a powerful economic and trade bloc, and all medium sized nations should desire to form some type of relationship with this organisation in their own interests; however, this does not necessitate membership or the signing of formal treaty arrangements, but may involve a relatively informal statement of co-operation on a range of topics for mutual benefit. Thus, it is these sentiments that this book seeks to explore.

Britain as an Awkward Partner

One aspect underlying the difficulty of the relationship between Britain and the EU arises from the fact that the former has tended to regard European integration as primarily (or entirely) an economic process, whilst leading federalists have taken a more holistic viewpoint, balancing moves towards economic integration with elements of political union. Thus, British membership of the then 'Common Market' has been transformed as the organisation has taken on more powers and trappings of a

super-national state, most powerfully recently reflected in the introduction of EMU, but also in moves towards the establishment of a federal system including a constitution and unified foreign policy stance. These
initiatives have moved ahead of the majority of British citizens, who
express surprise (and more than a little hostility) towards this policy drift.
This divergence between those seeking a narrow or broad direction for
the EU has therefore dogged its development, with moves to pursue a federalist agenda, rejected by a majority of British voters due to a failure to
first debate the future of Europe and thereby gain consent (or otherwise)
for the preferences of the political elite.

The importance of the EU for British economic development has, additionally, been called into question due to the increasing impact of
globalisation. The dramatic reduction in world tariffs on manufactured
goods and many types of services, together with international deregulation of controls on currency movements and national financial sectors,
have facilitated the expansion of international trade, greater financial
market integration and the development of the trans-national organisation of production facilities. The process has enabled the rapid economic
development of Asian economies, including Taiwan, Singapore, South
Korea, Hong Kong, China and India. In such circumstances, the question
has been raised over the relative importance that Britain, or any other
medium-sized economy, should give towards *regional* economic integration, as opposed to pursuing a policy of *global* trade and other economic
links. Indeed, it is certainly true that, in more recent years, the former economic dynamism associated with the EU appears to have declined, and
the burdens of economic failure (i.e. long-term, large-scale unemployment) have been keenly experienced in many continental European
nations.

Moreover, the issue of Britain's relationship with the EU is further complicated since it cuts across traditional political divisions, so that advocates and opponents of deeper political and/or economic integration can
be found on both sides of the party political divide. Neo-liberal conservatives may support the creation of a large free trade area, immune from all
political interference with the agenda of big business, but may oppose
most forms of regulation (particularly social policy) and discussion of
political integration that originate in Brussels. Similarly, a left-of-centre
supporters of European integration are likely to hold their views regarding the importance of establishing regional regulation of capital, and promotion of a social dimension to an otherwise narrowly economic
perception of European integration, whilst they may be less enamoured

by the power that the 'project' gives to trans-national corporations and the resultant weakness of trade unions and national governments. Consequently, the greater the emphasis all parties place upon the negative features, the more likely they are to be described as 'Eurosceptics', and the net advocates of the process 'Europhiles'. Yet, the important point to note is that honest commentators within each grouping accept that the debate over the future relationship between Britain and the EU is not wholly one-sided and that their conclusions are reached due to their analysis of the problem and preferred solutions.

Consequently, this book seeks to provide an analysis of the economic and political relationship between Britain and the EU and thereby facilitate discussion of the future direction in which this relationship might develop. In the process, it examines current trends and developments in seeking to arrive at an estimation of whether EU membership has been a burden or an asset for the UK economy. However, the primary intention of this edited collection is to provide a series of credible policy alternatives in contrast to the recent trend of EU integration, thereby illustrating that a looser form of relationship between the UK and EU is not only feasible, but also desirable. Such policy options may appear to be a radical and esoteric departure for those relatively unfamiliar to the UK-EU debate, however, with the introduction of EMU and the constitution/Lisbon Treaty, then a tipping point has been reached.

Hence, contributors consider alternatives to the current arrangements between Britain and the EU, whether involving a degree of re-negotiation of rights and responsibilities, or adopting some other means of relaxing the uniformity necessitated by current membership rules, so that, either Britain alone, or indeed the entire EU organisation, can enjoy enhanced flexibility and autonomy within a loose membership arrangement. In the terminology, this would create a united conglomeration of individual, sovereign states, and not a 'United States of Europe'. Additionally, a number of chapters examine the consequences that might arise if Britain withdrew from the EU, either to be free of the costs and restraints imposed by membership, or through desiring to create different forms of trade and/or macroeconomic strategy aimed at more optimally promoting national economic development than under the current EU model. Hence, conclusions are reached relating to a range of alternative economic policies that could be adopted, both within and without formal EU membership, which might improve the economic development of the British economy.

Structure of the Book

The book is divided into two principal sections reflecting that a comprehensive and successful long-term realignment of the association between Britain and the EU requires consideration of both economic and political aspects. Hence, the first section of the book seeks to explore the present and future economic relationship commencing with a chapter by Ruth Lea which outlines potential directions in which the UK could head in terms of both the EU and also with the rest of the world. Hence, Lee argues that although the rationale for initial membership in the 1960s and 1970s was understandable both economically as 'the sick man of Europe' and politically as a country that 'had lost an empire and not yet found a role'; the world has since moved on dramatically. In particular, firstly, the global economy and, secondly, the EU's political and legislative reach over member states have changed out of all recognition. The second chapter by Ian Milne explores a similar theme through focusing upon the global trading landscape and in particular concludes that a superior outcome for Britain would be to adopt the model of interlocking networks of user-friendly free trade agreements. Hence, Milne proposes that the UK joins a multi-country free trade agreement alongside the United States for its trade and investment with the world outside the EU and Swiss-style sectoral agreements for its relations with the EU.

John Mills further develops the economic analysis through considering the UK's experience inside the EU and considers what might have happened if we had been outside. From this counterfactual-type study Mills indicates that benefits would include the full savings on our net EU budget contributions and potentially half of CAP costs, together with a dividend from less regulation. However, there are potentially larger gains through an improved growth rate from shifting our vision and our trading patterns more towards the faster growing parts of the world which could well increase our growth rate by 0.5% per annum. In a wide-ranging chapter reviewing economic aspects of membership Philip Davies describes the EU as a failed system with a substantial cost to the British tax payer and business. Hence, to remain competitive through attracting investment and win business, the initial step is the freedom to form partnerships with the emerging economies of Asia and Eastern Europe. Davies argues that we built our wealth as world traders and our future economic prosperity depends on trading with economic power houses which were never considered as such when we joined the EU. This is followed by an econometric-based analysis of the estimated economic costs and benefits by a team of researchers (Le, Minford and Nowell) based on the Liverpool Model. This initially focuses on protectionism in trade, where the EU is supposedly in favour of competition and free trade, but where the reality is such that many are surprised when they see the extent of covert protection. Moreover, their chapter goes beyond traditional notions of the concept of protectionism that refer primarily to trade, to the labour market and welfare systems.

Following these broad analyses of the economic relationship between the UK and EU, the section subsequently focuses upon detailed discussion and evaluation of the microeconomic aspects of the UK-EU relationship. Firstly, in relation to the limits placed upon British tax policy Matthew Elliott notes that significant policy options are blocked as they would contradict supranational level decisions, whilst EU intrusions into tax policy are strengthened by the European Court of Justice, such that the EU seems likely to gain an even greater say over tax policy. Consequently, the democratic accountability at the EU level means that such policy is frequently formed without reference to the preferences of ordinary people, whereby innovative tax reforms, that might have broad social and political benefits, are unable to make headway.

The second detailed area analysed is trade policy in terms of both general issues (Brian Hindley) and relating to specific partners (Brent Cameron). The chapter by Hindley outlines the three possible forms of trade relations between Britain and the remaining EU member states: no formalised bilateral trade relations, just the WTO; a free trade area; and a customs union. The ensuing discussion reviews the legal, economic and political issues raised by these alternatives before addressing which would offer the superior economic alternative for the UK. The chapter by Cameron commences by reviewing the concept of the global economy which is in a state of evolution, whereby new rules, partnerships and markets are coming into the mainstream. However, the chapter specifically explores the idea of extending the trade promotion programme, *Commonwealth Advantage*, so that the UK becomes a conduit for Commonwealth firms to access the EU, whilst also facilitating Commonwealth companies and thereby the UK to use the cost benefit of doing business in Canada as a means of gaining access to NAFTA.

Thirdly, the unique position of City of London as a major global financial centre and the implications upon this from EU membership is then assessed by David Lascelles, whilst in a similar vein the manner in which EU regulations have impacted upon investment markets is also explored by Philip Booth. The chapter by Lascelles reflects upon the notion that although the Treasury's five tests concluded that joining the euro would be good for the City, in fact it is probable that London would have done less well if the UK had joined the single currency given its position within the wider EU. In particular, that despite its dominance of euro markets and its powerful position in Europe, the City's relationship with the EU is a highly complex one relating to discomfort with the EU's political aspirations, its urge to 'build' and regulate, and a sense that it is viewed with suspicion rather than appreciation across the Channel. In a similar critique of regulatory frameworks, Booth explores the EU's Financial Services Action Plan, which seeks to enable the creation of a single market in financial services. He argues that no convincing case has been made that it is necessary for the EU to regulate in this field, whereby as with much EU regulation, the focus has been on creating a single market when the creation of a free market should be the goal. However, this does not mean that EU countries could not regulate their investment markets if they wished, but that any regulation would have to be subject to the EU's desire to ensure freedom to trade goods and services. Thus, the EU role in financial regulation should be to ensure the freedom of movement of goods, services, capital and people and not to develop a unified regulatory framework for financial markets and services.

Finally, the Editors discuss the notion of developing an invigorated industrial strategy to boost the supply-side of the British economy, together with an overview of potential macroeconomic paths that the UK could follow upon loosening its ties with the EU. Our intention is to demonstrate, not only that national economic management is still feasible, but also that it is preferable to transferring the main levers of macroeconomic policy into the hands of the EU which is incapable of using them consistently in the best interests of all member states simultaneously.

The second section of the book seeks to complete the picture of what a looser relationship between Britain and the EU would entail through exploring the issue of sovereignty with particular emphasis placed upon the development of a credible alternative strategy beyond the confines of the EU. Thus, to place the changing pattern of sovereignty in a broader context, Marc Glendening explains why the democratic nation-state is in danger of disappearing without even a serious war of ideas taking place. He argues that EU member countries have been experiencing a slow-burning, quiet revolution which has seen periodic and major transfers of decision-making power to Brussels, whereby whenever an issue of international significance occurs a large section of the political and opinion-forming classes combines to demand that more powers are transferred to international institutions. However, it is rarely explained how such a further concentration of supranational authority will improve the situation and why voluntary, ad-hoc co-operation between sovereign countries cannot achieve positive results. To illustrate this shift in the Europeanisation of British foreign policy the chapter by Ian Milne analyses the three principles that have governed the foreign policy establishment's mentality: 'the bridge principle'; the 'EU integration works' principle; and the 'British ideas are prevailing in the EU' principle. Subsequently, the chapter examines various ideas of foreign policy that Britain could adopt upon exit from the EU, including international organisations such as the Commonwealth, which could play an important part in the post-EU world.

This section then returns to explore the central theme in the EU debate of how the key implication of Europeanisation relates to the issue of sovereignty. Hence, several chapters address this central theme from a variety of perspectives. Firstly, John Redwood then discusses how Britain was sold EU membership as purely a limited trading arrangement with no loss of sovereignty, being able to still run our own economic policy, set our own interest rates, conduct our own foreign policy and retain our unique common law system of civil and criminal law. However, successive treaties have built on what was already apparent in the original Treaty of Rome that our partners on the Continent wish to take more and more power to the centre and create a federal state. In his chapter, Roger Helmer develops this argument through suggesting that when making the case against political union in Europe the nomenclature of independence and self-determination, freedom and democracy, resonate more strongly than the rather old-world concept of sovereignty. Additionally, this chapter examines not only the undemocratic nature of EU institutions, but why they are incapable of becoming democratic; why the pro-EU arguments of influence within a larger entity ring hollow; together with what the alternative to EU membership might be, and why it is so much more attractive than the *status quo*.

In contrast, to the previous chapters, that of Andrew Mullen addresses the issue of sovereignty from a left-progressive perspective addressing the fundamental question as to what is sovereignty before summarising plans to reclaim sovereignty from Europe in terms of intergovernmental and Keynesian-socialist alternatives. Mullen then offers a number of options for reasserting sovereignty, but reminds left-progressive forces that implementing such a project would be far from easy; the restoration of economic and political sovereignty in a meaningful way would transform Britain and its place in the global economy and the world order.

Finally, the Editors then discuss how although federalist forces are trying
to build a United States of Europe such a process is the opposite of how
every other nation has been created. Hence, the chapter outlines the
importance of British parliamentary democracy based upon the sovereignty of the people and contrast this with the EU's integrationalist trend
which carries profound implications for the exercise of national sovereignty. However, the concept of 'sovereignty' has been much disputed in
recent debates, particularly with respect to the relationship between Britain and the EU; therefore the chapter also analyses this concept in detail.

In addition to reviewing the impact upon sovereignty from a diversity
of standpoints and advancing arguments for the repatriation of powers to
the UK, there is also the need, as with the economic policy options, to look
towards innovative relationships in an ever evolving global dimension.
Hence, in the penultimate chapter David Howell explores the notion that
Britain needs to broaden its political horizons whilst seeking to be the best
possible local members of our European neighbourhood. However, we
should not be transfixed by our geographical location and instead build
links with what are becoming the world's most prosperous and dynamic
areas, with the smaller nations as well as the large ones, the struggling
poor ones as well as the rapidly industrialising and increasingly high-tech
ones. In summary, this is what an enlarged Commonwealth can do for us
in a way that the EU can never achieve and for which it lacks the reach and
the right basic policy structure. Hence, Britain's external relations priorities need major re-alignment. Additionally, in the book's final chapter, the
Editors discuss how the UK-EU relationship has been juxtaposed
between periodic elite-level enthusiasm for closer European integration
and a general lack of enthusiasm for such measures on behalf of a majority
of the electorate. In particular, it makes little sense to allow a nation's
democratic self-determination to be undermined through participation in
further initiatives leading towards deeper economic and political integration without first considering a range of alternatives that exist for the UK.
Consequently, this chapter seeks to outline a number of these options.

Part I
Options for Economic Revival

Ruth Lea

Time for a Global Vision for Britain

Introduction

When Lord Blackwell and I set up Global Vision in 2007, we felt there was a need to open up the debate on just what sort of relationship Britain should have with the EU and, pari passu, with the rest of the world. We started from the position that it was understandable why Britain should seek membership of the EEC in the 1970s. Britain was economically 'the sick man of Europe' and as a country 'we had lost an empire and not yet found a role.' Meanwhile the countries of the EEC were prospering. To belong to the EEC club and be inside a customs union, at a time when tariffs were high, was an attractive idea. However, the world has moved on dramatically since the 1970s. In particular, firstly, the global economy and, secondly, the EU's political and legislative reach over the member states have changed out of all recognition.

The Changing Global Landscape

The relative shift in economic power to the emerging economies is indisputable. According to Gordon Brown (2005), when he was Chancellor of the Exchequer, the EU's share of global output fell from 26% in 1980 to 22% in 2003 and was expected to fall to 17% by 2015. The comparable data for China and India (together) were 6% (1980), 19% (2003) and 27% (2015). I know of no-one who challenges the view that the EU's share of global activity will shrink as the 21st century progresses, not least of all because of its declining demographics (Lea, 2008a).

Moreover, as the global recession developed in 2008, the geopolitical response was to acknowledge that G7, comprising the US, Canada, Japan and the four largest EU countries, was no longer the appropriate international forum to discuss these global crises. Instead the main forum of international debate has been the G20, a group of 19 of the most economically significant countries plus the EU[1], despite the fact that it is a more cumbersome group for negotiations. The rising significance of G20 was evident at their meetings in Washington in November 2008 and in London in March 2009. India and, especially, China are taking their rightful place in international forums. The influence of these countries can only increase notably at the expense of the US and, in particular, of the EU.

Indeed, such is the growing significance of China that there is talk about an emerging G2 comprising the US and China. Whilst this ignores the increasing multilateral basis of economic and financial diplomacy, it reflects the reality that on an increasing range of international issues little can happen without agreement between the US and China. Consequently, international forums for debate and decision-making are belatedly catching up with economic reality.

For many years analysts have commented that the tectonic plates of the global economy were inexorably shifting. The global economic crisis has proved the catalyst that is reconfiguring the geopolitical landscape in the 21st century such that it is simply inconceivable that future negotiations and discussions on global economic matters could omit China and other crucial emerging economies. We are living in historic times and the days of the hegemony of the 'west', with Japan as an honorary member, are over, being consigned to the history books. Certain events are catalysts of 'gear changes' in world history and the current global recession is one of them. It is therefore imperative that British businesses must be able to take full advantage of this changing global landscape, without the EU's restrictions and costs, in order to thrive in the 21st century. But Britain's continuing membership of the EU's political and economic union does not just impose restrictions and costs; rather it implies a Eurocentric view of the world which quite simply is no longer relevant or right. Britain therefore needs to reconfigure its focus from a European present to a global future.

The EU's Increasing Influence and Costs of Membership

When Britain joined the EEC in 1973, its policy reach was mainly concerned with the customs union and agricultural policy. Since then the reach of the EU has expanded into just about every area of policy (e.g. regional, industrial, financial, transport, health and safety, employment and social legislation, energy, environment, climate change, fisheries, justice and home affairs, foreign and defence policy and so forth). Moreover,

1   The G20 comprises 19 countries & the EU. The countries are Argentina, Australia, Brazil, Canada, China, France, Germany, India, Indonesia, Italy, Japan, Mexico, Russia, Saudi Arabia, South Africa, South Korea, Turkey, the UK & the USA. G20 was set up in 1999.

the EU's legislative activities are accelerating such that according to Open Europe (2009) the number of legal acts in force in the EU has gone from 10,800 in 1998 to 26,500 in 2008.

This EU extension of power seems to have taken some British politicians by surprise, but the ultimate goal of political union was always the objective of the EU's founding fathers. It should be remembered that the original Rome Treaty (1957) spoke of the 'ever closer union of the people's of Europe'. As the power of the EU and its myriad institutions has increased, the sovereignty of the individual member states has inevitably been curtailed. Transferring power to the 27-nation centralised EU, with its very considerable bureaucracy, can only restrict the ability of the member states to respond to changing circumstances in their best interests. Consequently, large centralised organisations have rigidity when what is required is flexibility and this is all the more true when the global economy is changing as it is.

The main integrationist developments since the Rome Treaty can be seen through the Single European Act (1986), which aimed to complete the Single Market, the Maastricht Treaty (1992), which created the European Union, and the Amsterdam (1997) and Nice (2000) Treaties. The 2003 Constitution marked another major transfer of power from the member states to the EU's institutions. Even though it was comprehensively rejected by the peoples of France and the Netherlands in 2005, it lives on under the guise of the Lisbon Treaty which is of huge significance for this country (Blackwell, 2008), which in the words of former French President Valéry Giscard d'Estaing (2008), grand architect of the Constitution: '… the Treaty of Lisbon, is simply a legal re-packaging of the Constitution, albeit unreadable, and scrupulously reproduces the innovations set out in the Constitution.'

Furthermore, the EU's powers and activities are, therefore, increasingly constraining Britain's ability to make decisions in the best interests of the country. But this is not all, they are also very costly. According to estimates by Craig and Elliott (2009), the EU costs about £2,000 for every person in the EU, some £100bn for the UK alone. Even the UK's contributions to the EU budget, a small part of the overall burden, are around £13bn a year, equivalent to over a third of the defence budget and a potentially very useful saving in financially straightened times. Another study conducted by Milne (2004) found that the current recurring annual direct net cost to the UK of EU membership was between 3% and 5% of GDP, with 4% of GDP the 'most likely', amounting to nearly £60bn. These are not trivial sums.

Britain's Trading Relationship with the EU Customs Union

Britain is a great trading nation. In terms of current account credits, including both visible trade and invisibles (services, investment income and transfers), the UK and mainland China tied in third place after the US and Germany in 2006. Of course trade with our EU partners is important, accounting for around 50% of good and services trade, but as the relative position of Europe shrinks the UK must be free and flexible to exploit its unrivalled worldwide business and cultural ties. This is not the case at present.

The UK, as a full member of the EU, is currently a member of both the EU's customs union and the Single Internal Market (SIM). It is frequently argued, if not assumed, that membership of the customs union and, especially, the SIM is a requirement for trade to flourish between the UK and the EU. But it is clear from Switzerland's trading success with the EU that membership is not a requirement for thriving trade (Church, 2007). Hence, it is not necessary to be a member of the outmoded customs union and it is not necessary to be a member of the SIM. Indeed, on the contrary, membership of the EU's customs union has negative ramifications for our trading relationships with the rest of the world and membership of the heavily regulated SIM has negative implications for our international economic competitiveness.

As a member of the EU customs union, the EU's Trade Commissioner negotiates trade deals and has a seat in the World Trade Organisation (WTO) on behalf of all EU member states including the UK. Britain, despite the fact that it is the 5th or 6th biggest economy and the 3rd largest trading nation, is, therefore, unable to unilaterally negotiate bilateral deals with favoured partners. These include the US (the UK's single biggest trading partner), China, India or the other members of the Commonwealth. In particular, the inability to negotiate trade deals with the Commonwealth countries, with their shared cultural and business ties, is especially disadvantageous to Britain (Cameron, 2008). In an age, arguably, of increasing bilateralism in trade deals and the resurgence of the Chinese and Indian economies the current situation is clearly sub-optimal for Britain.

Moreover, the EU's tendency towards protectionism, especially in agriculture, is not only disadvantageous to the UK in possessing a very small agricultural sector, but it can also damage the trading prospects of developing countries and, therefore, their ability to prosper. Thus, membership of the EU's customs union was probably economically positive for the UK in the mid-20th century, when tariffs were high. In the rapidly changing global economy of the 21st century, when tariffs are low, it is not. Customs unions are old-fashioned and, by restricting Britain's ability to exploit optimal trading opportunities, impose opportunity costs.

The Single Internal Market

It is frequently asserted that, even if we moved to a looser relationship with the EU, we should keep the SIM, with its four freedoms of goods and services and capital and labour, as the 'jewel in the crown' of the EU as it enables and opens up free trade. But this is to misunderstand its intrinsic nature which is only partly about opening up markets, but is also about regulating markets in order to achieve 'harmonized level playing fields' and ban 'unfair competition'. Hence, the employment legislation is specifically implemented to develop and underpin the European Social Model, which is characterized by heavily regulated labour markets such that the SIM and its regulations are, therefore, a package.

The regulations destroy competition and impose costs on businesses that our competitors outside the EU do not carry. Estimates of the costs bring this point home very forcibly. According to Open Europe (2009) the cumulative cost of regulations introduced over the past decade in the UK, and which had their origins in the EU, was as high as £106.6bn equivalent to 72% of the total costs. Additionally, the Commission has also calculated the costs with Günter Verheugen (Vice-President of the European Commission, responsible for enterprise and industry) estimating that the cost of complying with EU regulations is as much as €600 billion a year (The Economist, 2006), equivalent to 5.5% of EU GDP, or the size of the Dutch economy.

Meanwhile the benefits are much lower than the costs, which according to the EC Commission (2007) 'over the last 15 years the single market has increased the EU's prosperity by 2.15% of GDP. In 2006 alone this meant an overall increase of €240 billion, or €518 for every EU citizen, compared to a situation without the single market'. An alternative Commission estimate of a boost to prosperity of €225bn (for 2006) was quoted by the Treasury and the DTI (2007) in their analysis of the single market. However, whichever figure is taken, it is clear that the costs comfortably outweigh the benefits by a factor of about 2½ to 1. Moreover, it is clear that British business is unhappy with the heavy regulatory burden associated with the single market. In a poll of 1,000 Chief Executives conducted for Open Europe, 54% thought that EU over-regulation 'outweighed' the benefits of the single market and 60% thought that the UK should renegotiate to reduce its involvement in the EU to one of free trade only[2]. Consequently, membership of the SIM, far from being a costless panacea, in fact imposes huge and growing costs. It is a problem for Britain and not a solution.

The Need for a New Relationship with the EU

The way forward for the UK is to renegotiate a new, more modern relationship with the EU outside the customs union, so that Britain is able to negotiate its own bilateral trading relationships, and outside the SIM so that Britain would no longer be committed to adopting SIM-related legislation (Lea, 2008b). The new relationship should be based on trade and cooperation in mutually beneficial areas, whilst opting out of political and economic union. This is similar to the current relationship enjoyed by Switzerland which, as already pointed out, has a very close trading links with the EU countries (Church, 2007). It is frequently asserted that, if Britain were to leave the EU's political and economic union, the other EU member states would refuse to trade with us, but this ignores the basic truth that countries trade in order to prosper and create jobs. Given the huge trade imbalances between the UK, on the one hand, and for example Germany, on the other, it is clear that Germany prospers more from trading with the UK than the UK does with Germany (Lea, 2008c).

All the economic evidence outlined above suggests that a new looser relationship with the EU is the right way forward for Britain. But the political feasibility of negotiating a new relationship is frequently dismissed as impossible because, it is asserted, key Continental politicians would refuse to even consider such a development. This is, however, simply not true.

Former French President Valéry Giscard d'Estaing (2008) has, for example, proposed the idea of a 'special status' for Britain on several occasions, explaining, by way of background, that there were profound differences between different EU countries concerning the degree of integration they considered necessary for the future success of Europe. The majority wanted integration to continue which was regarded as necessary for the future of Europe. However, for others, especially Britain, this was not the case. Such differences, he said, created antagonisms which, if they were to end, would be better for all. One way forward, he proposed, was to recognise that Britain was a special case. If Britain did not want to integrate further, then Britain should, must, be offered a 'spe-

---

2   ICM surveyed 1,000 Chief Executives for Open Europe in September 2006.

cial status'. Britain could then opt out of any EU developments towards further integration. It would be a case of 'this far, but no further'.

The significance of these proposals is hugely important. Clearly some Continental politicians, at the most senior levels, are prepared to negotiate a new settlement for Britain with the EU. President Giscard d'Estaing, informed by his unrivalled knowledge and experience of European politics, has offered a potential solution and opened a door. It is clear that negotiating a new UK-EU relationship is politically feasible.

So a looser relationship with the EU is economically persuasive and politically feasible. The next question that has to be addressed is whether the British people would want it. The answer in poll after poll is a resounding yes. All our Global Vision polling shows that the majority of people are unhappy with the current relationship. Roughly a half want a looser relationship with the EU based on trade and cooperation and a quarter want to leave altogether, whilst a quarter wish to maintain the status quo. Similarly, a ComRes poll for BBC2's Daily Politics in March 2009 concluded that 55% of people agreed with the statement 'Britain should leave the EU but maintain close trading links', whilst only 41% disagreed.[3].

The British people know that our current relationship with the EU is a costly, old-fashioned and restrictive. They are right. It really is time for Britain to move into the 21st century and grasp the opportunities this century will undoubtedly bring, outside the EU's political union. Britain made the modern global world in the 19th and early 20th centuries (Ferguson, 2003). Europe's borders are too small for Britain. Britain must have a global vision.

---

3   Poll conducted for BBC2's Daily Politics programme by ComRes, sample of 1,004 voters between the 13–16 March.

Ian Milne

Backing the Wrong Horse

Introduction

The UK conducts its internal and external trade through the European Union's Customs Union/Single Market. That model, which was originally designed in the 1950s for economic and geopolitical conditions that were different from today's, is emulated nowhere else in the developed world.

This chapter reviews ongoing developments in the world trading system. It concludes that the UK would be better off if it adopted the model, used by the rising Asian superpowers and the entire developed world outside the EU, of interlocking networks of user-friendly free trade agreements.

It proposes that the UK joins a multi-country free trade agreement alongside the United States for its trade and investment with the world outside the EU (accounting for 93% of world population and growing); and Swiss-style sectoral agreements for its relations with the EU (7% of world population and shrinking).

An Overview of Trade Arrangements

In organising their international trade, states can choose between three basic models (Leach, 2004; WTO, 2004):

1. the customs union, where each participating country cedes to the union control of its own trade policy vis-à-vis third parties, adopts a common external tariff and accepts whatever trade policy the union decides;

2. the Free Trade Agreement (FTA), where each participating country keeps control of its own trade policies vis-à-vis third parties;

3. 'going it alone', where a country joins neither a customs union or an FTA.

In 1957 the Treaty of Rome established a customs union which was always more likely than an FTA structure to achieve the explicit objective of gradual political federation. This choice was made when tariffs were high, and when 'bloc-ism' as a way of looking at the world, especially during the Cold War, was understandable. Since then, the European Union (EU) has superimposed on the customs union a tightly-regulated single or internal market, with a cumbersome supranational bureaucracy which now includes the Commission, Parliament, Council, Court of Justice, the *acquis communautaire* and the single currency (presently used by fewer than half of EU-27) run by a European Central Bank.

Some fifty years on, it is now clear that the economies of the Single Market are failing. Four factors have to be taken into account:

1. The economic underperformance of the EU in general, and the Eurozone in particular, has lasted for ten years. The European Commission, among others, anticipates little improvement in future (European Forecasting Network, 2004), despite the boldness of the Lisbon rhetoric.[1]

2. Continental Europe's ageing demographic profile offers little prospect of its economic performance improving, even if France and Germany were to implement the supply-side reforms they so desperately need. Any productivity gains at the firm or sector level will be offset by sharp declines in working-age population and corresponding increases in the pensioner to worker dependency ratio in almost all of EU-27 (Deutsche Bundesbank, 2004; IMF, 2004).

3. The EU model has not been emulated anywhere in the developed world. The relatively few customs unions that do exist outside Europe are in poor African countries, former Soviet dependencies, Gulf States and developing countries in South America. Outside Europe, no major industrial trading nation has chosen to conduct its trade via a customs union. The EU's immediate neighbours, the countries which make up the European Free Trade Association (EFTA), with per capita GDP far greater than the EU's, have firmly stuck to the FTA model, for both intra-EFTA and EU-EFTA trade—including for their participation in the EU Single Market. Tomorrow's economic superpowers, China and India, have also chosen the FTA route. The evidence is clear: FTAs deliver the same benefits that EU members get from EU membership, but with very few of the costs.

---

1   At a summit in Lisbon in 2000 the EU set itself the objective of becoming "the most competitive and dynamic knowledge-based economy in the world" by 2010.

4.   Recent research has shown that EU membership imposes an annual
     net cost to the UK of 4% of GDP (Milne, 2004).

There appears therefore to be a prima facie case for considering whether
the UK's economic interests are best served by remaining in the Single
Market. Would not the UK (the third-biggest trading nation and the
fourth biggest economy in the world) be better off if it adopted the model
which appears to be associated with superior economic and trading outcomes? That is, after all, the model — interlocking networks of
user-friendly FTAs — that has been chosen by the entire developed world
outside the EU and, significantly, by the rising Asian economic
superpowers.

Developments in the World Trading System

Between 1980 and 2002, world trade has more than tripled while world
output has doubled. The world trade to GDP ratio has risen from around
16% in 1980 to almost 30% in 2002; the trend has been upward since the
end of the Second World War and seems to have accelerated in the last 20
years. Most trade takes place between structurally similar industrial
economies: for example, 80% of OECD trade takes place with other OECD
economies. World trade appears to have grown because of a combination
of reduced costs of tradeable goods (which make up two-thirds of all
trade), rising living standards and income per head and — especially in
the last ten years rising levels of Foreign Direct Investment. Productivity
growth in the traded goods sector and falling tariffs appear to have
accounted for two-thirds of trade growth (reductions in exchange rate
volatility seem to have had little impact) (Dean and Sebastia-Barriel,
2004).

The post-war multilateral trading system is supervised by the World
Trade Organisation (WTO), an intergovernmental body, for which
Regional Trade Agreements (RTAs), whether customs unions, free trade
agreements or hybrids of the two, are stepping stones to full
multilateralism.

The last ten years have seen an explosion in the number of FTAs, bilateral, regional, inter-regional and cross-regional.[2] This is partly in
response to the agonising slowness and relatively meagre outcomes of
'pure' multilateral negotiations such as the Uruguay Round (1986–94),
which lasted eight years and the ongoing Doha Round, which began in

2   See WTO publications such as its Annual Reports; its annual World Trade Reports; OECD,
    Regionalism and the Multilateral Trading System, 2003; and the World Bank's Annual Report,
    Global Economic Prospects 2005: trade, regionalism and development 2005, November 2004.

2001. The slowness and complexity of WTO multilateral negotiations are inherent in the wide membership and the consensual intergovernmental nature of the negotiating process. In contrast, FTAs are flexible, allowing countries to pick and choose between trade partners, industrial sectors and types of co-operation—for example the free movement of people or protection of intellectual property. Not least, FTAs allow countries to conclude negotiations relatively quickly—though it has to be said that the higher the number of participants (for example in a regional FTA), the slower the process.

Modern FTAs[3] are comprehensive, typically covering services, labour mobility, investment, competition, trade facilitation, government procurement, intellectual property rights, subsidies and (sometimes via side letters) the environment. Such FTAs provide members with all or most of the benefits that members derive from the EU Customs Union/Single Market, but with few of the costs.Customs unions themselves, especially the EU, have enthusiastically joined the fray negotiating FTAs not just with other customs unions such as Mercosur,[4] but also with individual countries (such as Mexico, which is itself a member of the North American Free Trade Agreement, (NAFTA)). The world trading system can now be characterised as a 'patchwork' of interlocking and overlapping RTAs, the bulk of which are FTAs. However, despite the proliferation of cross-regional RTAs, no agreement yet exists between the world's current biggest trading entities, the EU and the US.

When the UK joined the EEC in 1973 customs duties between industrial nations were high, typically in double figure percentages of imports by value. Since then, as a result of successive trade rounds conducted under the aegis of GATT and its successor the WTO, average tariffs are now very low and tending to zero. In the case of the UK, 92% of all UK imports (goods, services, income and transfers) in 2002 were tariff-free; and the average tariff on its imports of goods was under 1%. As a proportion of all taxes raised by the UK in 2002/2003 less than ½% came from tariffs on imports. The situation of other developed countries inside and outside the EU is similar. Transport costs now tend to be a bigger brake on trade than tariffs.

The eventual disappearance of customs duties (tariffs) will negate the raison d'être of customs unions: there is little point in them unless there

---

3   See, for example, the International Trade Agreements Database and Archive at the Center for International Business, Tuck School of Business; and OECD, Regionalism and the Multilateral Trading System, 2003.
4   Mercosur comprises Brazil, Argentina, Paraguay and Uruguay.

are customs duties to collect. However, until tariffs disappear completely, rules of origin are needed to determine the country of origin of an imported manufactured product, and how much tariff, if any, it should bear. Rules of origin are also used (though sparingly by developed countries, except for agriculture) to apply measures such as anti-dumping and countervailing duties, safeguard actions and quotas (WTO, 2004; European Commission, 2004; OECD, 2003; EFTA, 2004; Estevadeordal and Suominem, 2003).

Rules of origin are inherent in FTAs as each participant keeps control of its trade policies, including tariffs and quotas, vis-à-vis nonparticipating countries. Rules of origin are not needed within customs unions in respect of trade between members, so long as each member imposes a Common External Tariff on imports from outside the union (which the EU does but which, for example, Mercosur so far does not). Nevertheless, such rules are still needed in a country in a customs union to apply to imports arriving directly from outside the union.

Rules of origin involve administrative costs and can distort trade flows. To minimise such effects, work on harmonising rules of origin worldwide has gone on since the signing of the World Customs Organisation's Kyoto Convention of 1974 on the standardisation of customs procedures. These have been complemented by the work of the WTO's Committee on Rules of Origin, set up in 1995, and the Brussels-based World Customs Co-operation Council. Rules of origin are also dealt with at the OECD and at UNCTAD.

Progress in formal multilateral harmonisation has been slow. However, as a result of the 'free market' in FTAs, de facto convergence of rules of origin is happening through the voluntary adoption in most FTAs of either the NAFTA or the PANEURO models, which are similar. The NAFTA model tends to be the template in intra-Asian and trans-Pacific FTAs, and will be the blueprint for the future Free Trade Agreement of the Americas. The PANEURO model is used in FTAs between the EU and, for example, EFTA and North African and Middle Eastern countries.

The UK has no seat or voice at the WTO. It surrendered them to the EEC on accession in 1973. The EU Trade Commissioner, Peter Mandelson, negotiates on behalf of all EU member states as a bloc. Since trade policy is decided within the EU by Qualified Majority Voting (QMV), and no country has a veto, the UK, with only 8.4% of the votes in the Council of Ministers at present is to all intents and purposes an impotent bystander at the WTO. It should be noted that in the United Nations, the World Bank, the

International Monetary Fund and NATO, the UK shows no inclination to surrender its votes and seats to functionaries of a regional bloc.

UK leverage at the WTO is sometimes claimed to be stronger as part of the EU customs union than it would be if the UK spoke for itself in WTO councils. That claim has validity only in so far as British commercial interests coincide with those of all or a majority of its EU partners—all 26 of them. When British interests do not coincide, it follows that UK leverage is weaker than it would be if the UK were outside the EU.

Given that the structure and pattern of UK global trade is different from that of its EU partners, there is no a priori reason to suppose that, on balance, British interests and those of its EU partners coincide more often than they diverge.

Trading Options for the UK

Before say, 2010, it is possible that the UK will find itself, whether it likes it or not, at the margins of 'Europe'. First, domestic politics might evolve to the point where a British Government initiated a process of partial or wholesale detachment from the EU.[5] Second, British policy-makers might consider it to be dangerous for the UK to have over 40% of its trade with a regional bloc which has only 7% of world population and which is in marked long-term economic decline.

The question of how best to reconfigure the UK's global trading arrangements would then move from the theoretical to the practical. The UK, in that scenario, for the first time since 1972, would be free to choose its own trading arrangements as a function of its own best geopolitical and geoeconomic interests.

It seems unlikely, for the reasons set out above, that the UK would seek to create or enter another customs union, or to 'go it alone'. The practical way ahead would lie in some combination or variant of the FTA route for its trade both with the world beyond the EU and with the EU itself. The choices, broadly (they are not mutually exclusive) would be as follows.

Option One: the UK enters a multi-country FTA alongside the US

One possibility, often floated, is for the UK to join the US, Canada and Mexico in NAFTA, which itself will constitute the North American component of the hemispherical Free Trade Agreement of the Americas (FTAA).

---

5   At the time of writing, partial detachment from the EU, through repatriation of the Common Fisheries Policy, appears to be the official policy of the Conservative Party.

Another possibility would be for the UK to join a Global Free Trade Alliance (GFTA), an idea being developed by the Washington-based Heritage Foundation (Feulner et al., 2004). The GFTA would go beyond the traditional FTA, in that members would voluntarily (but not irrevocably) commit themselves to genuine reciprocal free trade—no tariffs at all, no quotas, minimum regulation—with the other members. The GFTA would not be a treaty; each member would enact national legislation to allow free trade with its partners. It would not be restricted to a specific region. Among 12 countries that would qualify initially according to Heritage's criteria are the US, the UK, Australia, New Zealand, Hong Kong, Singapore, Ireland and Iceland.Option Two:

UK enters bilateral FTAs worldwide on a case-by-case basis

The UK, currently the world's third biggest importing nation and fourth biggest economy, would be an attractive FTA partner for both developed and developing countries in and near Europe, in the Americas and in Asia. A starting point might be an FTA with its single biggest trading and investment partner worldwide, the US.

Option Three: With the EU itself

The EU will soon have different kinds of FTAs with half of all the countries in the world. Some (for example with Norway through EFTA-EEA) involve the other party 'opting-in' to the EU Single Market. Another (for example with Switzerland) is an *à la carte* arrangement providing selective *de facto* (but not *de jure*) opting-in to bits of the Single Market through sectoral bilateral agreements (Global Britain, 2004). Others (for example with Mexico) are comprehensive arms-length FTAs of the traditional kind. So, if and when the UK decides to reconfigure its trading arrangements with the EU, there would be no shortage of well-functioning models from which to choose.

Switzerland is not in the EEA, not in the EU Customs Union and not, except for one aspect of civil aviation, in the Single Market. For its trade with the EU, Switzerland has 'cherry-picked' the economic and political sectors in which it wants to co-operate, keeping full sovereignty in all other areas. There is no reason why the UK should not follow the Swiss model if it so chose.[6]

Alternatively, if the UK wished to continue being an integral part of the Single Market, the EFTA-EEA model would be one way of doing so. Three

6 Switzerland, surrounded by EU countries, does around 70% of its trade with the EU, compared with the UK's around 45%.

of the four EFTA members, Norway, Iceland and Liechtenstein, along
with EU-27, form the 30 member EEA, of which the UK is already a member. The UK, if it chose this model, would remain in the EEA, re-join EFTA
(which it left in 1973), and, like Norway, Iceland and Liechtenstein, stay
out of the CAP, the CFP, the Customs Union, Monetary Union and so on,
but opt-in to the Single Market. Formal institutions allowing EFTA-EEA
members to participate in the decision-shaping of EU EEA-relevant legislation already exist. The UK, like the existing EFTA — would have no vote
in the EU Council of Ministers — but after all, a zero vote in the Council of
Ministers is not that different from the UK's current situation as a full EU
member, with no veto on Single Market matters and its voting power
heading towards 5% as the EU enlarges further to the east.

In joining EFTA the UK would immediately become a party to EFTA's
numerous existing and soon-to-be-concluded FTAs with non-EU countries, if it judged that these best served its interests. The example of Switzerland, an EFTA member but not an EEA member, suggests that EFTA
would be flexible enough to accommodate British requirements vis-à-vis
the world outside the EU if these differed significantly from those of the
other members.

Finally, Mexico and the EU have a comprehensive FTA giving Mexican
companies practically the same access to the EU as EU members themselves, but with none of the costs. Again, there is no reason why the UK
should not build on such a model, since the UK is far more valuable to the
EU as a trading and investment partner than Mexico (Global Britain,
2002).

Conclusion

Two geo-political considerations should determine the UK's choice of
global trading arrangements for the next half-century. The first is the
probability that the US will continue to be the world's most powerful
nation — economically as well as in other respects — for at least the next 50
years. Over the long term, it will continue to be in the UK's interests to be
closely allied with that power. If, as widely predicted, the Chinese and
Indian economies become as big as that of the US by the middle of this
century, they will do so by being fully-engaged with the US in particular
and with the West in general. Their global influence is unlikely to rival
that of the US for some time after their economies have reached or over-
taken America's.

The second is that Continental Europe is in long-term economic decline,
partly because of economic and social rigidities hard-wired into its sys-

tem of governance, partly because of its demographics. Europe's global influence has already peaked. Eastward enlargement, far from solving the EU's problems, will exacerbate them. Its destiny, as a cohesive regional power, is to follow the Ottoman Empire into oblivion.

Those geo-political considerations indicate that the best foundation for the UK's future trading arrangements would be a combination, under the WTO umbrella, of Option One above (a multi-country FTA alongside the US) for its relations with the world outside the EU, and the Swiss Model, (sectoral FTAs) for its relations with the EU. That combination would give the UK economy the flexibility and agility it needs to prosper globally in the decades to come.

John Mills

Options for Economic Policy

Introduction

Would Britain benefit economically from being outside the European Union? A good starting point for answering this question is to consider what the UK's experience has been inside the EU over the last 35 years and to consider what might have happened if we had been outside. Of course, counterfactual analysis of this type is always open to criticism, but some of the patterns are so clear that it is difficult for anyone to argue against them.

Historical Costs of EU Membership

It helps that the period since Britain joined what was then the Common Market until now divides itself neatly into two fairly equal halves. There were the years from 1973 to 1992 when various efforts were made to harmonise Britain's economic policy with that of other Member States. This was done mainly through a succession of systems of exchange rate co-ordination, particularly the Snake (1969 to 1975) and then the Exchange Rate Mechanism (ERM) (1979 to 1993). Between 1973 and 1992 the British economy performed significantly worse than the EU average, growing cumulatively by 1.67% per annum compared to 2.56% for the EU as a whole.

After Britain left the ERM in September 1992, there was a sea change. Roles were reversed and Britain did much better than the rest of the EU, growing by an average of 2.85% between 1993 and 2007 compared to 1.75% for the eurozone. Efforts to co-ordinate Britain's fiscal, monetary and exchange rate policies with those of other Member States largely came to an end. The main driver for British economic policy ceased being the maintenance of any particular parity between sterling and the DM and subsequently the euro. Instead, achieving a sustained low level of inflation became the over-arching goal and one which for most of the last sixteen years has been successfully achieved. There was certainly a conjunction of economic forces which helped to keep inflation at bay, a flood of cheap imports from the Far East, weakened trades unions and low commodity prices, but these helped everyone, not just the UK, to keep inflation down. Britain, of course, stayed outside the euro.

It is no co-incidence that after 1992 the UK's relative position within the EU in terms of economic performance steadily improved. The lower exchange rate for the pound once we left the ERM and the less deflationary conditions which were thus made possible were major contributory factors. This experience certainly suggests that tying Britain's economic policy formation tightly into that of the other EU Member States has not generally in the past been a recipe for success. There are good reasons for believing that it is equally unlikely to be advantageous to do so in future. This is because the thrust of EU economic policy remains much as it was during the Snake and ERM periods. There is still huge pressure to co-ordinate economic performance, exemplified by the creation of the euro which, of course, happened during the later period when Britain was no longer trying to stay so closely involved with other Member States. The problems which in the end sank the Snake and the ERM, but which the euro was supposed to solve, have only really been suppressed, not cured. The German economy, having been through a difficult patch around the period of unification at the beginning of the 1990s, is now much stronger and more competitive than those of most other eurozone members. Consequently, the eurozone as a whole has a balance of payments surplus, but only because of the stellar export performance of Germany, which also has a balance of payments surplus with other countries with the euro as their currency. The resulting imbalances have been sufficient to tip the eurozone currently into a recession for all too similar reasons to those which in the end caused the Snake and the ERM to collapse.

The British economy may be in poor shape too at the moment, but it is at the end of a long period of sustained growth and low inflation, which gradually became the envy of many other EU members. There were undoubtedly elements of good luck as well as good management in the British performance over this period. The City may have had a negative influence on much of the rest of the British economy, particularly its manufacturing sector, but financial and related services contributed very strongly to Britain's growth record. Big increases in public expenditure, which would have been much harder to achieve inside the eurozone rules, also fuelled economic activity. However, both over-dependence on the City and public spending to keep GDP increasing, let alone all the borrowing required to sustain it, have left severe imbalances from which we are now suffering. Our difficulties, however, although somewhat different, appear to be no worse overall than those in the eurozone, but we have had a higher rate of growth in the meantime, at least over the last 16 years since 1992, than they have.

Co-ordination, or lack of it, of fiscal, monetary and exchange rate policies have not, of course been the only feature of Britain's economic relationship with the other Member States. At least three other major areas of policy have been affected during our years of membership since 1973, these being tariff reductions, budgetary costs overlapping with our involvement with the Common Agricultural Policy (CAP), and the regulatory regime in which both business and government have had to operate. We consider these in turn.

Without doubt, a major early achievement of the Common Market was to reduce the tariff barriers between Member States, although the case for doing this behind a common external tariff instead of on a multi-lateral basis is much more dubious. Although inappropriate exchange rates have often meant that the benefits secured from free trade were less than they could or should have been, the general trend towards lower tariff barriers has been one which, on balance has brought major advantages with it. There is considerable doubt, however, as to whether the tariff reductions and their eventual abolition necessarily required the existence of Common Market as it then was to allow this to happen. It very probably speeded up the process within the common external tariff, but the strong tendency towards free trade at least in industrial goods both across the whole of Europe and the industrialised world since World War II strongly suggests that nearly all the tariff reduction and abolition which occurred within the Common Market would have happened anyway.

Nor was the impact of the creation of free trade within the EU as great as it might have been. Language barriers, difference in technical and other standards and the complications caused by national VAT schemes all contributed to the Single Market not producing as much benefit as it was hoped it would. Much more serious a blot on the free trade record of the EU, however, has been the CAP. Originally designed to protect French farmers from the social strains of excessive numbers of people on the land in France, the CAP has developed a momentum of its own across the whole of the EU which it has proved impossible to contain. Serious reform is still a distant prospect, currently on ice until at least 2013. In the meantime, the CAP continues to be an extremely expensive and inefficient way of organising farming within the EU, with devastating consequences for the Developing World.

The CAP not only raises the cost of food for the average British family by some £20 a week, the way the CAP regime functions has also been a major contributory factor to the net budgetary cost to Britain of our membership of the EU. The relatively small proportion of the British economy devoted to agriculture has meant that the UK has never benefited that much from EU farm subsidies compared to other countries such as France, Ireland and Denmark. The pattern of British imports (higher proportionally than the average, so we pay more than our fair share of import duties to the EU), plus the way the VAT regime works (a higher proportion of UK GDP is VATable than the EU average); all produce an underlying bias towards relatively high contributions to the EU budget. Far from this being offset by high EU expenditures within the UK, the reverse condition applies. As a result Britain has had a significant net contribution to pay to the EU for its membership every year (except in 1975), perhaps not wholly without significance the year of the referendum on whether Britain should stay in the Common Market. In aggregate a huge net sum has been paid, now totalling some £125bn in 2008 prices. Nor are there any prospects of this burden being reduced. On the contrary, the agreement reached at Brussels in December 2005, means that a further steep rise is in prospect, as the rebate won by Margaret Thatcher in 1984 is eroded away, and the EU budget increases. The real cost is further increased by the fact that it effectively has to be paid in foreign currency by the British government, thus adding to the deflationary consequences of Britain's ballooning foreign payments deficit.

If the Single Market has still not achieved the benefits hoped of it, this has not occurred as a result of any sloth on behalf of the EU authorities in trying to introduce regulations across the EU, many of them designed to have the same impact in all countries thus producing a more even playing field for trade. Apart from the well known fact that some countries have always been much more assiduous than others in applying the rules, with Britain often regarded as generally unduly punctilious, there is now a mountain of evidence to show that the cost of excessive regulation has now become a major burden on all EU economies. Both in Britain and the Netherlands, studies have shown that the net cost of regulation (achieved by subtracting the cost from the benefits) is now of the order of at least 2% of GDP. This is a very large sum of money. Of course, not all regulations stem from the EU, but a high proportion do. Furthermore, all regulations benefit some people, who almost always form a vocal minority if there is any suggestion of regulations being watered down or removed, so regulations, once established, are notoriously hard to remove.

How much does all this add up to? Some costs are easier to quantify than others so that any attempt at precise accuracy is bound to fail. Tellingly, however, all the serious efforts which have been made to pull all these costs together come to broadly the same conclusions, clustering round approximately the following annual figures: Net Budgetary Cost: about £4.7bn in 2007, rising towards £6bn to £7bn a year in 2013; non-budget EU contributions: running at about £1.9bn a year, but likely to rise; Common Agricultural Policy: estimated to have a net annual cost to the UK economy of about £15bn; regulation: excess of costs over benefits now estimated to be about 2% of GDP, whereby if half attributed to EU, about £12bn a year.

These costs total to about £34bn a year, but are crucially on a fairly sharply rising trend. They do not, however, take any account of the dynamic effects on the British economy caused by both the heavy direct burdens on our economy on the one hand and the fact that our membership of the EU has bound us into a close association with one of the slowest growing parts of the world economy for most of the last half century. This is a much harder figure to estimate with any precision, but if it was 0.5% per annum, the impact over the last ten years alone would be to have reduced our current national income cumulatively each year by some £60bn per annum. Judging by the growth record of economies such as those of Norway and Switzerland, which are outside the EU, this figure may well be on the conservative side. If the cumulative dynamic costs are added to the current costs we incur every year, EU membership has indeed been a very heavy economic millstone round our necks.

Future Prospects for Britain and the EU

Given this starting position, what changes in economic prospects could we therefore reasonably expect to foresee if Britain were no longer to be bound by its current EU membership obligations? Surely, the first point to be made is that the current situation is so disadvantageous that the scope for change for the better is really very substantial. Some caution is needed; however, about both how long it would take to see the benefits coming through, how much could reasonably be expected to be retrieved over a relatively short period and how disruptive the major changes involved might be.

The most immediate gain is likely to be on our net contributions to the EU budget. It is difficult to see there being any case for any extended period while our net payments to the EU were phased out. There would then be a large and immediate net gain both to our national income, to our foreign payments position and to our public finances. Those who would feel the pain of a very awkward transition would not be in Britain, but our current EU partners who would have to find alternative ways of filling the large budgetary gap which would materialise in EU funding once our net contribution was removed.

If we were no longer EU members, there is little doubt that we would want to move away from the CAP's way of supporting agriculture, or from the Common Fisheries Policy (CFP) way of dealing with fishing. The likelihood is that we would want to move back towards the system which was in place before we joined the Common Market. This kept prices within the UK at world level, with production subsidies assisting British farming where it was deemed necessary, rather than keeping up prices through tariffs. It is likely that the cost of any such scheme would be rather lower than that of the CAP, but very unlikely that there would be no costs at all. Some of the funding requirements would remain, even if the funds were disbursed in a different way. There would, however, be big welfare gains to the Developing World if we were in a position to open our markets to their agricultural exports.

Would there be any danger of our former EU partners erecting tariff barriers against British exports, especially if we were no longer members of the CAP? It is extremely unlikely. The UK has a large balance of payments deficit with rest of the EU, so the erection of mutual tariff barriers would do much more harm to them than to us. Even if this unlikely scenario materialised, its effect would be very limited. Duties on nearly all of our exports to the EU, and theirs to us other than agricultural products, are capped by World Trade Organisation agreements to such a low level (less than 2% on average) that they are barely worth the administrative costs involved in collecting them.

We should also not be too optimistic about the benefits to be secured from getting rid of the excessive burden of regulations which has been built up in recent years. Not all of these arose from the EU in the first place. Once in place, as already noted, regulations are notoriously difficult to revoke as their benefits tend to be concentrated on a small number of people who would suffer from their absence rather than a much larger number who pay the cost. At the least, however, it should be possible to do something to reduce the flow of future regulatory burdens.

Conclusion

What, then, would the overall benefit be? Within a relatively short period, we should be able to achieve the full savings on our net EU budget contributions, which by the second decade of the twenty first century are likely to be well in excess of £10bn a year. Over a period of years, we might be able to save perhaps half of the £15bn cost of the CAP, another £7.5bn a year. With a bit of a dividend from less regulation, a figure of £20bn does not look unattainable.

Potentially, however, there would be even bigger gains if reducing our current EU burdens improved our growth rate. Shifting our vision and our trading patterns more towards the faster growing parts of the world and away from the EU at the same time might, as suggested previously, well increase our growth rate by 0.5% per annum compared to what it would be within the present EU constraints. Looking ahead to a growing economy, this could well be worth something of the order of £75bn cumulatively every year.

Whether an improved performance of this sort actually materialised would, of course, depend on the policies which the British government decided to pursue. They might or might not make the most advantageous choices. At least, however, the judgements they made would be on where they thought the British national interest lay. Especially against the background of the burdens which certainly would be lifted if we were no longer EU members, it is hard to see how we could be worse off than we are now and easy to see how our prospects might look a lot better than they do at the moment.

Philip Davies

It's the Economy Stupid

Introduction

£100,000 per minute; £50.6 billion per year; £347.3 billion in 35 years. These figures do not reflect spending on national defence, schools or policing. They are not about the value of food we produce or even how much we give in aid to developing countries. Instead, they represent the cost to the UK of the European Union.

In the days when ordinary families are feeling the pinch of the credit crunch ever more acutely it is important to reflect just how much of our national wealth is given over to the EU. I say given, but when one considers what we get in return for these vast sums of money, lost would perhaps be a better word. Billions lost to an inefficient, wasteful and reputedly corrupt body that, if it were a business, would have been shut down by regulators years ago. Despite the huge sums which we pump into this organisation the public, which foots the bill or even our elected government have no power to change or even effectively monitor this costly and bureaucratic monolith.

Indeed so much of what the EU does goes unnoticed. Occasionally the public will read in *The Sun* about some wasteful EU scheme or some barmy idea relating to straight bananas, but the public don't know the half of it. When hard working families in my constituency are finding it more difficult to stretch their over-taxed pay packets as the economy feels the strain I am sure they would find it inexplicable that any of their hard earned money should be used to subsidise French farmers.

We elect Members of Parliament and our Government on the back of promises about what they want to do to improve our country. We accept their laws and regulations so long as we feel that there is a chance that things are going to get better and when we feel that things are not getting better we vote them out and bring in a new lot, with a new set of promises.

Yet with so many of our laws emanating from the EU the Government is not even responsible for a good deal of the damaging regulations which affect British business and British jobs.

While we cannot hold our Government accountable for every law or regulation dreamt up by an unelected EU bureaucrat, what we can hold them accountable for is not challenging this undemocratic, wasteful and corrupt institution. When defence spending is at its lowest proportion of national wealth since the 1930s; when our hospitals are dirty and suffer from infestations and vermin; when there simply aren't enough police officers to police our increasingly lawless inner-cities and when the burden of taxation is higher than ever; surely someone should be questioning the money we hand over to the EU. Well these questions certainly aren't coming from Whitehall that is for sure.

When those few of us who raise the issue of a positive future for Britain outside of the EU in Parliament or elsewhere; Government Ministers treat it almost as heresy. There is no acceptance that in a democracy it is right to discuss something which takes away so much taxpayers' money. Instead we are told 'how dare we raise' something which would cause such untold damage to our economy and our prosperity. Yet their claims are entirely false. To suggest that our prosperity depends on EU membership is simply ludicrous. They shut down any discussion of how this organisation might actually be damaging to our economy.

In this chapter I intend to show that such arguments are not heresy and are in fact the right way forward for our country.

The Democratic Deficit

In 2004 the European Union was included in the CIA World Fact Book, the open source publication that tracks the key characteristics of every nation around the globe. It was the first time a supra-national body had ever been included in the publication dedicated to nation states. The reason the CIA gave for the EU's inclusion in the Fact Book was that 'it has many of the attributes associated with independent nations: its own flag, anthem, founding date, and currency, as well as an incipient common foreign and security policy in its dealings with other nations. In the future, many of these nation-like characteristics are likely to be expanded'.

The inclusion of the EU in the CIA's World Fact Book provides impartial third party endorsement of the fact that the EU has moved far beyond the idea of a common market which Sir Edward Heath and Harold Wilson sold to the British public back in the 1970s. The original Eurocrat, Jean Monet, the architect of the modern EU, first spoke of political union being the eventual aim at the time of the creation of the European Coal and Steel Community, a fact that must have been known to our political leaders who took us into the project.

The EU has moved further toward nationhood, dragging Britain along with it, than most members of the Government would care to admit. Consequently, 70 per cent of our laws now emanate from the Continent, yet the political machine that produces them is unelected, unaccountable, and essentially unacceptable.

This raises the fundamental question of how much longer can Britain claim to be a democratic country when more than two thirds of our law comes from an unelected and unaccountable supra-national state and which take precedence over those passed by our democratically elected Government? If we don't like what our governments do we can show our disapproval in the ballot box. But no such right exists with the EU. The EU can ride roughshod over the wishes of the British people and there is little we can do. We don't even have anyone to complain to. Only collectively, as a nation could we really do anything to stem this ebbing of our democracy and that is through withdrawal from the EU.

Now those who support the EU may meekly raise the European Parliament as evidence of how the EU is in someway democratic. But this fig leaf of democracy hardly addresses the democratic deficit. Firstly, the Parliament plays second fiddle to the unelected Commission which continues to be the engine of the EU. Secondly, there is little identification between the British public and the European Parliament. The result is that few people vote for it so MEPs cannot claim to speak for the vast majority. Thirdly, no matter which party you vote for British MEPs will always be in the minority. The result is that representatives from other countries can overrule British MEPs on an issue which may be against our national interests. This makes a mockery of the idea of our national sovereignty and our democratic institutions. Now we are told that we need to be at the heart of Europe because not to be would see us lose our cherished influence. However, this influence is negligible at best. The EU continues to lumber in a direction which is at odds with the UK's national interest and all the British Government can do is to try and spin defeats as victories for British influence. The wasteful and damaging Common Agricultural Policy continues to benefit French farmers and damage the UK farming sector unabated. As we're told by Gordon Brown to cut down on food waste, we're left to wonder what each family could do with the extra £20 per week that withdrawal from the CAP would save. As skilful a politician as Tony Blair was, it proved to be nothing more than bravado when he promised an overhaul of this policy and hours later not only lost part of Britain's rebate but agreed to increase spending on the CAP to 48% of the EU budget. Even he had a hard job presenting the exchange of this for assurances of his own EU standing as a victory.

No one has ever voted for the EU we have today. In 1975, people were given the choice about whether or not to remain in an 'economic union' (which Edward Heath had taken us into without a vote), what they did not vote for was the political union we have today. For those who have come of age after 1975, they have had no say at all. People now realise that the EU does not represent their interests. A poll for the independent think tank, Open Europe, conducted in March last year found that 68% did not believe that the EU represented ordinary people. The same poll found that 58% wanted the EU to have less power than it does today and that more decisions should be taken nationally.

An Economic Argument

Culturally and politically, the EU does not have the same place in British national life that it does in some countries. Its bureaucratic nature goes against our political traditions in a way which is simply not the case on the Continent. The reason why the British public are willing to acquiesce to this institution is because of the economy. It is widely accepted that millions of pounds are wasted every day by an inefficient and reportedly corrupt institution over which the UK has no sovereignty. If the British people were allowed the opportunity to voice their opinion on that in a referendum they'd vote to leave the EU by a landslide. However, it is on the economy that the argument over whether Britain remains in the EU will be won and lost.

People are primarily concerned with the issues that affect them on a daily basis. Most people see the EU as distant and impersonal with little impact on their personal lives. Thoughts of mortgages, bills to pay, schools and children being stabbed on the street leave little time to dwell upon Continental institutions. Proponents of the EU understand this and they present their arguments in terms people can understand and appreciate; jobs and trade.

By presenting Britain's membership of the EU in economic terms, they know that they can sell to the British people what is essentially a political project. It is unfortunate, if understandable, that people and small businesses will unquestioningly accept government reassurances of economic stability when they are 'preoccupied' with supporting their families and livelihoods.

People are told that if Britain were to withdraw from the EU then trade with our European neighbours would suffer, our economy would suffer, and we would experience an immediate loss of jobs and prosperity. We are told that over 60% of our trade is with the EU; that withdrawal would mean massive losses for our markets and the disappearance of three million jobs. Our political leaders repeat this mantra over and over again. In November 2006 Tony Blair went as far as to claim that: 'I can't see a single good reason for Britain not being at the centre of Europe and every good reason why it should be. Europe gives us weight and strength.'

However, when you examine these issues in detail it becomes clear that the EU is in fact detrimental to trade and employment. Britain is worse off by being in the EU and withdrawal would give Britain a more flexible global position from which to meet the challenges of the 21st Century. Let us look at these areas: Trade will not be lost because it is a bilateral relationship; European states make money from us too. Indeed, they actually make more money from us than we make from them. Britain has been running a trade deficit with the EU since we joined in 1973. According to the House of Commons Library, between 1973 and 2007 the cumulative trade deficit between the UK and the EU amounts to an astonishing £347.3 billion, meaning that our EU 'partners' have made £347.3 billion more from us than we have from them. This deficit continues to rise at an alarming rate as our surplus in trade with the US rises year after year and it is well worth noting that even Switzerland, a non-EU state, enjoys a healthier balance of trade than we do. European businesses with any sense are highly unlikely to end this relationship on a mere principle of wounded pride. Britain was trading with Europe long before we were members and it is currently unimaginable that we will not continue to do so long after we leave. The UK does not need to be a member of the EU to have a free trade agreement with the EU as Switzerland, Norway and even Mexico all demonstrate. If we wish to develop a trade agreement with China we are not allowed to do so; we have to get Peter Mandelson to agree one with the whole of the EU; this is ridiculous in a fast moving world.

The EU currently accounts for around half (not 60%) of the UK's exports given the inclusion of services, with total exports making-up around 21% of GDP. This means that EU trade totals around 10% of UK GDP, not the 60% again claimed by those with a vested interest in keeping us in the EU. With the EU, the regulatory red tape infiltrates and ties up nearly every aspect of business dealing. Multinational corporations may be well placed to shoulder this burden, but for small businesses, this can be crippling. With the rising economic power of India, China and Russia and a globally unstable economic market, the UK needs to ensure that it as flexible and competitive as possible if it even hopes to compete with the cheap labour and efficiency of these emerging powerhouses. Miring itself in the bureaucracy, restrictive employment laws and high taxes of this monolithic supranational state is not the way to do this.

This leads us onto the jobs market. Accepting for the sake of argument the figure of three million jobs Britain would lose on leaving the EU which depend upon trade with Europe. However, as outlined above, trade with Europe is not dependent on our membership and consequently neither are these jobs. The only jobs dependent on the EU are those of EU civil servants based here; they may well need to search for alternative employment but this hardly accounts for three million jobs. It's not just the beleaguered British who have something less than glowing to say about the EU; the European Commission itself admits to the inefficiency and waste that many proponents and beneficiaries of the system are keen to turn a blind eye to. In 2006 Enterprise and Industry Commissioner Gunter Verheugen stated that EU regulations were costing the European economy 600 billion euros a year, amounting to around 5.5% of Europe's total GDP!

It is staggering enough that each year European businesses are losing the equivalent of the entire GDP of Holland due to EU regulations, but when you compare it with what the EU estimates to be the financial benefit of the single market, then the case for the EU is damaged even further. Commission estimates for 2002 put the benefits at 165 billion euros, quite substantially less than the costs. Even when you take account of inflation the costs of EU membership to business is around three times the benefits. Far from being good for business the bureaucratic EU is actually profoundly harmful to business. Whilst a very small proportion of businesses in the UK get any benefit from the EU single market (because they don't trade with the EU) all businesses are saddled with the cost of EU regulations whether they trade with the EU or not and it is usually our smallest businesses who suffer the most from this. With this in mind it is no wonder that 52% of Chief Executives canvassed by an ICM/Open Europe poll now think the cost of implementing EU regulations now outweighs the benefit of the Single Market and 60% believe we should leave the EU and just have a free trade agreement.

Since 1970 the United States has enjoyed net growth of around 25% yet the EU, a much heralded economic powerhouse has enjoyed net growth of around zero. When you compare the EU's stifling levels of regulation and high taxes with the business friendly low tax economy of the US, you are forced to conclude that the EU's social democratic model has contributed to this sluggish growth. Gordon Brown is fond of stating that the UK has just enjoyed the longest period of sustained growth; but what might this have been if we had not had the drag of the EU? The answer is too depressing to dwell on.

Britain contributes far more to the EU economy than it gets out of it as British tax payers fund inefficient farmers across the EU, any number of wasteful EU social projects and a huge budget simply for self promotion.

Since we joined the EEC in 1973 Britain has contributed over £211 billion in membership fees. In 2007 the full cost to the UK, both direct and indirect, worked out at an astonishing £50.6 billion. Over the financial period 2007–13 the UK will hand over an additional £71 billion. Think of the hospitals that sum could build, the policemen or nurses it could fund, or the difference it could make to a person's pay packet through lower taxes as the annual cost of the EU for every man woman and child works out at £873.

This money would make a world of difference hard working family on a tight budget, especially in the face of rising food, fuel and mortgage costs as every minute of 2007 the EU cost the UK £100,000. If Britain were to come out of the EU we could afford tax cuts, increased defence spending and spending on the public services that other European states are so proud of. In contrast, over the financial period up to 2013 Britain will receive only €770 per person in EU spending – the lowest of any member state.

Thus, there is no wonder that the government refuses to carry out a full cost/benefit analysis of our membership of the EU. If membership of the EU was so beneficial, you would have thought the government would have jumped at the chance to carry this out!

Lies, Damn Lies...

EU Commission workers freely admit millions of British taxpayer's money is being wasted by the EU, but there is no independent means of proving this. Here in the UK we have the National Audit Office, so when the Government wastes inordinate amounts of taxpayers' money on unwise or badly managed projects there is a body that holds it to account. No such body exists within the EU. The EU is left to police itself. The European Parliament takes on much of the burden within the EU but as is common in the political cultures of certain European countries, a certain level of waste and corruption is seen as inevitable and therefore there is little anyone can do about it.

Most member states are unlikely to do anything to expose this corruption. Those who are net receivers are unlikely to raise objections about an inefficient and wasteful system that directly benefits them. They know the EU doesn't work, but it works for them. For net contributors like the UK the bad deal they receive is something they do not want to admit to, much less advertise. The last thing the British Government want is for the British people to see just how many hospitals, schools or prisons could be paid for with the money wasted in Brussels. The European Parliament occasionally raises specific incidences of waste or corruption, but this falls far short of the structural waste and inefficiency of this political union. Apart from the sporadic interest demonstrated by certain sections of the media, the British people remain oblivious to the staggering waste of the EU. Brave whistleblowers such as former Commission Chief Accountant Marta Andreasen or Assistant Auditor Paul Van Buitenenen are sidelined and silenced, allowing these practices to freely continue.

The endemic corruption that is merely hinted at in the press cover foreign holidays, luxury housing, and security equipment. Entire cities are accused of inflating rents to benefit from merely having Parliamentary buildings in their country. For thirteen years the European Court of Auditors has refused to sign off accounts that they know are riddled with misunderstandings and mistakes at best, and downright frauds at worst. Would anybody in their right mind keep giving more and more money each year to an organisation that hasn't had its accounts signed off by auditors for 13 years? Would the government ever recommend giving more and more money to any other organisation in that situation; of course not ... so why should we with the EU?

Conclusion

The indictments against the EU as outlined above are devastating. It is a failed economic system which costs the British tax payer and British business billions. If Britain is to remain competitive in the 21st Century, if we are to continue to attract investment and win business, then we will need to start by freeing ourselves from this stifling political union. With the emerging economies of Asia and Eastern Europe it is not a time for uncompetitive protection rackets and inflexible economic and political rules. Business is global and if we are to compete then we must be too. The barriers of nation states are of much less relevance than they once were. On any given day someone can operate a business from their living room in Doncaster and trade with an artisan in Jakarta online. Government must reflect this with a light regulatory touch and the main impediment to this is the EU.

The credit crunch and the sight of further economic woes ahead will focus people's minds on the economics of the issue. When they have to make cut backs in their daily lives, they will be less sympathetic about a body which receives more of our national income than our Armed Forces. When the Government looks for funds to increase spending on health or education or even looks to ease the burden by lowering taxes, the EU pot presents huge potential for funds. We built our wealth as a country as world traders; and our future economic prosperity depends on trading with countries like China and India, and even with emerging economies in South America, Africa and the Middle East, economic power houses which were never considered as such when we joined the EU. It does not depend on being part of a backward looking, inward facing protection racket which the EU has become.

Europhiles try to caricature those of us who wish to leave the EU as out of date 'Little Englanders'; however, it is they who are out of date 'Little Europeans'. We have to adapt to a new global economic environment. When asked why I think we should leave the EU, I always think back to Bill Clinton in his 1992 US Presidential campaign, when he said 'it's the economy stupid".

Vo Phuong Mai Le, Patrick Minford and Eric Nowell

Measuring the Economic Costs and Benefits of EU Membership

Introduction

In this chapter we set out the costs that face the UK through its continued membership of the EU. We focus first on protectionism in trade, where the EU is supposedly in favour of competition and free trade, but where many are surprised when they see the extent of covert protection and we then consider other areas, briefly because they are better known.

Although protection is a word that refers primarily to trade. But at the heart of the political economy of the current 'sick men of Europe' (Germany, France and Italy) lies the fear of unemployment; so protection also extends to the labour market and to the welfare system designed to buy off the unemployed. In the labour market this protection covers limits on hours (designed to share work around), strong powers for unions, minimum wages, high unemployment benefits of potentially indefinite duration, workers' councils designed to stop job cuts, and much else. Because this protection is not enough to stop firms closing factories, if they could not be controlled somehow by local politicians, it has led to protection against take-over by foreign firms. It is now usual to hear worries about 'economic nationalism' breaking up the single market. Finally, we conclude with a discussion of what policy options are available to deal with these issues.

Protectionism in Manufactures

It is usually assumed that since the various GATT and WTO rounds have brought manufactured trade tariffs down across the world then EU protection is light in this sector. However, in the wake of retreating tariffs governments have been given wide discretion to reach agreements on trade quotas, to impose anti-dumping duties or to threaten them and negotiate pre-emptive price rises by importers. Furthermore, these processes reinforce the power of cartels to be established and to survive (see Messerlin, 1990); thus what starts as temporary protection against 'dumping' ends *as* the equivalent of a permanent tariff. Tariffs are transparent; but these measures are hard to monitor. While we know how many duties have been imposed and what trade agreements have been made, we cannot easily find out what pre-emptive measures have been taken, nor can we tell whether agreements which have notionally lapsed have done so effectively (especially if a cartel of producers has been implicitly allowed to perpetuate it, as noted above). Calculating the tariff-equivalent has to be done by looking at the price-raising effect of all the various interventions.

Fortunately there is data on prices now on a wide scale owing to the purchasing power parity calculations being done by international organisations. A pioneering study by Bradford (2003) of the price differentials between major OECD countries and their least cost OECD supplier suggested that the EU was substantially more protectionist in impact than the USA even though the latter has resorted to a similar number of anti-dumping duties. Averaging across the EU countries studied (Germany, Netherlands, Belgium and the UK) Bradford's figures, which are adjusted for distribution margins, tax and transport costs, are 40% tariff-equivalent for the EU against 16% for the US (see Table 1). These percentages are not much different if one looks at 1999 instead of his original 1993.

We have updated these figures to 2002 and extended the comparison more widely now that OECD membership has risen to include Korea in particular; we also cover all EU countries and have made an attempt to update the figures relative to China. The figures for the EU weighted average against lowest-cost non-EU trade partners are somewhat lower in 2002; the US, followed by Korea, are the lowest price alternatives. For the EU *as* a whole the 2002 figure comes out at 21%, against 30–40% on the narrower basis for the 1990s. For the US, which has also embraced policies of non-tariff protection, the 2002 figure is 6.5%, against middle double digit percentages in the 1990s.

If one attempts to include China, possible in a crude way for 2002, the implied protection estimates become much larger: 68% for the EU and 48% for the US. These numbers should be treated cautiously because we do not have prices in separate commodity categories for China and indeed China as yet does not produce for export a whole range of advanced products competing with western countries. The estimates rely on the manufacturing wage cost comparisons made by the US Bureau of Labour Statistics (which estimates Chinese manufacturing wage costs per hour at 7% of Korea's); we also assume that unskilled labour represents 30% of total costs, a percentage deliberately put on the low, cautious side. Nevertheless even these crude estimates indicate just how China's products are being kept at bay by various means, at least in finished form. Even as protection may be coming down on the products of the more developed emerging market countries such *as* Korea, we can see that it is rising in response to the penetration of Chinese products.

Table 1: Estimates of Tariff-Equivalents on Manufactured Goods Due to All Trade Barriers (%)[1]

	1990	1996	1999
Belgium	42	65	42
Germany	39	60	29
Italy	38	36	21
Netherlands	42	58	41
UK	41	41	50
US	16	14	15

Protectionism in Services

Throughout the UK debate on the EU it has been implicitly assumed that somehow the UK would gain from the Single Market in services. We are after all large net exporters of services. It might therefore seem that we must benefit from a customs union in services where we are net exporters just as we lose from one in food and manufactures where we are net importers.

However there is little parallel between the arrangements in food and manufacturing on the one hand and services on the other as there is no EU customs union in the vast mass of service sectors. Instead there is a patchwork of national protectionism, with the UK having relatively free mar-

---

1   Data are expenditure-weighted average ratios of imputed producer prices to the landed prices of goods from the country with the lowest level of price in the sample. *Source:* Bradford and Lawrence (2004).

kets within it. Some survey-based measures of the extent of protectionism across countries and industries are presented in Table 2.

Table 2: Survey Indicators of Service Barriers (Scale 0–6 From Least to Most Restrictive)[2]

	1978	1988	1998
UK	4.3	3.5	1.0
REU	5.4	5.1	3.4
US	4.0	2.5	1.4
Australia	4.5	4.2	1.6
Canada	4.2	2.8	2.4
Japan	5.2	3.9	2.9
Switzerland	4.5	4.5	3.9

The idea of the Single Market is to replace this patchwork with a free deregulated market across the EU; in principle this might be accompanied by some sort of barrier against non-EU service companies which could parallel the customs union in food and manufactures. However service markets within the EU are individually often penetrated by foreign (notably US) firms through FDI and other arrangements (especially in the UK which in practice has liberal access for US firms). Hence, once there was EU-wide deregulation it would inevitably allow free access to foreign firms lodged in national markets which cannot be practically distinguished from their national counterparts, indeed in many cases have merged with them.

Moreover EU-wide deregulation would, independently of such penetration, unleash strong competition between a large swathe of European national firms. Such competition would be deliberately boosted by EU competition authorities whose aim would of course and rightly be to ensure that prices were pushed down to competitive levels. Indeed, they

---

2   Simple averages of indicators for seven industries: gas, electricity, post, telecoms, air transport, railways and road freight. Depending on the industry the following dimensions have been included: barriers to entry, public ownership, market structure, vertical integration, price controls. For the REU, simple averages of individual EU countries (Nicoletti and Scarpetta, 2001).

would welcome any assistance in that regard from foreign competitors located in the EU.

Hence, the prospects for services sectors would appear to consist of two main possibilities:

a) the single market fails to make much progress at all in the face of strong producer vested interests in national markets; national protection thus remains as now;

b) it is highly successful in the end and produces competitive price levels.

The aim of the EU Commission appears to be to move steadily towards the second by the progressive dismantling of national service barriers.

What of a third option where the EU established a customs union in services? Under this the Single Market would establish EU-wide regulative barriers which put EU-wide prices somewhere between the most liberal and the most restricted regimes currently in place typically somewhere between the restricted Rest of the EU (REU) average and the current liberal UK regime. We find that such a service customs union would involve substantial transfers to the UK from the rest of the EU as UK service producers displaced REU home producers within the customs union. UK producers of services would receive higher than world prices, this amount on UK net exports being paid for by REU loss of tariff revenue. Such a transfer is unlikely to appeal to the REU majority within the EU's Council of Ministers. If protection is to fall, they would prefer it to fall without a customs union being formed.

Assessing the costs to the UK of these arrangements is rather easy in cases (a) and (b) and those between them. Under both of them the UK's leaving would make no difference on the assumption the UK's regime *is* already liberal. Under (a) the UK continues in its liberal regime if out just as when in; the REU too carry on *as* now. Under (b) if the UK stays in it is part of a competitive market; but if it left it would also enjoy a competitive market, exactly the same situation for its consumers and producers. Thus, contrary to the popular perception the UK faces no prospective gain from being within the EU Single Market in services; it would be as well off under free trade. On the other hand it is plain that other EU countries would gain considerably from the reduction of national protection of services since this would usher in competitive prices for consumers and either a rise of efficiency in service production or a displacement of resources out of services into other areas of greater productivity.

The Cost of EU Protection

In this section we use these estimates of protection to estimate their welfare implications for the UK and for the EU. For this, we use a CGE world model built by Minford et al. (2005) to generate estimates of changes in trade that result from this protection. Firstly, we examine the gains and losses were the UK to withdraw from various parts of the EU's trade arrangements (see Table 3), which is relevant to the decision of the UK to withdraw or not from individual parts of the trade treaties. We note that the UK has a strong incentive to withdraw whilst for the REU the UK's withdrawal creates marginally negative effects.

Table 3: Net Gains to the UK and to the REU if the UK Withdraws from Status Quo Trade Arrangements and Adopts Unilateral Free Trade (% of GDP)

	UK	REU
Agriculture	+0.3	-0.06
Basic manufacturing	+1.4	-0.06
Hi-tech manufacturing	+1.6	-0.1
Traded services		—
Total	+3.3	-0.22

We can also ask whether the UK and REU have any incentive to liberalise EU markets and move to free trade, with the UK remaining a member of these common arrangements. For this we create Table 4 of net gains and losses for the UK and the REU, comparing a post-liberalisation situation with the assumed benchmark.

Here we can see that there is a strong incentive on welfare grounds for the REU to liberalise. Notice, however, that if we want to know what the sum total is of doing all these things together we have to re-examine the estimates under that precise assumption. In practice UK withdrawal would occur across all the areas of trade; to leave one area would probably not be negotiable. Essentially you must 'leave or not leave'; having left, certain treaty areas might be restorable under a completely new relationship (see Table 5).

Table 4: Net Gains to the UK and to the REU if the EU Replaces Status Quo Trade Arrangements with Unilateral Free Trade (% of GDP)

	UK	REU	REU[3]
Agriculture	+0.3	-0.03	
Basic manufacturing	+0.8	+0.54	+0.6
Hi-tech manufacturing	+1.4	+1.5	+1.6
Traded services	+0.2	+1.3	+1.3
Total	+2.7	+3.3	+3.5

Table 5: UK and the REU Simultaneously Move to Free Trade

	UK	REU	REU[4]
Sum of partial effects	+2.7%	+3.3%	+3.5%
CGE full estimate	+17%	+14%	+14.2%

The gain of welfare to the UK here is dramatically larger at 17 percent (this amount is not greatly affected by whether the REU simultaneously liberalises or not). What is going on is that with agricultural prices at home greatly lowered by the elimination of the CAP tariffs, land prices drop substantially (26%) *as* demand for land in agriculture contracts sharply, and land is switched into traded services and non-traded activity (with the implicit permission of the planning authorities). These latter two sectors are therefore able to expand considerably: services by 35%, non-traded by 15%. Notice that both agricultural output and manufacturing fall by about a quarter. One may legitimately have doubts about the political feasibility of this solution, which is why we do not use it as our central estimate. However, it does indicate that, in the presence of some planning flexibility, the central estimate we have used, based on partial substitution effects only, could be a significant underestimate with how much so depending naturally on the extent of such planning flexibility.

---

3   REU if UK has already gone to free trade; this is column 2 plus transfer effects (these are already eliminated by UK liberalisation)

4   REU if UK has already liberalised does not include liberalisation of services

In this case of the EU as a whole, liberalising services alone in the first step, we have not attempted to assess using our CGE model. The reason is that the outcome depends on a complex of factors, not merely the drop in general external protection but also the role of inward investment in services, reconstituting local suppliers with the help of external expertise. An example would be the effect of the liberalisation of airlines on airline provision by continental European airlines; this has resulted in a steep drop in prices but also a surge in domestic operators, drawing on the experience of low-cost airlines from outside the European continent such as Easyjet. Thus, based on such an example, one might expect liberalisation to strengthen local service providers through competition and expand the market. Our CGE model assumes that competition already exists, albeit at high prices, and that the industry's structure is given; both assumptions are unlikely to hold.

With the liberalisation of services EU protection then becomes identical with that of the UK, consisting entirely of the EU's external tariff-equivalents. We can now assess the effects of removing protection in an orthodox way. Thus, turning to the liberalisation of trade in the EU the effects are naturally highly similar to those in the UK as is the rise in welfare at 14% (or 14.2% if the UK has already liberalised by leaving.) Again we find that there is the same large drop in land prices and a switch of land use into services (up by 35%) and non-traded industries (up by 10%). Politically, as in the UK, this raises questions of realism, in particular with planning consent. Planning is a highly complex phenomenon in the REU, differing both across countries and across regions within countries. On the other hand, given the huge pressures to create employment under the REU conditions of generally high unemployment, the popular pressure might be greater for liberalisation. The essential point we make here is not that the full simulation should be believed but that it reminds us that the central case calculation based on partial substitution effects alone is a minimum which could be added to depending on the extent of land liberalisation.

Assessing the Overall Economic Costs and Benefits

In this final section we briefly consider the broader economic costs and benefits of membership of the EU (see also Cecchini, 1988 and NIESR, 2000) from the UK's viewpoint although the argument can be generalised to other EU members with suitable data. There is every reason to believe that the EU as a whole is being damaged, in particular by excessive social intervention, which has caused both unemployment and slow growth. In considering the economics of the EU, we interpret the thrust of future EU policy in the light of recent policy actions by the EU (for example the decision by France and Germany to scrap reform of the CAP) and of the general thrust (in favour of protectionism and social rights) of proposed new policies, such as those recently envisaged in the draft constitution and its successor the Lisbon Treaty.

Using the Liverpool Model of the UK economy we have examined what might be the effects of these social policies, which amount to the reversal of the reforms brought in by the UK government from 1979. On the assumption of rather moderate changes (a minimum wage raised to 50% of male median wages, union power restored to mid-1980s levels, social cost rises worth 20% of current wages), the model predicts that they would raise unemployment by 5.7% — that is 1.8 million — and cost 6.4% in reduced output. It could of course be either more or less depending on just how extensively this harmonisation was pursued; but the draft constitution indicated clearly enough that what we have seen so far — including the working time directive, the social chapter and the works council directives — is just a beginning.

A further (`bail-out') cost comes from potentially insolvent state pensions on the Continent. Extensive estimates were made of these pension deficits in an OECD study in the middle 1990s. Recent attempts (eg OECD, 2001) to recompute these prospects suggest little change. If we take these 1995 OECD projections as illustrative at least, the deficits projected are: for Germany 10% of GDP by 2030; for Italy about the same; and for France a little bit less. Add up these deficits as a percentage of UK GDP, which is of similar size to each of these countries, and you come to some 30 percent. If the UK were to pay a quarter of that, for example via some federal system of burden-sharing, then the bill would be some 7% of GDP. Again, like harmonisation, the extent of this is rather uncertain; it could be a lot more or a lot less, depending on both the extent of reforms undertaken by these countries and the extent to which the progress of federalism enables burden-sharing between countries. But this is certainly a burden the UK does not want to risk sharing, at even a modest level.

Policy Options

The basic dilemma faced by the UK is that on the one hand it would gain from leaving the EU at this point in time, were EU policies to remain fixed and were a departing UK government to choose to pursue policies of market liberalisation and free trade; but that on the other hand EU policies are unlikely to remain fixed because the REU's own interests are the same as the UK's viz free trade and market liberalisation while there is also no real guarantee that UK governments will embrace free trade and market liberalisation. UK voters have traditionally been cautious about making large institutional leaps; the one exception was the decision to join the EEC as it then was in the early 1970s but then it was not seen a a leap, rather as an adoption of a limited and purely economic relationship. The EU framework has evolved greatly since then, very largely because of the adoption ironically at the UK's insistence of the 'Single Market' directives. These have been used to generate many of the costs enumerated above. But it needs to be understood that these 'costs' are computed on the assumption that the alternative is a UK run independently outside the EU on entirely free market principles; if that alternative is not available, then some 'costs' evaporate and indeed some 'benefits' appear.

Forecasting how institutions will develop is a hazardous business. One can recognise that many functions exercised by the EU, such as preventing unfair subsidies to 'national champions', are beneficial compared with the likely independent national alternative. National politicians are only too prone to give in to home vested interests when existing industries and jobs are threatened. The free market in capital and labour also brings benefits to the UK which would be unlikely on its own to pursue such a liberal regime. The current EU Commission is in fact anxious to promote freer trade but is held back by opposition from powerful EU member governments, notably that of France. Yet ironically French citizens stand to gain *as* much as UK citizens from free trade; so one might reasonably assume that eventually some political group would rise up and form a coalition of French votes in favour of just that.

There are policies the UK could adopt within the EU that would strengthen the hand of those pushing for free trade and other reforms in the EU. However, one of the problems is that the losers from reforms are not easily compensated in an EU context; hence national governments fight against EU reforms that would damage their own vocal vested interests. Yet a useful use of EU collective tax revenues would be to help adjustment by such vested interests. In a quiet way this is happening in agriculture, as farmers are being paid to adapt. But there the EU has revenues that can be used fairly flexibly. The UK could press for other EU money to be useable in a more flexible way: some of the Objective 1–3 money for example might be reserved for this purpose. An incentive could thus be created for governments to be more reform-orientated as they would receive more EU money to help them compensate losers.

Another way of assisting from inside the EU would be to improve public education in matters of the economy. Many REU politicians and certainly many voters simply do not understand how an economy is improved by market forces when in the short term some industries and jobs are 'lost'. The UK government could help to promote a 'mission for economic education' within the EU.

One of the UK policies that has been enormously successful in changing the climate of opinion in the EU has been enlargement. The new joiners are generally in favour of reform. They are potential allies in the policies suggested above. Further enlargement would strengthen us and them still more very probably.

All the above is true but the Lisbon Treaty has altered the terms of the discussion. It is a retrograde development because it gives much bigger powers to EU judges to make new law according to 'fundamental rights' that amount in parts to a socialist shopping list. The UK government's failure to alter the document in a free market direction or else to block it is a setback for good economic policy. Should this Treaty go through in spite of the Irish referendum rejection then a new and more threatening environment will be born in the EU. This creates both a necessity and an opportunity for the UK to redefine its relationship with the EU, in the form of one that retains areas of EU competence where it promotes free trade and competition, but draws a line in other areas of intervention. The objective should be for the UK to continue as a member but to remain outside new integration of the form mandated by the Lisbon Treaty. Given the Irish concerns (shared by far more countries than the shotgun ratification process has suggested) a way will have to be found to accommodate divergent views about the EU; the UK should be active in promoting the 'new variety' that will enable both a wide EU membership and progress in market reform, while allowing those who want closer political links to have them in addition.

Conclusion

In this chapter we have attempted to estimate the costs, both to the UK and the Rest of the EU (REU), of the EU's protectionist trade policies in agriculture, manufacturing and services. Contrary to the popular impression that the EU is a mechanism for creating a 'competitive single market', it turns out that the EU is levying costs in wasted resources of the order of 3% of GDP (or under favourable planning assumptions a large multiple of this) by protecting its industries from world competition. These costs apply to UK and REU citizens more or less alike and on a similar scale. The economic damage created by the EU does not, however, stop there: because of the widespread welfare lobbies within member countries on the Continent, the majority coalition within the EU has pressed for social protection and spending to be 'harmonised' at a fairly high level. It also faces a prospective pensions crisis, in the sense that it cannot be assumed necessary cuts in pensions promises or rises in the taxes to pay for them will be politically feasible. Thus those member states whose pension plans are affordable and whose social regulations are the least burdensome on business, face the prospect of a potentially severe burden from the pensions problems elsewhere in the EU and from the pressure of harmonisation. We have been able to quantify this potential cost for the UK; but it is also a real threat to many other members, such as those recently joining from the East.

In summary, the EU brings gains as well as costs, with UK citizens gaining from the wide market in goods, services, people and capital that is opening up, guaranteed by EU institutions. However, in the future the UK could help to promote reform in the EU in various ways, but the Lisbon Treaty if it *is* passed will give the forces of reaction far more power, and of an undesirable sort. The main policy conclusion for the UK is that it should use the opportunity presented by the Irish No to inject more flexibility into the EU's structure. The UK should participate in the EU as a process for economic market opening but not for other purposes.

Matthew Elliott

The Effects of the EU on British Tax Policy

Introduction

Membership of the European Union (EU) limits British tax policy in many, critical ways. Significant policy choices are closed to us as they would contradict with major decisions made at the supranational level, particularly with Value Added Tax (VAT) and import duties. The EU's intrusions into tax policy are strengthened by the European Court of Justice (ECJ), which favours less flexible interpretations of the various directives. Over the coming years the EU seems likely to gain an even greater say over tax policy. European politicians and officials frequently argue for greater tax harmonisation and new EU taxes.

These limitations on our tax policy have numerous harmful consequences. The weakness of democratic accountability at the EU level means that tax policy is too often formed without reference to the preferences of ordinary people. Our ability to encourage behaviours we see as having broader social merit, through tax breaks, is limited. Innovative tax reforms, that might have broad social and political benefits, are unable to make headway.

VAT

Across the EU there is a minimum rate of VAT set at 15 per cent (European Commission, 2008). Some countries set their rate higher than that; the UK rate is 17.5 per cent. There are reduced rates allowed on certain products, such as domestic fuel and power which must be at least 5 per cent. Some exemptions are also allowed; books are not liable for VAT in the UK, for example (HM Revenue and Customs, 2008).

This leaves very little room for manoeuvre if a country wishes to make changes to its VAT system. The first thing this clearly rules out is major cuts in the headline VAT rate. This may not seem like much of a policy restraint as many countries have moved towards taxes on consumption, rather than income or capital, in recent decades. A move towards consumption taxation is felt to deliver superior economic performance by attracting international investment (KPMG, 2007). That has meant that there is relatively little impetus to prioritise cutting VAT rates.

There are, however, two reasons this situation could change. Firstly, there could be some change in the weight of evidence over which kinds of taxes are economically preferable. For example, the European Central Bank recently estimated the effect of the size of government on economic growth and one finding they came to was that indirect taxes such as VAT have a particularly large effect on growth (Afonso and Furceri, 2008).

Secondly, the economic analysis that direct taxes on income and capital are more economically harmful may not change, but it might be felt that the distributional effects make cutting VAT a priority. VAT, like most consumption taxes, imposes a particularly heavy burden on the poor. In Britain, those from the bottom quintile, by income, pay 11 per cent of their gross income in VAT whereas those in the top quintile pay 4.5 per cent (Office for National Statistics, 2008). The benefits system compensates for this difference; but it would be legitimate to argue that taking such a large share of the income of the poorest in tax is still a decidedly bad idea. The benefits system is unreliable, wasteful and often traps people into dependency, making it harder for them to improve their standard of living. Cutting VAT to below the 15 per cent minimum could be a relatively efficient means with which to improve the conditions of the poor, but it is not an option available under current EU law.

Another set of policies ruled out by the inflexibility of EU rules on VAT is in the provision of exemptions to encourage the consumption of particular socially useful goods. Member states cannot easily carve out new exemptions that can encourage socially useful consumption. For instance, the Federation of Master Builders and the TaxPayers' Alliance have, since early 2008, been running a joint campaign for a cut in the VAT levied on home improvements and repairs. At the moment VAT is charged on home improvements but not on new build, encouraging people to build new houses instead of improving existing ones. Improvements and repairs to existing homes are less aesthetically disruptive and energy intensive than building new ones. Charging VAT on home improvements also creates opportunities for unscrupulous 'cowboy builders' who avoid the tax. As a cut in the VAT on home improvements would make it cheaper to have energy saving measures installed it would also help the fight against fuel poverty (The Federation of Master Builders, 2008). Targeted cuts in VAT could support such social objectives but cannot be put in place without specific changes to EU law.

A harmonised VAT regime makes root and branch reform of consumption taxation impossible. This rules out policies such as the Local Sales Tax, billed as a potential replacement for VAT and Council Tax (Carswell, 2004). A Local Sales Tax aims to reduce Britain's fiscal centralisation in order to give local government a greater ability to make independent decisions.

Indeed, just 25 per cent of local government funding in the UK is derived from local sources, against 62 per cent in the United States and 66 per cent in France and Germany (Carswell, 2004). This fiscal dependence on the centre reduces the ability of local government to act independently. Central government can ring fence funds, impose statutory obligations and set out how they expect local authorities to deliver services with the implicit or explicit threat of financial sanction if local government does not co-operate. A local sales tax is a fairer way of providing councils with fiscal independence than increasing council tax or creating some new poll tax, more practical than a genuinely local income tax, and possible to collect on a local level unlike value added tax. This could be a genuinely important tax reform, addressing broader problems with the structure of British government, but again it is ruled out by EU rules.

Import Duties

While member states collect import duties their rates and base are determined by the EU and revenues are handed over as Traditional Own Resources (EU Commission, 2004). The tariff structure is complex but constitutes a significant premium on the price of importing a wide range of goods. For example, at the time of writing the import duty on a walking stick is 2.7 per cent of its value. A spacecraft faces a tariff of 4.2 per cent of its value. A live bull of the Schwyz, Fribourg or spotted Simmental breeds carries a duty of 14.2 per cent of its value, plus €93.10 per hectokilogram in weight (Business Link, 2008).

The EU is a customs union, rather than a free trade area, which means that it imposes a common tariff on imported goods. This prevents Britain embracing free trade. New Zealand has, since the mid-eighties, not just eliminated almost all subsidies but most import duties. Apart from a free trade deal with Australia these moves to reduce protection have been made unilaterally and have therefore gone far beyond what is required by the World Trade Organisation (The Economist, 1999).

There is good reason to think significant moves toward free trade might be politically feasible in Britain, where attitudes to free trade are relatively positive. A YouGov poll in March 2008 found that 52 per cent of people had a positive attitude to free trade, agreeing with the statement 'Free trade is generally a good thing because consumers benefit from cheaper goods and services, we can sell more abroad and, in the end, our economy is better off.' By contrast, just 30 per cent had a negative view, agreeing with the statement 'Free trade is often harmful because too many workers here in Britain are liable to lose their jobs to foreign competition, and our economy suffers', whilst 19 per cent of people did not answer the question (YouGov, 2008). Both main political parties profess to a commitment to free trade. Prime Minister Gordon Brown told the Chamber of Commerce in Delhi that he desires a 'globalisation that is founded on open markets, free trade, flexibility and investment in the skills of people and in a new relationship between rich and poor countries working together' (Brown, 2008). David Cameron told business leaders in Davos that 'We must be clear about our position. Yes to free trade. No to protection' (Cameron, 2008).

If Britain could move substantially towards free trade there would be significant benefits. Prices would fall for consumers, particularly on food products, economic distortion would be reduced and many poor people in developing countries would be able to make a better living exporting to Britain. Falling food prices would be particularly beneficial for poorer British families. The poorest ten percent of families spend 12 per cent of their income on food and non-alcoholic drink whereas the average family spends 6 per cent and the richest ten per cent under 4 per cent of their income on food (Office for National Statistics, 2008).

The EU has shown some willingness to adjust duties in order to ease the pressure on families caused by high prices for basics like food. In response to severe rises in food prices driven by worldwide subsidies for biofuels (Chakrabortty, 2008), cereal import duties were suspended in December 2007 and are likely to remain suspended untill June 2009 (European Parliament, 2008). However, with decisions made centrally there is clearly the possibility of a conflict of priorities between member states, where another member state desires greater protection and Britain is facing significant social or economic costs from high prices. In that scenario import duties could make significant price shocks to the British economy significantly worse.

The ECJ

The European Court of Justice (ECJ) can intervene in member states' tax policy. There are two key mechanisms: Interpreting directives on taxation, such as the VAT directives, and ruling on whether tax laws violate broader EU principles.

The ECJ's interpretations of directives on VAT play an important role in determining the flexibility that countries have within the harmonised system. For example, in 2008 the Court ruled that an Italian plan for a form of VAT amnesty constituted a failure to fulfil obligations under the VAT directives (ECJ, 2008). Such judgements reduce the freedom of member states to decide how they should enforce VAT and constitute a considerable strengthening of the EU's role in tax policy.

Many of the cases that have strengthened EU control are brought by the Commission against member states. ECJ case law since 1997 reveals that the Commission has won the vast majority of the cases that they have fought against member states[1] with 72 per cent of judgements in the Commission's favour, 24 per cent decided in favour of the member states and 3 per cent of cases ended with no clear victor. Most of the 9 judges on the ECJ are not tax experts, and in around 80 per cent of cases take the decision recommended by the Advocate General. The Advocate General, as part of the EU organisation, may be biased towards decisions taken at the EU level.

The ECJ is also charged with enforcing freedom of establishment and free movement of capital. It has the power to strike down any national tax law that breaches those principles, and already has done so in a number of cases. For example, the British Government is currently struggling to create new rules to avoid the double taxation of foreign profits (Teather, 2008) after losing a case to Cadbury Schweppes at the ECJ (ECJ, 2006). While the ECJ may have improved the final outcome in that case it is quite possible that the Government would have been forced to take the same decision itself anyway in order to prevent firms being forced to move to other countries that taxed their foreign profits more fairly. However, it would be preferable if these decisions were taken democratically.

New Proposals

There are a series of proposals that could increase the EU's role in tax policy dramatically in the coming years. For example, there are proposals for

---

1   Results based on searching the Curia database, http://curia.europa.eu/, for cases on taxation in which the Commission is a party.

a Common Consolidated Corporate Tax Base (CCCTB) that would establish a single set of rules for calculating a company's tax liability.

It has been suggested that the establishment of a CCCTB would be a
particular priority for the 2008 French Presidency. It appears likely that
attempts at corporate tax harmonisation will be delayed following Ireland's rejection of the Lisbon Treaty as they imperil its progress by alarming Irish voters concerned for their country's tax sovereignty (Sovereign
Group, 2008). However, this delay could easily be temporary, and efforts
to harmonise the tax base could resume, particularly if the Lisbon Treaty
comes into force or is abandoned. The momentum for an EU corporate tax
could well be strengthened by Britain's slow progress in cutting the tax.
This might plausibly shift Britain from opposition to support for corporate tax harmonisation as British governments try to prevent corporate
tax revenues being eroded.

A CCCTB would be likely to lead to higher average tax rates. Profits
would be apportioned to different countries artificially, and sales by destination would be likely to feature heavily in the formula apportioning
profits. Eastern European countries that tend to supply the Western economies would lose out and, as Eastern European corporate tax rates are
generally lower, businesses would face higher overall bills. This would
undermine the competitiveness of EU economies and lead to investment
being diverted outside Europe (O'Sullivan, 2007).

Businesses have backed the idea of a CCCTB on the basis that the
scheme remains optional but that is not likely to remain the case. The
point of the scheme is supposed to be to simplify the tax system and running two systems in parallel hardly advances that objective. The Commission has already suggested that the CCCTB only initially be optional
(EUR-Lex, 2006). Beyond that, harmonising the tax base is a necessary
first step on the road to tax rate harmonisation. France and Germany have
already pressed for the EU to go beyond the CCCTB and harmonise corporate tax rates (Castle, 2004). That would undermine the tax competition
that has brought down rates across the developed world and would
endanger the competitiveness of EU economies.

Furthermore, there have been a number of proposals for direct EU
taxes. The Austrian Chancellor, Wolfgang Schüssel, has argued for a tax
on flights or short-term financial transactions (Castle, 2006). Alain
Lamassoure, a French MEP, has even argued for a tax on mobile phone
text messages and e-mails (Libbenga, 2006). The Commission, in a 2004
report, argued that tax-based own resources would help form stronger
links between EU citizens and the EU institutions as well as enhancing the

transparency of the EU budget. They propose taxing energy consumption, corporate income or existing national VAT bases (which are already harmonised, as discussed above).

An EU tax would almost certainly lead to reduced accountability for EU spending. There are already problems with a lack of scrutiny and transparency in the EU's spending. The European Court of Auditors has refused to sign off the EU's accounts for thirteen years in a row, citing numerous accounting errors and possible cases of fraud (BBC, 2007). The lack of genuine European democracy means that what little accountability there is generally comes from member states' governments. Collecting taxes directly from citizens would weaken accountability, as governments would be bypassed.

An EU tax is also likely to lead to higher overall taxes. The EU would feel less risk from tax competition that erodes the revenues of individual states that push up taxes on mobile economic activity. That competition would still exist, particularly if the new EU tax were on corporate income, but would be less politically obvious, as all member states would suffer together.

Unless the tax is a simple one, or hypothecated from collections by member states, it may also require a new collection apparatus, which would involve considerable expense and further increase the burden on taxpayers. Beyond that, there is little reason to think that national politicians would entirely use the relief resulting from reduced contributions to the EU to reduce taxation; a large portion may be used to boost spending, leading to a net increase in taxation (Caesar, 2001).

EU Commissioner Michaela Schreyer has argued that an EU tax might resolve the debate over states that are net contributors or net receivers from the EU budget and lessen criticism of the EU (Caesar, 2001). Britons who do not want to see greater EU integration might not see that as a good idea. Beyond that, it is unlikely it would be practical to collect the tax in a way that would not make establishing the contributions coming from each nation an easy task (Mutén, 2001).

Conclusion

The EU has a considerable influence on British tax policy. The VAT regime is largely controlled by the EU, with member states allowed to vary rates above a mandated minimum but little flexibility beyond that. Import duties are set as part of the EU's rules and member states have no ability to vary their base or rate at all. The ECJ is ever present to enforce a rigid interpretation of these rules, leaving little room for member states to make allowances for local conditions. New proposals would further extend the EU's reach into British tax policy in several harmful ways.

Firstly, ceding control over tax policy to a supranational organisation has a number of important consequences. Ordinary people have almost no ability to democratically affect vital decisions. They have to take, for example, high rates of value added tax as a given. There is no European demos that can hold the EU to account and national voters are unable to control significant areas of tax policy. This is a violation of the democratic principle.

Secondly, Britain is unable to adopt new, innovative tax policies. For example, if Britain were to follow New Zealand's example and become the first major economy to scrap import duties we could be a powerful example for the rest of the world. The effect on the worldwide progress of free trade and, as a result, prosperity at home and abroad could be dramatic. That option is not open to us thanks to the strictures of EU membership. On a smaller scale, the need to have a Value Added Tax prevents us adopting a Local Sales Tax and making local government fiscally independent. Our centralised politics is being locked in place by the EU's restrictions on our tax policy.

Thirdly, our tax policy cannot respond flexibly to new conditions. Both VAT and import duties set at the European levels have a significant impact on our ability to reduce taxes that push up the prices of essentials and social goods. An important example is the charging of VAT on home improvements, encouraging the building of new homes rather than the renovation of old ones.

Finally, new EU taxes and corporate tax harmonisation threaten to increase the total tax bill. This would leave consumers and businesses worse off. It would also leave European nations less able to compete with the rest of the world, hurting economic performance, future prosperity and tax revenues.

Our ability to form flexible, innovative tax policy, and keep down the overall bill, is hampered by our involvement in the EU. Taxes may be one of life's certainties, but setting our own tax policy would give us a much better chance of making them less of a burden.

Brian Hindley

British Trade Policy Outside the EU

Introduction

Outside the EU, British options for trade policy towards non-EU countries will depend on the form of its relations with the remaining EU. Broadly speaking, three forms of trade relations between a departed Britain and the remaining EU are possible. They are:

a) no formalised bilateral trade relations, just the WTO;

b) a free trade area; and

c) a customs union.

I first discuss the legal, economic and political issues raised by these alternatives, then turn to choosing between them.

No Formalised Bilateral Trade Relations

The first option is attractive to those extreme Euro-sceptics who want institutional forms that are utterly separate from the EU. Institutional forms are one thing, however, and trade flows another. EU tariffs are currently low on average, at least on most non-agricultural goods; and while that situation continues, a large fraction of British trade (currently around one half) will be with the EU whether Britain is in or out of the EU, or whether formal bilateral trade agreements are in place.

To some observers, the brute fact of EU-British trade flows suggests that a Britain departed from the EU should try to create a formal bilateral trade relationship with the remaining EU. If trade between the two is going to be large in any event, they say, why not put in place institutions that facilitate it? Moreover, substantial trade flows are inevitably accompanied by trade disputes and a formal relationship between Britain and the remaining EU might offer a faster means of resolving disagreements than is provided by the WTO and might even reduce the number of disputes.

Others, concerned with worst cases, observe that to leave the EU without securing bilateral ties is in effect to rely on the WTO for legal protection in trade matters. That, they say, is risky. They regard the WTO as being too weak to offer much help against aggressive actions of the EU especially a vengeful EU, or one that wishes to impress upon remaining members that resignation is expensive.

Moreover, they add, continuing in worst-case mode, the world economy might suffer cataclysmic change. Low EU tariffs are not necessarily forever. If the world found itself in economic crisis, and/or the WTO collapsed, protectionist sentiment always latent in the continental EU could lead to major increases in EU trade barriers. A Britain without bilateral ties to the remaining EU could then find itself out in the cold, without favoured access to EU markets or to any others. Hence, they say, the diplomacy of a departing (or departed) Britain should aim to create a formalised trade relationship with the EU: both to guarantee trade peace with the EU and as an insurance policy against hard times.

On a more positive note, the freedoms of movement within the EU (of goods, services, capital and persons) are, for many in Britain, its best feature. Such persons would wish to maintain as much of these freedoms as possible; and it is difficult to see how this could be done without a trade treaty between Britain and the EU.

The threatening possibilities noted above, also produce other responses. A Britain without a bilateral trade relationship with the EU would be free to establish formal trading relationships with powers other than the EU. The idea that Britain could form a free trade area with the United States has a following; as does the idea of a free trade area or customs union with the Commonwealth or some part of it. Some see the possibility of a relationship with the US and the Commonwealth — the notion of an Anglo-sphere.

A UK-EU Free Trade Area

If a departed Britain opts for formal bilateral ties with the remaining EU, the trade aspect of those ties will take the form either of a free trade area (FTA) or a customs union. A principal difference between these two arrangements is that a custom union has a common external tariff, adhered to by all of its members; while members of an FTA are free (at least formally) to set their own tariffs.

Among those who believe that Britain should preserve some form of formalised trading relationship with the EU, an FTA finds supporters. 'In an FTA', they say, 'we can have free trade with the EU *and* the freedom to set our own tariffs—especially on agricultural goods—*and* to join other FTAs'.

The term 'free-trade area', though, is misleading on several levels. In this context, it is wrong to simply *assume* that the range of goods that would be freely traded between Britain and the EU under an FTA would be the same as the range freely traded under current arrangements. That will depend on the negotiations that lead to an FTA; but their outcome is quite unlikely to mimic current trading relationships.

An FTA needs 'rules of origin'. These are rules that tell customs officials in one member when a good arriving at the national border should be deemed to be the product of another member—and therefore admitted free of import duty—and when it should be treated as the product of a non-member and therefore charged duty.

Rules of origin are complicated; but the mere fact that a good has some British content is not sufficient to make it 'British'. Moreover, the WTO has no jurisdiction over rules of origin within FTAs—the EU can make up the rules it applies without hindrance from that source. Finally, most FTAs in which the EU is involved impose quotas on exports to the EU—especially on agricultural exports from the FTA partner to the EU.

It is not true by definition, therefore, that an FTA between the EU and Britain would give Britain free trade with the EU, or even a close approximation of free trade. That depends upon the outcome of negotiations between Britain and the EU. Were something like free trade with the remaining EU available, a UK-EU FTA would be attractive. But it is far from clear that such an agreement would be on offer.

A UK-EU Customs Union

Nor is there any guarantee that a UK-EU customs union would continue free trade in all goods. The WTO (GATT Article XXIV) requires tariffs and other restrictions on trade between partners to be abolished on 'substantially all' trade; but usage—and particularly the usage of the EU—has pushed that condition quite far in the direction of 'most'.

A UK-EU customs union, moreover, would restrict British policy towards the non-EU world in ways that options (a) and (b) do not. In particular, membership of a customs union would prevent Britain from joining preferential trading arrangements with other countries—unless the whole of the EU did so. Britain could not enter an FTA with the US, or with the Commonwealth, for example at least, not without leaving the UK-EU customs union. Furthermore, Britain would have to join preferential trading relationships that the EU joined. Britain's options, in other words, would not in this respect change from current arrangements.

Moreover, in such a relationship, the economic weight of the remaining EU makes it likely that the UK's role in the determination of tariffs or in choice of trading partners would be minor.

Choosing a New Form of Trade Relationship

There is no uniquely best choice among these three situations. Different observers will stress different features of each to arrive at a preference for any one of the three.

A sensible place to start thinking about the issue, however, is first principles. In the first place, it is necessary to recall the issue at stake. Whatever Europhiles allege, Euro-scepticism is not Europhobia. The core objection to the EU is not that it is European, but that it seeks to create a state or quasi-state that would incorporate Britain. If Britain does in fact leave the EU, it will most likely be to avoid absorption into such a European quasi-state.

Once that fate has been avoided, however, there is no reason why there should not be all manner of cooperation between a departed Britain and the remainder of the EU. Indeed, since much of British trade is likely to be with the EU, and since Britain has many interests in common with other states in its vicinity, most of which are in the EU, there is a very strong case for cooperating with the remaining EU

Oddly, however, that strong case does not automatically extend to trade, at least so far as the economics of the issue is concerned. Despite widespread enthusiasm for customs unions and free trade areas, economic analysis gives no ground for any presumption that countries participating in such arrangements are economically better off as a result. Indeed, possibilities of FTAs or customs unions underlie much discussion in this area, and are often talked about as though they have no downside. But they do.

The downside is that such arrangements distort choices among the origin of goods. Goods from partners in a customs union pay no duties when they are imported: similar goods from countries outside the customs union do pay duty. Thus, a widget from a fellow EU member, say France, and a widget from the US may both cost £100 in Britain. But if the real price of the US widget is £75, if the rest of its £100 UK price is a £25 import duty that goes either to the British government or the EU, purchase of a widget from the US gets us the widget and £25 of governmental revenue;

whereas a widget bought from France just gets the widget. The UK price is the same, but the French widget costs more.

If Britain charged the same tariff on widgets from all foreign sources, US widgets (at the prices in the example above) would be purchased in preference to French widgets; and the real resources that Britain expends on importing any quantity of widgets would be less. On this account, Britain would be better off outside the EU, or any other customs union or FTA, than inside.

Of course, there are benefits to being a member of a customs union; but in popular discussion, the putative export advantages of belonging to a customs union completely overwhelm this distortion on the import side, in a way that has no intellectual justification. The economic benefits of FTAs or customs unions in discussion of British options outside the EU, or in the widespread notion that Britain has no options other than the EU, are greatly exaggerated. There is no evidence that Britain has made substantial economic gains from its membership of the EU customs union, especially when the Common Agricultural Policy is taken into account, a gross example of the import distortions noted above.

Economic gains by themselves, therefore, are unlikely to make a compelling economic case for joining any FTA or a customs union. A case that is deemed to be compelling is likely to depend on politics or on circumstances left out of simple economic models. Politics, of course, has provided the central stated rationale for the EU. That rationale has been that European economic union would prevent a recurrence of war between France and Germany. The success of the EU is often proclaimed on the basis that no such war has occurred, which assumes, of course, that in the absence of the EU, there would have been. Opinions on the probability of war between France and Germany had the EU not come into existence are likely to differ. Most people would agree, however, that if the EU prevented war, it was worth it.

In terms of circumstances left out of the simple model, several propositions about states of the world were important in the brief earlier discussion in directing attention from one set of arrangements to another. They were that:

a)   the EU might be vengeful towards a departed Britain;

b)   the world might undergo cataclysmic change, so that a Britain without formal ties to a major trade bloc would find itself out in the cold; and that

c)   outside the EU or a customs union with the EU, Britain could seek to
      establish FTAs or customs unions with parts of the Commonwealth
      and/or the US.

Each of these is worth extended discussion.

EU Attitudes Towards a Departed Britain

Some in the remaining EU might be vengeful towards a departed Britain.
Such a feeling might be akin to religious difference, the hatred of the
orthodox for schismatics; but people who would be better off without
British competition, and anxious to block it, might also join in.

Two things are clear. The first is that the expression of such feelings in
policy would be inimical to the wider interests of both parties: both have
more to gain from cooperation than conflict. The second is that EU actions
that discriminated against Britain, as compared with other non-EU
sources of imports such as Japan and the US, would be illegal under the
WTO. There is therefore a solid and objective foundation that diplomacy
might use to build cooperation.

No doubt care should be taken, if possible, over the manner and timing of
Britain's departure. But a long campaign by the EU to make life in Britain
unpleasant seems unlikely and therefore should not have a heavy weight
in thinking about departure.

Britain Out in the Cold?

Were Britain shut out of EU markets that would be painful but not devastating. Were Britain shut out of the markets of all of the major economic
groupings in the world, that would be even more painful, but still not
devastating.

In the first place, if all of the major economic groupings in the world
went on a protectionist rampage, that would not bode well for the quality
life inside them; so that attractions of being inside would be much
reduced. In the second place, 'all of the major economic groupings in the
world' do not at the moment, and will not in the foreseeable future, cover
100 per cent of the world economy. For countries outside these blocs,
therefore, opportunities for beneficial trade would continue to exist, even
in the event of a relapse into 1930's style protectionism.

The likelihood of such a relapse, moreover, is open to question. At the
time of writing (April 2009), the world is in what is arguably its greatest
economic crisis since the 1930s. So far, however, the movement to protectionist policies has been at the margins, not at the centre of the policy of
any WTO member. If the current situation does not improve over several

years that position would certainly come under greater pressure; but there is at the moment no obvious cause for pessimism.

FTAs with the Commonwealth or with the US?

Attractive as it may be to some in Britain, the idea of FTAs with the US and/or the Commonwealth has two problems. One is whether such FTAs would in fact give rise to economic gains for Britain. The second is whether they are feasible — whether partnership with Britain offers sufficient benefits to partners to interest them in the idea. Unfortunately, neither question can be answered with a clear positive.

The United States International Trade Commission, 2000, calculates costs and benefits of an FTA between NAFTA (North American Free Trade Area), which contains the US, Canada and Mexico. Naturally, its primary focus was on the effects for the US; but it calculated impacts on the UK in passing and found them to be small. The USITC (2000) calculates the impact on the UK in two situations:

(a) Britain remains part of the EU and joins NAFTA; and

(b) Britain leaves the EU and joins NAFTA.

It concludes: 'The effects of the contemplated FTA [on] each country's GDP are very small'. About situation (a) it says that: 'the UK's GDP increases by less than one tenth of one per cent ......' (p.xiv); and about situation (b): '... UK GDP falls by 0.02 per cent' (p. xv). There is, in other words, no great economic benefit to Britain from joining the US, Canada and Mexico in NAFTA.

If Britain left the EC, of course, Commonwealth trading links that were broken in 1972 could be restored. Commercial relations with the UK, though, will not fill the sails of a revitalised commonwealth, as some hope, the UK market is simply not big enough. Moreover, of course, Britain obtains the major benefit to it of such an arrangement (e.g. the potential of cheaper food supply) merely by leaving the CAP.

Conclusion

My own conclusion is that the downsides of going it alone are probably exaggerated, and that at least one aspect of the upside, the possibility of trade deals with other countries, is also probably exaggerated. Going it alone is feasible.

Britain's interests are so heavily correlated with those of other countries in the EU, however, that should British departure from the EU be seriously contemplated, real effort should go into maintaining a situation in which cooperation between Britain and the remaining EU is possible. Britain should inspect with care what the EU is willing to put on the negotiating table. So far as the trade aspects of departure from the EU are concerned, there is no reason to be dogmatic about what we will and will not accept.

Brent Cameron

Building the Transatlantic Bridge

The Potential for Canada-UK Trade

Introduction

When most people refer to the 'global economy', it conjures up images of
an orderly and organised system of trade and commerce, with set rules
and understood conventions. While not a wild free-for-all indicative of
the American Old West, we must appreciate that the global economy does
not possess the same level of structure and regulation as we expect in
national economies. Indeed, the global economy is in a state of evolution.
New rules are being established, new partnerships are being forged, and
new markets are coming into the mainstream. What commentators refer
to as 'globalisation' is actually the process by which the world economy is
evolving. Like biological evolution, however, it is impossible to know
with any certainty what the end result will be, or if the process has a defi-
nite end at all. We may not know what the result of this process of
globalisation will bring, but we know what it has done so far, and what
trends are for the immediate future.

First, we are experiencing a contraction of time and distance through
faster transportation and communications networks. In the 1800s, personal and business transactions between Britain and Canada took weeks
and months to complete, today they are done in less time than it will take
to read this book. Second, we are seeing the rise of non-traditional economic powers, the so-called BRICs (Brazil, Russia, India, and China).
Between them, we find the majority of humanity who, until recently, were
outside the world's economic system. This addition of 3 billion new consumers represents a shift of economic power not seen since James Watt
developed the steam engine. Third, we see the transformation of our own

national economies to accommodate this expanding frontier, either through regional alliances like the EU and NAFTA, or through mergers of large corporations with those from other jurisdictions. In my own country of Canada our oldest brewery, Molson, merged with Coors of the USA to form a company that is avowedly neither American nor Canadian, but both in terms of its corporate governance, its stock listings, and in its production and marketing. In Europe, the Airbus consortium may be the most established example.

These moves might appear to be part of a conscious strategy to deal with a globalising world, but I am somewhat sceptical of that explanation. Forcing economies and industries together is no more a strategy for globalisation than saying that 'buy low, sell high' is a strategy to make money in the stock market. Surely no one would suggest it would make good business sense if all of Britain's financial institutions should merge into some über-bank and set up shop on every High Street on the planet. The truth is that we are still struggling to understand the rules of globalisation and tend to improvise when we cannot read the tea leaves. We fail to appreciate that there are no rules because globalisation is a means to an end, and not an end in itself. Some of us believe that if nations and corporations are truly concerned about their future, they will focus not on the nature of globalisation, but what they want to get out of it.

Consequently, globalisation is best seen as an evolutionary process, meaning that it follows a natural course based on its environment. Governments can help the process along, through trade agreements and treaties, but many times this has not been necessary. The UK trades as much with the United States as with its EU partners, and yet no free trade treaty with the US exists. Canada's exports to the UK in 2004 were 25 percent higher than the year before, and again, no free trade treaty exists between us. Australian exports to Canada have increased at an average rate of nearly 4 per cent each year for the last decade whilst again no free trade treaty in place.

What is the explanation for this? Why, in the absence of a comprehensive deal at the WTO, or the establishment of free trade agreements, are we seeing impressive growth in both the quantity and quality of trade between these countries? Is there something unique about these countries that encourage trade and commerce? The answer to the last question is, of course, yes.

In 1997, the Commonwealth Heads of Government commissioned research into the nature of trade between its member states. The suspicion was that Commonwealth countries had a natural advantage in trade with each other that did not exist elsewhere. The result of this inquiry was a study that identified a 'Commonwealth Effect' in trade (Lundan and Jones, 2001). By their estimates, Commonwealth countries trading with one another experienced business costs that were 10 to 15 percent lower than similar dealings with non-Commonwealth countries of comparable size and GDP. Specifically, according to the study trade between Commonwealth nations was enhanced because of such things as a common language of business, education and scientific research, common legal and political structures, and historical links. An alternative way of expressing this that we do business in English, according to rules based on the English Common Law, passed by legislatures based on the Westminster model, and interpreted by jurisprudence influenced by the British tradition. Hence, these shared attributes reduce impediments to trade, and therefore, also the overhead in conducting business. Comparing the way in which Commonwealth nations do business is, in many respects, a case of comparing apples to apples. And so, it should be obvious why companies in our respective countries find natural markets and natural partnerships from amongst our ranks.

Another study attempted to measure the impact of certain factors on international trade which estimated that the lack of a free trade agreement between two countries reduced potential trade by 33 per cent, the same as the impact of using separate currencies (Frankel, 2000). Additionally, the study also measured the impact of using different languages, and lack of geographical proximity which were each found to reduce potential trade by 50 per cent. What does this say about Commonwealth trade? Firstly, in terms of trade between Canada and the UK, the common use of English nullifies the impact of the ocean that separates us. Secondly, the use of a common language and legal structures has more of an impact on our bilateral trade than the adoption of a single currency has had for the eurozone. Just as important, if the impact of the 'Commonwealth Effect' is greater than the impact of a trade treaty, then a *de facto* free trade deal already exists, whether or not Brussels cares to negotiate with Ottawa, or vice versa. So, the reality is that the global economy is both a formal and informal creature.

Although nations sign official treaties, they also gravitate to those partners to whom we have an affinity. What does that mean for us today? Well, a great deal, for us and for the world economy as a whole. We are citizens of two Commonwealth countries who share a natural and historical bond that gives us all the advantages of free trade without the formal treaty. We are also respective members of the two largest trading blocs on the planet, NAFTA and the EU. Between these blocs, over US$25 trillion of GDP is generated, roughly half the world's economic output. While Brussels and Washington argue and squabble over tariffs and duties, the truth is that businesses and investors on both sides of the Atlantic already have a bridge to one another. As gatekeepers on respective ends of the bridge, Britons and Canadians have a powerful role to play in shaping the evolution of globalisation, and our own futures. We do not need to wait for a WTO deal, or a truce between the EU and the US. We do not need to wait for a change in the policies of governments or political parties. All we need to do is open our eyes, open our minds, and get on with the business of doing business.

For example, the trade promotion programme, *Commonwealth Advantage*, is working to help Commonwealth companies use the cost benefit of doing business in Canada as a means of gaining access to our NAFTA partners, the United States and Mexico. I would suggest that this concept needs to be expanded so that the UK becomes a conduit for Commonwealth firms to access the EU. As someone from outside Britain, it would be impolite of me to state any opinion as to Britain's prospects in Europe. I realise that any discussion of trading alternatives does run the risk of being pulled into the debate over EU membership, but it is an unnecessary entanglement.

However, if you want a different relationship than the one currently offered vis-à-vis the EU, this model offers a ready alternative since it illustrates Britain's opportunity to be Europe's bridge to both North America and to the Commonwealth. If you care about Britain's economic prospects in the coming decades, you see the promise of new trade and investment opportunities. Britain and Canada have a proud and positive past. Over generations, we have evolved our relationship from that of an empire and its colony, to proud sovereign nations who have been partners in prosperity, and allies in adversity. This partnership is not a relic of a bygone era, it has prevalence in today's world. For whatever reasons, we have failed to appreciate its value and its potential to transform, the virtual bridge between America and Europe, and a guarantee of continued relevance in a changing world. Canada-UK trade is not just about two sister nations of the Commonwealth deepening our ties. It is about constructing the two end points to the bridge that unites Europe and North America, and opens access to our broader family, nearly 2 billion of us in total.

Conclusion

Let me conclude with my own bit of prognostication on the future of globalisation and the world economy. It is a world economy of regional trade blocs that are interconnected into a much larger network, the Commonwealth economy. Whether it exists in some official capacity, as I would hope to see, is a point to be debated and discussed. What cannot be denied is that it exists unofficially, and that it impacts business decisions around the world every day. Whether or not it lives to be something more is a matter for each and every one of us to decide.

David Lascelles

The City

Introduction

Back in 2000, when Britain was considering whether to join the euro, one of Gordon Brown's famous five tests was the impact such a move would have 'on the competitive position of the UK's financial services industry, particularly the City's wholesale markets.' As it turned out, it was the only test to which the Treasury gave a positive answer: joining the euro would be good for the City.

A decade later, it is hard to see what all the fuss was about. Even though Britain did not join the euro, the City's fortunes have swelled beyond its wildest dreams. Recent shocks notwithstanding, banks and markets have flocked to its soaring towers, bringing thousands of ambitious bankers keen for a share of its fast-expanding markets. Today, London ranks beside New York as one of the world's only true international financial centres, with a share of financial business almost equal to that of Paris and Frankfurt combined. London has even evolved into the prime centre for trading in euro currency and euro-denominated assets, despite its location outside the eurozone.

This outturn is particularly impressive given the dire warnings that were made at the turn of the century about the imminence of London's demise if the UK did not join the euro. If the Treasury was right in its answer to the fifth test, all that can be said is that London would have done *even better* inside the eurozone, though a greater degree of success than that already achieved is hard to imagine.

But an opposite view is also possible: that London would have done *less well* if the UK had joined the single currency. This is not merely a provocative view, but one which touches deeply on London's position within the wider EU. Despite its dominance of euro markets and its powerful position in Europe, the City's relationship with the EU is a highly complex one, marked at its most explicable level by feelings of love-hate, but deeper down by discomfort with the EU's political aspirations, its urge to 'build' and regulate, and a sense at the end of the day that it is viewed with suspicion rather than appreciation by its friends across the Channel.

What Does the City Get Out of the EU?

These feelings lead to a question: what does the City actually get out of the EU? Or to put it more neutrally, does the EU deliver net benefits to the City? To be sure, the EU creates opportunities for the City's international markets through its efforts to break down national barriers and open up cross-border trade. But do these benefits outweigh the huge amount of costly regulation that Brussels heaps on the finance sector, the europolitical wrangling that provides a constant distraction, the general feeling that the 'Anglo-Saxon culture', of which the City is arguably the most powerful example in Europe, is unwelcome?

This chapter argues that the answer to all these questions is no: the City derives few if any measurable net benefits from the UK's present relationship with the EU. The chapter goes on to explore the question that follows: would it actually do better outside EU regulation? Is the natural place for an institution like the City — huge, unique, international — beyond the confines of a structure made up of such widely differing and often conflicting political and business interests as the EU?

The City's Uniqueness

The uniqueness of the City is a good starting point to address these questions. The City is unique in the context of the EU in two ways.

First as Table 1 illustrates, it is in a class of its own in terms of the size and diversity of its markets, the number of banks, its international reach, the daily volumes traded in its markets; hence, it is the only European centre that can claim world status.

In fact a recent ranking of world financial centres put it ahead of New York thanks to the international scale and quality of its business environment. By contrast, Frankfurt only made it to 6th position (behind emerging centres such as Hong Kong and Singapore) and Paris to 14th (see Table2).

Table 1: Share of Key Markets (% 2007)[1]

	UK	US	Germany
Cross-border bank lending	21	9	11
Foreign equities turnover	46	43	4
Foreign exchange turnover	34	17	3
Derivatives turnover			
- exchange traded	6	40	13
- over-the-counter	43	24	4
International bonds	70	-	-
Hedge fund assets	21	66	-

Table 2: Competitiveness of Global Financial Centres[2]

1) London
2) New York
3) Hong Kong
4) Singapore
5) Zurich
6) Frankfurt
7) Geneva
8) Chicago
9) Tokyo
10) Sydney

But the City is also unique in a different way: there is no comparable concentration of economic activity anywhere else in Europe. All the EU's other big international industries – pharmaceuticals, chemicals, IT etc. – are much more widely dispersed. This creates a particular complication for the City in EU politics.

Although there is plenty of evidence that the existence of the City provides benefits not just for the UK but for the EU as a whole (through the efficiency of its markets, as an employer of EU nationals, through its eco-

1   Source: International Financial Services (2008)
2   Source: The Global Financial Centres Index (2008)

nomic influence etc.) this fact counts for little in the corridors of EU power. Any concessions made to the City tend to be viewed as 'gifts to the UK' for which reciprocal concessions are exacted, rather than as measures to boost an asset which is good for the whole of the Union. This distinguishes the City sharply from other major EU industries whose dispersal among many member states makes it easier for them to obtain political backing. For example, where the City can count on only one member to push its interests, the engineering industry can count on more than a dozen.

This means that the City tends to lose out when new laws and rules are being put together. The last five years have seen an immense amount of new EU financial regulation, contained in the so-called Financial Services Action Plan (FSAP), a package of 42 measures covering almost every aspect of the finance industry. Although originally touted by Brussels as 'pro-market' and light touch, the FSAP turned out to be enormously heavy-handed and bureaucratic—a common denominator for Europe's 27 financial services industries which made few allowances for London's exceptional position. Indeed, it has been argued that EU regulation is to blame for the Northern Rock debacle by tying the hands of the Treasury and the Bank of England (Congdon, 2008).

The FSAP has been bad for the City, imposing massive costs and extra layers of unnecessary regulation, as well as replacing time-tested City institutions such as the Takeover Code with untried regulations devised by eurocrats. According to the Financial Services Authority, 70 per cent of the rules it enforces are now made in Brussels. Yet the UK was virtually powerless to prevent it. Numerically, the UK was outvoted by other members who feared that the single market for financial services would be a licence for the City to overrun Europe. Although the EU is supposed to be about promoting points of excellence, the political reality is that jealous members have an interest in preventing others obtaining competitive advantage, so excellence is ground down in the name of 'harmonisation'.

The political weakness of the City within the EU is likely to be worsened by the Lisbon Treaty. If passed, the redistribution of voting power will make it even harder for minority interests to promote their agendas and block undesired laws and regulations. What little influence the UK has over the EU's regulatory initiatives will be further diminished, with damaging consequences for the City's unique interests (Lascelles, 2007).

The Global Context

There is one more sense in which the City is exceptional: its global reach. While Continental centres are essentially regional, serving their home markets and those in the vicinity, much of London's business is far away from Europe. Such things are hard to calculate, but it has been estimated that the City's business divides into three roughly equal parts: Europe, North America and the developing world. London is, for example, the global centre for emerging world finance, it has huge interests in the Far East and former colonial territories, it provides stock exchange listings for the new industrial giants of Russia, China and India, and it is the world's foreign exchange capital.

The effect of EU regulation has been to subject these non-European businesses to rules devised in Brussels to regulate intra-EU commerce. Many people in the City ask why they should submit to EU rules when all their business is outside. This could become a key consideration when banks consider where to locate their global operations. The risk of excessive regulation has regularly topped the polls of bankers' concerns For example, the annual *Banking Banana Skins* survey of banking risk by the Centre for the Study of Financial Innovation, London.

What is the 'Passport' Worth?

The imposition of a common EU regulatory regime would be acceptable if it represented the price paid for a greater good, namely the creation of a single market in financial services, something much in the City's interests. The famous 'passport' that would allow banks to move freely across borders has, however, been disappointingly slow to materialise. Even the EU Commission admits that national barriers still stand in the way of cross-border movement of financial services: local regulations maintained in the name of 'consumer protection', obstacles to takeovers of foreign banks, restrictions on what foreign suppliers can do. These are all illegal, but can be justified if they exist 'to protect the national interest'.

It could be argued, of course, that the City's weak position within the EU, and the imposition of the FSAP, have done little to prevent its headlong growth. This is true. But part of the reason for this is that other centres have also been hampered, and the City has been able to preserve *relative* advantage. Within the EU itself, Paris and Frankfurt are subject to the FSAP, and further afield New York has been hit by tough new controls which have driven business away from Wall Street, mostly to London. Reverting to the initial point about the UK's membership of the euro: one of the benefits of not joining the single currency has been to put a certain distance between the City and Brussels. Political independence is a key attribute of successful financial centres, and this has helped reinforce it.

The fact remains, however, that Britain's loss of control over the design and implementation of financial regulation has been bad for the City because it has forced it to accept an ill-suited regime which was tailored to fit all-comers and may even be intended to hold the City back. And this trend is certain to continue. The 'streamlining' of EU governance will further erode Britain's ability to influence financial regulation. Down the road, there may also be moves to create a 'single regulator' for the EU which would represent the complete transfer of rule-making and enforcement to Brussels, and deprive the UK of what little regulatory initiative it still possesses.

The City's success is, therefore, also its problem. Its pre-eminence has elevated it to a point where it no longer fits the EU context: it is one of a kind for which the EU has trouble making allowance, it is easily demonised by those who resent its success, and it risks being tied down by a regime which is certain to become more centralised and intrusive. What is to be done?

Is There an Alternative?

One point needs to be made straight away: there *is* a choice for the City as it looks ahead, in the sense that its future does not have to be locked in to Europe. It is truly global. Having a good regulatory and trading environment is far more important than being part of a large political/economic bloc, no matter how impressive its membership or persuasive its political leaders.

Two broad routes present themselves. One is to stick with the EU regulatory system and try to make it better. The other is to step outside it and reclaim the initiative on financial regulation.

If the UK stays inside, one option might be to renegotiate all or part of the FSAP and hope to secure a deal that was better tailored to City interests. There were hopes that Charlie McCreevy, the Irish Commissioner in charge of financial services, might bring a more free market approach to many of these issues. But he has been thwarted by the Brussels political machine, and is now under fire for treating London too lightly. So the chances of reform must be rated nil. The more radical, route lies outside the FSAP, or outside the EU altogether. We shall consider the narrower of these options since the broader involves many more policy issues than the City.

There would be two major considerations if the UK opted out of the FSAP: how the UK managed its domestic financial markets, and how it positioned the City internationally.

At home, the UK would regain control of financial regulation and would be free to institute a regime that was more appropriate to its needs. Some of this could be based on FSAP measures (they're not all bad), but others would be tailored to the specifics of the UK market, which is relatively more diverse and competitive than Continental markets. The British consumer would probably notice little difference, though the cost of financial services might go down if the new regime proved less costly than the FSAP. But the financial sector would see big changes: a shift towards a more UK-flavoured system with a return to the more flexible approach that existed before.

The more difficult question is how the City would mesh in with foreign markets. But this is less daunting than it looks. It is worth recalling that the largest banking presence in the City is not European but American. The absence of FSAP type arrangements with the US has not prevented British and American financial markets developing close relations – possibly the most active between any two financial centres in the world. And these cover not just wholesale markets but the whole spectrum of financial services at the retail end: personal banking, credit cards, stockbroking, insurance and fund management, all of which operate for the most part very smoothly – and without huge regulatory paraphernalia. The same goes for the City's relations with more than 100 non-EU countries whose banks are represented in the City. Switzerland, which arguably has Europe's second most successful international finance industry after the UK, is outside the FSAP but operates within the EU on the basis of a 1972 free trade accord and a series of sectoral treaties, one of which covers financial services (Hannan, 2004). Swiss banks, insurance companies and fund managers have a huge presence in the FSAP zone. You do not need an FSAP to create active and healthy cross-border financial markets.

The City's relations with the outside world which have made all this possible are governed by agreements at two levels. The overarching one is the World Trade Organisation's 1995 General Agreement on Trade in Services (GATS) under which the EU, the US and more than 100 countries committed themselves to open up their financial sectors to free trade, subject only to local prudential and central banking considerations. Furthermore, the GATS covers not just cross-border trade in financial services (where a bank in country A sells to a customer in country B) but the commercial presence of banks in foreign countries (where a bank in country A opens up an office in country B to sell services). This provides a very effective framework to promote the movement of services as well as institutions from one country to another — precisely what the FSAP set out to do.

Specifically, the GATS provides for 'national treatment', i.e. incoming institutions can do what local institutions can. The FSAP was meant to go a stage further and allow institutions to do in a host country what they were permitted to do in their home country, even if locals were not allowed to. But this is where the FSAP tends to fall down: host countries are unwilling to allow foreign institutions to do more than national ones.

At a more technical level, the GATS is supplemented by a web of voluntary inter-governmental accords which ensure that banks are fit to trade in world markets, and that none of them fall between the cracks when they move from one market to another. So the framework — though still rudimentary and imperfect — is already in place. International finance is extremely adaptable: it does not need supra-national 'harmonisation': it works best through voluntary agreement, as the City's impressive record amply demonstrates. Seen in this light, the FSAP looks not just harmful but superfluous.

A Cost-Benefit Analysis of the City Leaving the FSAP

The City would gain in shedding a costly and ill-suited regime, and recovering the freedom to set its own regulatory agenda and style, one which recognises its strengths, in particular the requirements of its professional wholesale markets. This would quickly add to the City's appeal, and make it more competitive within Europe and on the world stage.

It may be objected that the UK is irrevocably heading down the route of international unification of financial regulation because that is the global trend, so the FSAP only represents what would be happening anyway. This is only partly true. Yes, the UK is involved in a large number of international regulatory initiatives which include not just the EU but countries like the US, Japan and Switzerland. But most of these — like the Basel 2 Accord on bank capital or the new international accounting standards — are being negotiated for the UK through the EU rather than directly by the UK authorities. This disadvantages the UK in a number of ways: it means we have to adopt a common negotiating position with our EU partners, which may not suit us, and that our influence on the outcome is reduced. It also means that the accords are then implemented via EU directives which are designed to fit the EU as a whole rather than the City's unique needs. The US, which is outside this process, intends to implement Basel 2 in a much more selective way than the EU, and will thereby gain a useful competitive advantage.

When British regulators want to discuss global markets, they are just as likely to talk to their counterparts in Switzerland, the US and Japan as those in France and Italy. Today, the world's leading financial institutions are not regulated through local accords like the FSAP but through Memorandums of Understanding (MoUs) between regulators all over the world. At the latest count, the FSA had over 150 such MoUs. This makes the FSAP look very parochial.

Where the City would lose is in not being part of the EU's single financial market, and thereby no longer able to issue the 'passport'. UK institutions which had their sole European base in London would not automatically be able to offer their services through the rest of the EU, and EU banks would not automatically be able to 'passport' into London. On paper, that looks a severe disadvantage, but in practice it is not.

On the outgoing side, we have already seen that the passport is costly in terms of regulation, and offers dubious access to the rest of the EU, so its net value is small. However, virtually all the institutions in the City already have a presence elsewhere in the EU which they could use as a base to procure their passports. On the incoming side, EU banks would have to obtain authorisation to be in London. But not necessarily: there would be nothing to stop the UK unilaterally recognising the FSAP passport, so EU banks could remain in the City on exactly the same terms as before, and enjoy a lighter regulatory touch.

Some people might fear that international banking confidence in the City would be shaken if the UK opted out of the FSAP. This is understandable: the FSAP is, after all, the regulatory rock on which the City now stands. But it is just as easy to see the opposite happening: a surge of enthusiasm as London regained its traditional autonomy and began to strip down the excesses of the FSAP (remember that EU regulation is viewed as a cost). Nor is dissatisfaction with the FSAP confined to 'Anglo-Saxon' institutions: many Continental banks are frustrated with it too, and would welcome the chance to escape to an FSAP-free zone. As happened with the euro, an FSAP opt-out might actually produce an *increase* in the foreign banking presence in the City.

This is all speculative, of course. It is not clear how the UK could opt out of the FSAP, particularly since it might involve EU treaty renegotiation, and then unravel the FSAP's complex skein. But the practice of opting out is not new, and it is increasingly finding its way into the EU debate. The UK has had several opt-outs: the Social Chapter, the euro, the Schengen agreement, the Working Time Directive. Now there is talk in Opposition circles of extending opt-outs to areas like fisheries and foreign aid. The more the idea of a 'multi-speed' Europe gains ground, the more likely it is that there will be different levels of regulatory convergence, with some countries bound into tight accords, others having a looser involvement. It is possible to see the UK agreeing broad sets of regulatory principles with the EU (and the US and other countries too) so that the doors remained open, but running its own regime on the ground.

If opt-outs are being considered, the FSAP should be added to the list. As we have seen, there would be a net benefit to the City: it would lose little but gain much by repatriating regulatory initiative. Such a move would not only have very positive practical consequences: it would also be highly symbolic. It would send a clear signal to the EU that excessive regulatory unification can be harmful, and that there are alternatives.

The Lessons of the FSAP

The FSAP experience contains several messages which should make us wary of further attempts to centralise rules on an EU-wide basis, not just in financial services but more generally. One is that, for all its protestations about harmony and cooperation, the EU remains at heart a selfish project in which initiatives are viewed by many member countries more in terms of what they can get out of them individually than as a contribution to a greater good. So long as this remains the case, a best-all-round outcome will never be possible.

A second message is that, for all its claims to be on the side of deregulation, the EU is incapable of resisting the urge to regulate. As we have seen, the FSAP grew from a simple system of mutual recognition into possibly the greatest regulatory monster the world has ever seen, and no one was able to stop it.

But the third message is the most worrying: if the EU cannot recognise and encourage a point of excellence within its borders such as the City, what hope is there for other world class assets in the EU which may face the same treatment? Top quality industries and services, world competitive technologies, cutting edge research? If they are also to become the victims of intra-EU rivalries, to be levelled down by 'harmonisation', or simply snuffed out by regulation, they will all eventually die or leave. The EU single market needs diversity not uniformity, to be outward- not inward-looking. It is concerns such as these which make one wonder whether the EU can ever achieve its goal of becoming the world's most competitive economy, and should spur us to explore alternatives.

Philip Booth

EU Regulation of Investment Markets

Introduction

The EU Financial Services Action Plan (FSAP) attempts to bring sufficient uniformity to EU financial regulation to enable the creation of a single market in financial services. However, no convincing case has been made that it is necessary for the EU to regulate in this field. Indeed, as with much EU regulation, the focus has been on creating a single market when the creation of a free market should be the goal. A free market in financial services would not be a market without regulation but a market in which regulation was generated by the market itself. This is not a fanciful idea. Indeed, it was the norm in UK investment markets until the Conservative government opened the door to detailed, heavy-handed statutory regulation in 1986. This does not mean that EU countries could not regulate their investment markets if they wished. However, any regulation of those markets would have to be subject to the EU desire to ensure freedom to trade goods and services. Thus, the EU role in financial regulation should be to ensure the freedom of movement of goods, services, capital and people and not to develop a unified regulatory framework for financial markets and services.

To its credit, aspects of the FSAP do, indeed, try to limit financial regulation in those countries where it is most overbearing and restricts trade. However, at its heart is a desire to make regulation as uniform as possible, based on a belief that, in order to function properly, markets have to have regulation imposed on them from above and that, in order for competition to be effective, this regulation must be uniform.

It should be noted that this chapter relates wholly to the regulation of investment market transactions — trading, providing wholesale investment services and so on — and not to the prudential regulation of insurance companies or the regulation of the banking system.

Approaches to the Development of EU Regulation

On top of the regulation of investment markets by the Financial Services Authority (FSA), we also have EU involvement. There are two basic approaches to the development of regulation at EU level. The first involves harmonisation of all EU regulation at the same level. The second approach involves harmonisation of some common standards and then a process of mutual recognition whereby institutions that fulfil the regulatory requirements of one EU country are assumed to fulfil the requirements of all EU countries. There is, of course, an alternative to both 'harmonisation' and 'mutual recognition' – that of liberalisation.

Under the so-called Lamfalussy initiative, the basic approach to the development of EU regulation of investment markets has been to develop some core principles by which harmonised regulations are formulated. These form the basis of a 'common passport' which can be used to issue and trade securities under the regulatory framework in any EU country. National markets can build further regulations on top of the core harmonised requirements.

A number of EU Regulations and Directives[1] in this field were brought in under single market regulation. However, due to concern about the slow speed with which the single market programme was developing in the financial services sector, the European Commission published a Communication containing a Financial Services Action Plan (FSAP) that was designed to fill gaps in the single market process by 2005. Both regulations and Directives can be used to implement FSAP. A number of revisions to existing EU regulations and Directives, as well as new regulations and Directives, have been developed under the auspices of the FSAP. These include the following initiatives (see HM Treasury et al, 2003, for a user-friendly guide to FSAP and FSA, 2005 for the timetable for these initiatives, which are now more or less fully implemented):

- A Market Abuse Directive was adopted in January 2003 with an implementation deadline of October 2004. In practice, it was not fully implemented in the UK until the second quarter of 2005. The Directive harmonised rules on insider dealing and market manipulation.

- A Prospectus Directive was adopted in July 2003 designed to require all issuers of equity and debt securities to meet certain requirements when publishing prospectuses. The prospectus could then be used as a 'single passport' to allow securities to be issued and sold anywhere

---

1   Directives require implementation action by member states, regulations are implemented directly in all member states.

in the EU. This directive is based on harmonisation rather than on mutual recognition. Therefore its requirements have to be adopted by the UK. Member states were required to implement the directive by July 2005.

- A revised Investment Services Directive has been implemented that regulates the authorisation, behaviour and conduct of business of securities firms, including exchanges. This is known as the Markets in Financial Instruments Directive (MiFID) and had to be implemented by November 2007.

- A Transparency Directive was proposed by the commission in March 2003 to impose on issuers an obligation to meet continuing disclosure requirements after issue. It thus complements the Prospectus Directive and measures relating to fair value accounting. It had to be implemented by January 2007.

- A regulation relating to accounting disclosures requires listed companies to use international accounting standards (effectively fair value accounting methods) for reporting purposes from January 2005.

Because of the technical difficulty of many of these measures The 'Lamfalussy process' was developed whereby framework legislation was proposed by the Commission and European Parliament and then detailed regulation is developed and implemented by special committees with reference back to the European Parliament.

There is not space to discuss all aspects of EU regulation, but the tenor is clear in each case. The EU is standardising regulation and creating regulatory floors in areas where it simply has no business regulating. There is a legitimate role for the EU to prevent member states implementing regulation that prevents freedom to trade, but that is not the main purpose of the FSAP. In the following sections we show how regulation is a set of services that can be provided by investment exchanges themselves.

Exchanges Can Regulate Markets

There are many bodies other than the FSA that have made rules and regulations about conduct of business, listing, trading and so on in UK financial markets. Indeed, since the development of sophisticated financial markets in the nineteenth century, investment market conduct has been governed by the common law, the criminal law, the civil law, contract law, rules developed by exchanges and professions and other ad hoc bodies that have been set up or that have evolved in the market from time to time. The FSA now deals with nearly all aspects of financial regulation, hamstrung by EU rules, including some aspects that might be regarded as matters for the criminal law. In the remainder of this chapter, we argue that rule-making within financial markets is a process that can be developed within markets themselves. We do not need a statutory regulator either at the UK or the EU level.

The London Stock Exchange, in a document discussing the implementation of MiFID (London Stock Exchange, 2006), states:

> The London Stock Exchange's commitment to providing a trusted infrastructure for fair and transparent trading and competitive execution is long established.
>
> Whether conducted on or off-book, all Exchange business is monitored and published by the Exchange and benefits from:
>
> - A reliable and transparent trading environment providing best execution.
> - A well-regulated environment that publishes accurate price and trade information in real time.
> - Post–trade transparency of off book trades enabling investors to benchmark performance.
> - A highly reliable and fast trading platform enabling efficient trade execution.
> - A dedicated supervision team which ensures data integrity via real time monitoring.
> - Competitively priced trade reporting fees.
>
> As well as a centralised and well-regulated market, the Exchange is also able to provide investors with significant protections as a result of its stringent rules. These rules cover:
>
> - Terms of contract between trading counterparts.
> - Transparency.
> - Administrations of default procedures in the event of member failure.
> - Enforcement of settlement rules.
> - Structure for the market making system.

In other words, it is very clear that the London Stock Exchange is competing on the basis of the regulation, transparency, efficiency and security that it offers those who are transacting investments. If it were not effective in providing appropriate regulations for that purpose, then the Exchange would not be regarded as a worthwhile entity on which to list and trade securities.

The London Stock Exchange faces competition from other markets. Competition operates across a number of aspects of the services that the Exchange offers. As in any other competitive environment, some competitors will try to offer similar but better services. Other competitors will offer a differentiated product. Indeed, the London Stock Exchange itself offers an 'Alternative Investment Market' to provide differentiation within its own suite of products. Companies can have multiple listings on different Exchanges each of which have different listing rules and regulatory frameworks. New trading platforms, such as Chi-X and Turquoise, also provide competition for existing exchanges. Unfortunately, however, because the service of providing the package of rules and regulations to govern trading has been taken over by the government, the one thing these markets cannot do is compete according to their regulatory frameworks.

An economic case can be constructed for the regulation of investment activity such as that which takes place through stock exchanges. Regulation can be justified because of the potential for externalities where the behaviour of parties on an exchange affects other parties. For example, poor behaviour by an individual or firm can raise suspicions about other individuals or firms. There is also the potential for information asymmetries between clients and firms and for investors to 'abuse' markets by trading in 'thin' markets in a way that intentionally distorts price signals.

In theory, these problems can be overcome by regulation, although whether they should be overcome by *government* regulation or can be overcome in practice are different matters. Therefore, to accept that there is a case for regulation is not to accept that there is a case for such regulation to come from statutory bodies. If externalities are more or less contained within parties that operate on an exchange, there is an incentive for exchanges to develop mechanisms to resolve the problems. Market mechanisms may therefore evolve to deal with problems that are today dealt with by statutory regulators. There may be a case for statutory regulation if there are factors that prevent effective private regulatory bodies evolving[2] or if externalities go beyond those parties that can efficiently contract with each other. But even here, the case for regulation is weakened when one considers the issues highlighted by public choice economics.[3]

---

2 These factors could include problems created by the provisions of law in other fields. For example, it is possible that laws relating to the restraint of trade might prevent an exchange from imposing a particular punishment, even if the mechanism that gave rise to that punishment was agreed between the parties.

3 Public choice economics, which cannot be discussed in detail here suggests that, even if there is a prima facie case for statutory regulation, the pursuit of special interests of voters, politicians and bureaucrats will prevent the desired outcome from being achieved.

Is There a Case for Statutory Regulation?

Externalities from investment transactions

As noted, externalities may arise from the behaviour of firms involved in
the securities business. It will suffice to give two examples. Investment
transactions often involve the assimilation of a considerable amount of
information regarding the probity of the parties involved. Indeed, reputation is important in financial markets because of the costs of analysing
information relating to the probity of individual firms. If one firm in a
market behaves badly it may damage the reputation of other firms and
reduce investor confidence more generally. Thus regulation might help
maintain market confidence, which is, in fact, one of the objectives of the
FSA. A second example follows from this. Standardisation of contracts,
types of information offered to investors, and so on can reduce transactions costs significantly. If investment contracts are standardised, it will
benefit other firms who are using the same contracts thus creating a positive externality as firms have to accumulate less information to design
and understand the contracts.

   In the case of the regulation of investment transactions, it is by no
means clear that externalities significantly affect those who are not party
to investment transactions. Thus, in principle, market mechanisms can
regulate investment transactions. This could happen, for example, as a
result of exchanges developing standardised contracts, regulating information provision and regulating aspects of market conduct. Indeed, the
economic gains from the development of standardised information provision and standardised contracts are some of the prime motivating factors
for the development of exchanges. It is also important to note that statutory regulation itself is an important source of negative externalities. The
costs of regulation are imposed on parties that do not necessarily benefit
from it and, insofar as regulators' responses to the problems that they seek
to solve are sub-optimal, they will impose policies the costs of which are
greater than the benefits. Statutory regulation does not resolve and
externality problems, but private regulation might do so.

Information asymmetries

A second set of problems can arise as a result of 'information asymmetries'. Simply put, these arise where one party to a transaction has more
information than the other party and the costs of resolving the asymmetry
are non-trivial. The potential for information asymmetries in financial
markets is considerable. However, no market operates without informa-

tion asymmetries and there is no limit to the regulation that could be imposed to try to remove them. Financial markets are said to be prone to information asymmetries because information is costly to collect, is complex, subjective and often closely held by a small number of parties. Also, transactions often involve large sums of money changing hands infrequently rather than small sums frequently.

There is no question that information asymmetries exist in securities markets and that their impact can be serious. However, it is certainly not clear that statutory regulators are necessary to deal with the problem. Indeed, in the UK stock market, principal and agent functions were separated for investment transactions on the UK market until 'big bang' in 1986 to try to deal with this very problem. An exchange has an incentive to develop regulations regarding information provision to help overcome information asymmetry problems as it makes it a more attractive institution for trading. Such regulations existed on stock exchanges before the Financial Services Act 1986 and still exist today. Private stock exchanges can be regarded as one example amongst many were issuers of capital who wish to overcome information asymmetries, pay to demonstrate their integrity (in this case by paying for a listing and abiding by listing rules) because by doing so they will reduce the cost of capital by extending the range of investors who are willing to contract with them.

Is statutory regulation justified by conflicts of interest?

The FSA has taken an interest in conflicts of interest (see FSA Discussion Paper No. 15, for example). One form of conflict of interest highlighted is that which arises when an investment research house is giving buy/sell recommendations for a particular type of security and has a relationship with the company that has issued the securities. The question arises as to whether the broker has an incentive to provide 'biased' advice to help maintain good relationships with the company or, for example, to aid the process of underwriting a new securities issue.

It is not clear why regulation here is necessary. Where conflicts of interest are inherent in the nature of a particular investment institution's business (for example because they provide investment advice and hold securities on their own book in a company on which they give advice), impartiality would have a market value. Lightfoot (2003) suggests that there is strong historical evidence that universal banks in the USA in the late 1920s were penalised because the securities they underwrote might be subject to conflicts of interest. If this is so, it is difficult to see why this should not apply more generally to conflicts of interest. *All* market transactions have conflicts of interest, as do all transactions with government. A number of other studies provide evidence for this: see Crockett et al (2003) page 66 for a summary.[4] It is possible that monopoly power, concentrating investment research in a small-number of diversified investment banks may prevent market mechanisms from alleviating conflicts of interest effectively (see Congdon, 2003). But, surely competition issues should be tackled on their own merits rather than by using a special class of 'financial regulator'.

In general, institutional competition is a potential way to deal with potential conflicts of interest. Some institutions might give totally independent advice (research boutiques). Others may not be independent but have established and well publicised mechanisms for dealing with conflicts of interest. Still others may have conflicts of interest but reveal them to clients. Finally, some institutions may choose to remain opaque and not to reveal conflicts of interest. Investment houses might also decide to employ people who have signed up to a particular professional code to which they can be held accountable. One would expect investors to take into account the potential for conflicts of interest when purchasing investment services. Insofar as an institution seeks to mislead a client, this would be a matter for general law rather than for special financial regulation. Indeed, FSA (2002, para 4.8) recognises that institutional competition exists, even in the current regulatory environment. It could be argued that institutional competition is inhibited by the existence of a statutory monopoly regulator. Indeed, we should remember that statutory regulators have conflicts of interest too. For example, economic efficiency may demand a liberal approach but the self-interest of the bureau may demand that the regulator is cautious to avoid an event blowing up that may be blamed on the regulator.[5] Participants in a market economy have an incentive to resolve conflicts of interest – even if the structure of a market leads to some conflicts persisting, whereas there are few effective incentives for regulatory bureaus to resolve their conflicts of interest.

---

4   The papers in this publication also suggest ways in which the market can overcome conflicts of interest though the authors conclude that regulation to deal with conflicts of interest is appropriate in a range of financial markets. The authors also note that research-only investment houses, which do not have conflicts of interest also produce more 'buy' recommendations, thus suggesting that this widely recognised phenomenon may not simply be caused by conflicts of interest.

5   Of course, this conflict is exacerbated by the fact that the beneficial economic transactions that do not happen because of over regulation are not noticed because they never take place whereas problems that arise because of regulator inaction are obvious.

Monopolies and cartels

If the prior assumption is that regulation of investment transactions, and of those involved with transactions, can be undertaken by private exchanges, there might be concern that economies of scale and the necessity for exchanges to have a physical location might lead to a natural monopoly in the provision of stock exchange services. Also, because exchanges can limit access, in the same way that clubs can limit membership, they can act as cartels. Indeed competition and fair trading enquiries led to the break up of the pre-1986 system of private regulation in the UK.

These arguments may have been valid at one time, but are much less true today. Electronic trading significantly reduces costs and allows international competition (see, Davis and Steil, 2001, for some discussion of this). Indeed, one of the drivers of the EU single market programme in this area is the desire to allow cross border competition although, ironically, the FSA (FSA, 2001, para 3.9) argues that pan-EU competition requires a common approach to regulation.

Competition can also take place between recognised exchanges and non-exchange trading systems. The FSA suggests (FSA, 2001) that this may require the introduction of comparable regulatory standards across exchange-based and non-exchanged-based trading systems. There seems to be no recognition that the existence of competition lessens the need for regulation.

It is certainly true that there are network effects and therefore advantages of scale economies in stock exchanges. However, it is increasingly true that workable competition, if not perfect competition, is undermining the natural monopoly argument for regulating financial markets. The existence of electronic trading, non-exchange-based trading systems and international competition undermine monopoly power. The provision of exchange services is, in fact, a very competitive business. Indeed, as one of the functions of an exchange is to provide regulation, statutory regulation institutionalises monopoly power.

Regulatory Competition

We do not know the best structure for delivering regulation, the best regulatory framework for financial markets, or the best sets of detailed rules, ex ante. We can make some educated guesses and we can use economic theory as a guide, but we do not know in advance what the best structures, frameworks and rules are. We currently have a state, monopoly provider of regulation — the FSA which, to a large extent, is answerable to

EU law. Top-down, state-created structures cannot determine the optimal regulatory structure. This may seem like a glib point, an effort to use terms such as 'optimal' and 'competition' developed by economists for analysing decisions such as those relating to the number and type of bananas consumers may wish to buy in the wrong context. It is not. There are some issues relating to regulation that naturally belong with the criminal and civil law and with the statutory authorities. However, for the large part, financial regulation is, in fact, the provision of a set of services in the same way that railway through-ticketing and timetabling (including the invention of time zones), developed by private train companies in the nineteenth century, are sets of regulatory services in a different context. The notion of competition is highly relevant.

Arguments are often put forward to suggest that regulatory competition leads to a 'race to the bottom'. There is no evidence for this. Indeed, former Chairman and CEO of the FSA, Howard Davies, said (Davies, 2002):

> The argument that we hear is that regulatory competition cannot be allowed in the EU. Why not? Because, I am told, we would see regulatory arbitrage and a 'race to the bottom'. That seems highly unlikely to me, especially at a time when investors are, not unreasonably, nervous about unconventional corporate structures and opaque accounts. Furthermore, our regime, tougher in these respects than others in the EU, has attracted mobile capital, far from repelling it.

These arguments surely apply at the level of private regulators, such as exchanges, if they apply to competition between state regulators. Surely they also apply to issues such as accounting (see Myddelton, 2004), disclosure and corporate governance (see Sternberg, 2004).

Competition should lead to the evolution of appropriate standards rather than an erosion of all standards. Indeed, evidence that different investors value different forms of regulation rather than necessarily wanting tighter or looser regulation comes from a recent report published by the City of London (London Stock Exchange/Oxera, 2006). Oxera found that small and early stage companies preferred more liberally regulated environments (as they have no track record and satisfying additional regulations would be expensive). On the other hand, for other companies, a more stringent listing regime may have offsetting advantages (signalling quality and investor confidence) resulting in a lower cost of capital.

Competition is even required to discover the best form of regulation. Different methods of regulation impose different costs on market users and constrain innovation to differing degrees. The objectives of regulation can be achieved by direct regulation, supervision or monitoring. Direct regulation can involve rules to restrain behaviour or to require certain forms of behaviour or to the creation of incentives for firms to behave in a particular way (Llewellyn, 1999). It is by no means clear which approach is appropriate for achieving the different objectives of regulation and a competitive process may be the best way of discovering the best approach.

For many years, the London Stock Exchange had an effective monopoly of investment trading business. However, as a result, inter alia, of deregulation of capital flows, freer trade in services and changes in technology there is greater competition across exchanges. Such competition could facilitate the development of different optimal regulatory frameworks for those dealing in investments. Competing exchanges exist in the form of NASDAQ, pan-European exchanges, AIM and the London Stock Exchange main market. All these are in competition with off-exchange trading.

Conclusion

There are many benefits from exchanges providing systems of rules for investment market activity (see Pritchard, 2003). Exchanges can help create trust that leads to deep and liquid securities markets by designing transparent trading mechanisms, monitoring trading, imposing disclosure standards on quoted companies and enforcing rules. These features, as well as integrity and reputation, are important marketing tools for an exchange. Such functions do not have to be performed by a statutory monopoly regulator.

Indeed, the case for the statutory regulation of stock exchange transactions is weak. Such regulation should be provided by exchanges and other trading platform providers. There is certainly no case for regulation at the EU level. The role of the EU in the regulation of investment transactions should be to prevent member states bringing in statutory regulations that are a restraint on the free movement of capital, labour, goods and services: including the provision of investment services. Trading would, of course, be subject to criminal and other laws within individual countries but the regulation of investment transactions should firmly belong with competing exchanges.

Mark Baimbridge, Philip B. Whyman, Brian Burkitt

A New Policy Framework

Introduction

Participation in further EU integration will place an additional straightjacket upon UK macroeconomic policy and increases the difficulty of pursuing its national interest, largely due to the political desire to tie members more closely together. Thus, the EU is seeking to progressively replace economic autonomy for a nation state by the requirement to co-ordinate its economic strategy with the EU norm, or else be subject to sanctions levied by the EU Commission (Pennant-Rea *et al.*, 1997).

A decision to reject such developments would restore to national government those economic instruments essential to the management of its economy. Governments will be able to devise different economic programmes and, once endorsed by the electorate, will possess the means by which to pursue their chosen objectives. Democracy will, therefore, be restored, so that citizens can once again enjoy the opportunity to choose the economic strategy pursued by the government of the day. Moreover, governments will be able to pursue a more balanced economic programme, pursuing the multiple objectives of full employment, high economic growth and a sustainable balance of payments as well as low inflation. The opportunities are substantial.

To illustrate the broad range of macroeconomic policies that could be enacted, this chapter firstly outlines a number of broad alternative economic strategies that could be pursued. The intention is to demonstrate, not only that national economic management is still feasible, but also that it is preferable to transferring the main levers of macroeconomic policy into the hands of the EU which is incapable of using them consistently in the best interests of all member states simultaneously.

Additionally, in this chapter we focus upon the development of complementary industrial strategy that can only prove effective if supplemented by fiscal and monetary policies that target growth and reject deflation we outline. Historically, attempts to grow the British economy through macroeconomic policy initiatives alone have usually ended in accelerating inflation. However, inflation is not the British disease, but the symptom of an economy that cannot produce enough to satisfy domestic demand. Britain's basic economic problem is insufficient production. The solution is to boost demand, but channel it to UK industry thereby improving profits, stimulating production and hence productivity, and providing the incentive to invest. The prize from such a strategy would be the cutting of unit costs and inflation through a considered policy of economic expansion. It can be achieved, free from EU constraints, through control of the exchange rate and the accompanying interest rate changes. Such a policy makes it profitable to produce in the UK, by utilising the price mechanism to boost exports, encourage import substitution and lure British industry back into sectors it has abandoned, whilst a tax on imports would provide crucial support.

Tight Monetary Policy/Low Interest Rate Strategy

The first potential economic strategy seeks to follow the framework established by Alan Greenspan and the US Federal Reserve Bank, whereby national monetary authorities seek a higher long-term growth rate by providing a favourable climate for industrial expansion through low inflation and hence reduced long term interest rates. Fiscal policy is used to support the more dominant monetary policy by restraining inflationary pressures, thereby reinforcing the low interest rate objective.

In 'hard' versions of this strategy, the government endeavours to maintain a high value for the currency in order to squeeze inflation further. The objective is comparatively easy to accomplish if the country enjoys a trade surplus, because the pressure on its exchange rate is upwards due to the country's competitive position, assuming the absence of speculative motives to counter this fundamental relationship. Although the UK typically suffers from a current account trade deficit, the adoption of the other policies outlined in this chapter, in particular concerning an industrial strategy and active exchange rate policy would reverse this trend.

A Fiscal-Based Strategy

A second distinctive economic strategy involves the more active use of fiscal as well as monetary policy in order to pursue both internal and external balance for the economy. Internal balance refers to more than just low inflation, but also to low unemployment and to high rates of economic growth. Accordingly, a mixture of demand-side reflation and supply-side labour market policies, particularly measures encouraging re-training and labour mobility, could reduce unemployment. Thus, the net stimulative effect is targeted upon specific sectors of the economy that most require assistance, rather than raising aggregate demand *per se* and creating inflationary bottlenecks. Economic growth could be facilitated by the maintenance of a competitive exchange rate through managed floating, perhaps based upon a trade-weighted basket of currencies, together with tax incentives for firms that increase productive investment.

A mixture of fiscal and monetary policy could restrain inflation; if this proved difficult to achieve, rather than abandon the other internal objectives, governments could enact additional measures to restrain inflationary pressures. These might include the temporary re-introduction of credit controls, an incomes policy (tax-based or otherwise) or co-ordinated national bargaining. Although currently unpopular amongst economists who prefer the allocative efficiency of free markets, the reality of sticky wages and prices, due to oligopolistic markets as much as the existence of trade unions, gives rise to the possibility of market failure resulting in persistently high unemployment and slower-than-trend output growth. In this case, government intervention is justified to achieve a superior outcome. Finally, external balance can be achieved through the provision of a competitive exchange rate, although structural problems in export sectors may require supplementary supply-side measures to improve product quality, reliability and to encourage a shift of resources to provide goods and services in growing rather than stagnant markets.

Exchange Rate Policy

Export-led growth occurs because the firms that are competitive in world markets commence with the advantage of costs at least as low as their competitors given that an economy is usually required to sell its output to the rest of the world at a competitive price. Moreover, once export-led growth is established a number of forces operate to keep fast growing economies moving ahead. Particularly significant is the impact of successive waves of investment, which tend to reduce the cost of goods in the internationally-traded goods sector so rendering export prices increasingly competitive. However, a key determinant of competitiveness is to establish and maintain a competitive exchange rate, i.e. one that achieves balance of payments equilibrium at full employment.

There is always a rate of exchange that enables each country to employ its productive resources fully. In an ever-changing environment, the rate frequently alters to secure simultaneous full employment and trade balance. Therefore, when formulating British economic policy outside the EU, any suggestion that the pound should 'shadow' the euro must be rebutted. Such targeting makes domestic objectives harder to achieve; in any case the pound moves more closely with the US dollar than with any European currency. Whilst an exchange rate system to suit all economies for all seasons is an impossible reality given the complexity of determining the exact exchange rate regime for a country in light of the arguments concerning flexible and fixed exchange rates (Baimbridge and Whyman, 2008). Two systems, however, offer the greatest potential for combining an exchange rate that secures balance of payments equilibrium with full employment.

Firstly, managed floating does not involve parities that the government is obliged to preserve. Instead the currency is free to float, but the authorities intervene to avoid what they regard to be undesirable consequences of excessive appreciation or depreciation. A weak currency may lead to excessive depreciation that the government may wish to avoid because of its repercussions on the domestic price of imports and the internal cost structure. Alternatively, countries with a strong currency may seek to avoid appreciation if they want to accumulate reserves and are indifferent to the effect on the money supply. Moreover, a country may even attempt to engineer the depreciation of its currency that would otherwise appreciate if the foreign exchange market were left to operate freely.

Secondly, multiple exchange rates offer a system whereby different exchange rates are enforced for different transactions either on the current or capital account and can be viewed both as a form of exchange control (particularly over capital transactions) and as a rational response to the fact that different classes of goods have different price elasticities in world trade. Many countries, including Britain in the past with the 'dollar premium', charge a higher domestic price for foreign currency than the prevailing market rate for investment abroad in capital assets such as shares and property. Such a device acts in essence as a form of exchange control.

Misplaced Criticism

Supporters of continued EU membership argue that the degree of economic autonomy for the nation state outlined here is illusory, because globalisation and the integration of financial markets will not allow differences in economic policy to persist. However, this viewpoint is over-stated. For example, departure from the ERM and the subsequent 20% depreciation in sterling resulted in the resumption of economic growth, which facilitated a fall in unemployment to levels last experienced two-and-a-half decades earlier. A further argument for maintaining EU membership is the suggestion that the UK's European partners would engage in some form of trade protection, however, the argument is implausible. Firstly, the UK has suffered a substantial trade deficit with the rest of the EU since accession in 1973, therefore in the event of a trade war, our EU 'partners' would lose the most. Secondly, any such protectionist measures would fall foul of numerous international treaties, binding their signatories to respect reciprocity of trade.

In reality, Britain enjoys an effective long-run choice concerning its future strategy; it can embrace an essentially European identity, or it can pursue a global strategy. It need not fear that a long-term disengagement with movements towards further EU integration will lead to a powerless isolation. Britain is a member of the 'G8' industrial nations; its economy ranks as one of the largest in the world and the third largest in the EU. It is a member of the World Bank and the International Monetary Fund. It possesses a seat on the United Nations Security Council and remains the head of the Commonwealth, whose potential for expanded trade has recently been grossly neglected (West, 1995; Burkitt et al., 1996). Moreover, Britain enjoys a substantial portfolio of overseas assets and investments, and attracts the highest level of inward investment in the EU. It is the world's second largest financial centre and global investor. It has more companies in the world's top 500 than any other EU country. The UK is well placed to be one of the most dynamic and innovative global economies (Taylor, 1995).

Fundamentals of Industrial Success

An active industrial strategy must be based upon understanding of what promotes industrial competitiveness. Porter's (1990) exhaustive research demonstrated that economic success is achieved through the development of 'clusters' of mutually reinforcing internationally competitive industries. Britain once enjoyed the benefits of clustering, as one sophisticated industry spawned and reinforced others; British goods pulled British services into overseas markets and vice versa, its multinationals served as loyal customers abroad, and the cluster of financial services and trade-related industries was highly self-reinforced. However, a gradual unwinding of industrial clusters occurred, with only pockets of competitive advantage remaining. The spiral continues downward, cushioned only by long tradition and the remnants of technological innovation. Thus, many British manufacturing companies lag behind those of other industrial countries such as Germany, Japan and Sweden in process technology and in their willingness and ability to invest in new plant, undermining competitive advantage in industries producing manufacturing equipment such as machine tools and process controls.

The sectors where British firms sustain competitive advantage partly owe it to a cluster of related, supporting industries. In consumer goods and services, a vibrant retail industry creates pressures to innovate. Britain was among the first countries to permit television advertising, which created a fertile environment for companies to build skills in modern marketing. The City of London provides another sector where British strength relies upon the advantages of clustering. Britain's international position in financial services such as trading, investment management, insurance and merchant banking is concentrated in the City, along with supporting activities like information and telecommunications facilities, financial journalism, printing and publishing, legal services, financial advertising and public relations. The dynamism of this cluster attracts firms worldwide to locate in London.

However, British industry overall lacks dynamism and the ability to upgrade its competitive position unaided, due to cumulative disadvantages which reinforce each other negatively in the spiral of relative decline. Problems in one industry hurt others. Falling competitiveness reduces relative living standards, making consumer demand less sophisticated. Downward pressure on government revenue leads to cutbacks in resource creation and social services, weakening still more industries. Britain's remaining competitive advantages are insufficient to generate sufficient well-paid jobs for all its citizens. Therefore it is caught in the downward spiral of clustering and its relative living standards suffer accordingly. Loss of competitiveness creates its own momentum, which, once established, is hard to reverse without a major policy initiative. Indeed lingering market positions and customer loyalties allay any sense of urgency about the need for change.

A significant proportion of growth in skilled and value-added UK employment has occurred from investment by foreign firms. Much of this, however, is attracted by relatively low production costs. Foreign investments are largely in assembly facilities, taking advantage of poorly paid, mostly unskilled labour, or in service industries such as hotels, golf courses and retail outlets. While overseas capital benefits British industry, an economy whose growth depends on assembly outposts of foreign companies will be constrained in terms of productivity increases. Certainly such investment alone cannot break the vicious circle between a weak balance of payments, slow growth and declining manufacturing, which has developed in the three decades since UK accession to the EU.

Strategies for Industrial Success

Britain demonstrates the problems facing an economy needing to restart the upgrading process. A number of fundamental problems must be tackled by a coordinated industrial strategy if recovery is to occur:

- The UK cannot regain innovation-driven competitiveness without a world-class educational and training system encompassing all socio-economic and ability levels. The rate of investment in human skills must rise substantially, standards must be improved and technical expertise must be stressed. This is perhaps the most pressing issue facing Britain over the next decade, for the need to improve the quality and quantity of its labour force is great. Research conducted in France and Germany by the National Institute for Economic and Social Research (Prais and Wagner, 1988; Steedman, 1988; Prais and Jarvis, 1989) demonstrated that the level of technical qualifications of craft workers is far superior in those countries to that achieved in the UK. A further report (Prais and Jarvis, 1989) on training in the retail industry concluded that the UK was creating a certificated semi-literate underclass'. Moreover, training trends are deteriorating in the UK; in 1964 240,000 young people were in apprenticeships and 148,000 in industrial or mercantile training, but some 20 years later these figures had dropped to 55,700 and 36,700 respectively.

- British companies, as well as the government, face a busy skills agenda. They need to realise that without a broader pool of trained human resources, their competitive advantage will be limited. This need embraces managerial staff, where British firms have traditionally employed far fewer university graduates than other industrial economies. Unless companies accept greater responsibility for internal training of all workers, they will make little progress relative to their competitors. The multi-skilling of the industrial workforce provides the route to productive flexibility, quality and innovation, while enhancing individuals' occupational status. The inability of individuals to contribute to their full potential is reflected in the stunted economic performance of many sectors. Narrow vocational training is a contradiction in an economy that seeks to place workers at the forefront of innovation. Consequently the emphasis must be on quality training to reflect new economic requirements.

- UK investment levels need to increase to match the improved labour force, primarily in manufacturing but also in the infrastructure of essential services. Machinery and plant in many sectors are currently antiquated, so that the development of advanced technologies as a basis for expanding into modern high value-added production is held back. The future competitive advantage of British firms can only be based on innovation in new products and new processes of production. Government aid to industry enabling the maintenance of high investment can play a crucial role in this process.

- The UK lags behind other industrial nations in the share of GDP allocated to research and development (R&D). Government investment in R&D is among the highest as a percentage of GDP across OECD countries, but half is focused on defence that possesses limited spin-offs for civilian industry. Even more troubling is the low rate of overall R&D spending in firms. A reallocation of both government and company resources towards commercial R&D is necessary for successfully reversing the spiral of relative decline, by stimulating both the generation and the diffusion of innovation. Supporting reform of the accounting treatment of R&D expenditure would also prove beneficial.

- Without sophisticated buyers, innovation and dynamism will be stunted. Britain already enjoys demand-side advantages in luxury and leisure-related commodities. The challenge is to upgrade industrial demand to broaden the sphere over which British companies benefit from well-informed buyers. Improvement of managers' and workers' education contributes to this objective. The prosperous London and South East markets can be the cutting edge of new consumer demand conditions.

- Some of the operations of London financial markets have become a barrier to British competitive advantage. Institutional investors often do not possess commitment to companies nor do they play an active role in corporate governance. A group of large British conglomerates has emerged, which buy and sell unrelated companies, but whose financial orientation does little in the long-run to upgrade competitive advantage in domestic industry. The result of such trends is that US-style earnings pressures threaten to dominate UK management thinking. However, a long-run bias in industrial decision-making is in the interests of national prosperity.

- British economic prosperity will never be complete without a faster rate of new business formation to make headway in reducing unemployment, because revitalisation of established industries sometimes reduces the size of the workforce. However, new business formation depends on skills and ideas, on appropriate motivation and goals, on active competition, and access to capital. One of the urgent reasons for upgrading British education, especially in universities, is to seed new ventures. The UK cannot rely on foreign investment for job creation and prosperity (The Economist, 1991).

These measures should reduce the level of joblessness, leading to the long-term restoration of full employment. By reducing, and eventually eliminating, the long-run growth of imports and by stimulating an expansion in exports, the strategy aims to reconcile full employment with the simultaneous achievement of payments equilibrium.

The EU as Stumbling Block

However, such an industrial strategy can be reconciled with current EU regulations, let alone its future federal aspirations, thus Britain's essential interests' conflict directly with EU moves towards greater integration. However, with determination and imagination, there is no reason why Britain cannot acquire again the significant comparative advantages in the production of goods that once made it the workshop of the world. Services are a crucial complement to this process, but do not alone provide the growth momentum of manufacturing industry nor can they be relied upon to substitute for the deficits in overseas visible trade. The construction of such a competitive economy in the UK involves the complete unravelling and reconstruction of its relationship with the EU. It is to this relationship that we now return.

The policies required to revitalise British industry run counter to current EU rules and would be frustrated by movement towards economic and political union. Major historical trends cannot be reversed quickly; a permanent increase in the British rate of productivity growth, for instance, requires sustained economic expansion, a difficult endeavour given the deflationary tendencies of EMU.

UK membership of the EU tends to frustrate the achievement of these objectives through three fundamental mechanisms. Firstly, Britain's relatively weak competitive trade position with other EU nations prevents market forces from generating unaided the profits required for industrial regeneration. Experience demonstrates that market operations tend to accentuate strengths and deficiencies rather than eliminate them. Secondly, The Treaty of Rome severely limits aid to industry, whilst the public expenditure needed to complement the price mechanism in promoting industrial regeneration is circumscribed by the TEU convergence criteria and SGP. Thirdly, the current functioning of EMU limits the scope for dis-

cretionary national economic policies. Therefore, both markets and governments are prevented from addressing the UK's basic problems by the
very essence of EU operations and developments.

Conclusion

The design of a macroeconomic framework for a complex advanced economy depends upon a multiplicity of diverse factors, including recognition
of its unique industrial structure, monetary and fiscal policy transmission
mechanisms, the practice of wage formation, propensity for owner-occu-
pation, national savings rates and technological progress. A combination
of differences in consumer tastes, political choices, natural resources and
centres of competitive excellence, together with the actions of institutions
established to implement economic and social policy, necessitates differences in economic policy between nations. Moreover, exchange rate
regimes tend to have a greater impact upon smaller, export-orientated
nations than upon their larger neighbours, where only a relatively small
proportion of GDP is traded. Consequently, it is extremely difficult for
one international economic authority to replace national macroeconomic
management by one common interest or exchange rate. It is simply that
many economies of EU member states are too divergent cyclically and
structurally from their neighbours for any claim of prior convergence to
be convincing and, without such evidence, a common economic strategy
is unlikely to be simultaneously in their individual interests.

In view of such fundamental weakness at the heart of the EU project,
the decision to reject participation retains for national government the
economic instruments vital to successful macroeconomic management.
Exchange rates can fulfil their function of equalising the demand and supply for a currency by the variation of its price, thereby preventing a basic
uncompetitive imbalance from causing mass unemployment and falling
standards of living. Fiscal policy, freed from the twin restrictions of the
TEU convergence criteria and the Stability and Growth Pact, can smooth
cyclical fluctuations, avoiding periodic unemployment that wastes productive resources and generates associated human misery. The purpose
of monetary policy is, then, to prevent unstable boom and slump conditions in housing and financial markets, whilst seeking to ensure a low
interest rate for investors in productive capital.

In view of the overwhelming evidence supporting the maintenance of
national self-determination of economic policy, two factors remain to provide the momentum towards further integrationalist economic participation. The first relates to the determination of a small political elite to

complete the European integration project. However, these small elites are neither representative of the wider British electorate, nor even of the majority of business. In a democracy, governments should act in the interests of all the people, which requires the rejection of abandoning national economic policy. The second factor undermining the vigorous assertion of national independence is the fear of failure. The notion of the UK as a declining nation has long sapped its resolve to follow its own interests, yet as illustrated in this chapter, there is no reason for such defeatism. Fear is the enemy of innovation and as the one of the largest economies in the world; the UK possesses a significant number of advantages.

The scale of deindustrialisation is uniquely intense in Britain requiring the implementation of a solution geared specifically to British problems rather than a blunter, less sensitive EU-wide programme. However, any strategy designed to confront the UK's deep-seated trading crisis within the EU will take many years to come to fruition. Therefore a danger arises that such a strategy could be jettisoned before it has had sufficient time to be effective, in the face of short-term pressures. This consideration suggests that government funds for industrial restructuring should be exempt from any immediate requirement for reducing public expenditure. Consequently a programme to stimulate industrial investment, boost jobs creation, and improve the quality of education and training must be rigorously maintained in the face of potential short-run problems. The benefits from such a programme would be reaped over a five to ten year period, if the constraints imposed by EU integration are prevented from undermining its potential. Survival in the interim requires the creation of a breathing space for the British economy until the programme becomes effective. The preservation of this essential space depends upon the UK government possessing an active exchange rate and trade policy, with discretionary control over movements in the external value of sterling and freedom to pursue independent fiscal and monetary policies.

The question remains whether these can be better realised within an EU model of deeper economic and political integration, a looser relationship with the EU, or through a more independent arrangement, possibly involving withdrawal as a first step towards this reorientation of priorities. This is an important question since it goes to the very heart of what Britain will make of itself and whether it places artificial limitations upon its ability to deliver the priorities espoused by its citizens.

Part II
Options for Political and Sovereignty Renewal

Marc Glendening

Thinking Inside the Box

Restating the Case for the Nation-State

Introduction

The democratic nation-state is in danger of quietly disappearing without even a serious war of ideas, let alone anything more dramatic, taking place.

EU member countries have been experiencing a slow-burning, quiet revolution which has seen periodic and major transfers of decision-making power to Brussels. According to the German Justice Ministry, the only governmental agency to have attempted a forensic audit of the percentage of national laws that are based on EU directives, approximately 80% of the laws of that country passed since 1998 have been mandated by Brussels.[1] The think-tank, Open Europe (2009) have conducted their own study relating to Britain and concluded that over 50% of legislation relating to economic activity is based on directives and regulations. Whatever is the actual figure now, it is safe to assume that with the passing of the Lisbon Treaty the percentage of laws that are EU-initiated will soon account for a clear and accelerating majority of all national statutes passed since the Single European Act kicked in.

Whenever an issue of international significance rears its head, be it the credit-crunch, disputes over energy supplies, conflicts between east European states, threats to the environment, among other issues, a large section of the political and opinion-forming classes combines to demand that more 'urgently required' powers are transferred to international institutions. Very rarely is it explained how, precisely, such a further concentra-

---

1   See *democracy-international.org*, 19 September, 2005.

tion of supranational authority will, in practice, improve the situation and why voluntary, ad-hoc co-operation between sovereign countries cannot achieve positive results.

The Emergence of Transnationalism

There can be little doubt that transnationalism is now in the intellectual and real-world, political ascendancy. This is a consequence of the theoretical and positive case for states based on national communities of people simply not having been articulated in Britain, certainly not post our entry into the EEC. Because of this failure to engage on the ideological level against transnationalism, we have allowed a defence of the nation-state to become misrepresented as an aggressive, *volkish*, nationalism. The enemies of national sovereignty have thus been able to present themselves as progressive and liberal when, in reality, the opposite is the case.

There are several reasons why I characterise the political revolution we are being subjected to as 'Post-Modern Authoritarianism' (PMA), in addition to the fact that a number of leading transnationalists have themselves described the system of governance we are being subsumed by as post-modern. The PMA description refers both to an empirically observable institutional condition and to the ideological techniques used to help advance the transition away from national democracy.

The modern era was concerned, as Marshall Berman[2] put it, with 'visions and ideas that aim to make men and women the subjects as well as the objects of modernisation, to give them the power to change the world that is changing them.' A key aspect of its liberating agenda was the collectivisation of the idea of sovereignty; the capacity of a people to both define themselves as a distinct political community and to impose a favoured course of political action. In the heyday of parliamentary government it became clear where ultimate decision-making lay, who was responsible for what. There was one unambiguous central focus of authority within each society.

By contrast, in the post-modern period the political process is becoming arcane once again as powers are transferred to and fragmented between a range of non-directly accountable agencies at the domestic level as well as to various transnational bodies. This dispersal of power away from accountable government has been accompanied by a simultaneous centralisation of legal supremacy with institutions that sit above and beyond the nation-state.

---

2   Quoted in Boyne and Rattansi (1990), p6.

Moreover, the PMA transformation has been complimented by a political and cultural propaganda campaign designed to undermine the foundations of the nation-state and liberal democracy whilst refusing to spell out the true nature of the transnationalist alternative. The Post-Modern Authoritarians (PMAs) are therefore making the political world a mysterious place once again in order to draw a veil over this new epoch of elitist power.

A further reason why this new elitism should be classified as post-modern is that whereas the anti-democratic upholders of the Ancient Regime offered explicit traditional, religious based reasons for opposing popular sovereignty, their transnational counterparts still rhetorically insist that they are in the broad liberal tradition. By virtue of the subtle strategy they are pursuing, the PMAs are working to create a system that has the outward appearance of still being politically pluralist and free, but which in reality restricts important decision-making to delegated committees of remote, unaccountable officials at the international level. Political differences are debated within a very restricted, mainstream realm and can be negotiated away through consensual deal-making behind closed doors. Elections give the emerging system a veneer of legitimacy, the appearance of democracy, but in reality they are of declining significance. If 'outsider' political forces emerge that seriously threaten to break apart the emerging system then heavier mechanisms come into play. So, for example, the PMAs justify suppressing the right of peoples to vote in referenda on the grounds that this is necessary in order to defend democracy. This bewildering contradiction of form and content, this twisting of logic, is, of course, itself highly characteristic of post-modern times.

For example, Lord Neil Kinnock[3] famously declared the result of the French referendum on the European Constitution to be a 'victory for ignorance' . Valerie Giscard d' Estaing[4] commented that 'It is the method [a referendum] that has provoked the rejection … he people might consider that they made a mistake' . Andrew Duff[5], the Liberal Democrat MEP, said that 'the experience [of the French and Dutch referenda] begs the question of whether it was ever appropriate to submit the EU Constitution to a lottery of uncoordinated plebiscites' . Chris Bryant,[6] Labour MP, thought that 'Although a referendum might be appropriate for 'Pop Idol' … it is unsuitable for examining a treaty.' Whilst writing in the aftermath

3   Quoted in BBC website, 2 June 2005.
4   Valerie Giscard d'Estaing, *The Times*, 23 May 2006.
5   Andrew Duff MEP, quoted in *Liberator*, issue 303, 11 July, 2005.
6   Chris Bryant MP, quoted in *The Sun*, November 13, 2005.

of the Irish 'no' vote on the Lisbon treaty, the New Labour economist Will Hutton (2008), without any apparent sense of irony, attempted to associate the idea of democratically consulting the people with fascism: '...referendums work best for the demagogue, the dissimulator and scaremonger, as Hitler and Mussolini, lovers of referendums, proved.'

Until Britain's entry into the EEC, national independence was taken for granted. Since the start of the process of handing over power from Westminster, the mainstream EU-critical forces have necessarily had to focus on fighting rearguard and short-term populist campaigns designed to prevent the next seizure of law-making authority. If the situation is to be transformed it will be a necessary, if not a sufficient condition, to wage a war of ideas, starting from first principles. There are two main challenges facing defenders of the national-modernist legacy:

The first, is to do what the PMAs want to prevent from happening; namely, the exposure of the 'big picture' . This means initially labelling and describing the particular way in which national democracy is being superseded by transnational governance. Part of the reason national-modernists have failed to mobilise greater opposition to what has been happening is because of the disingenuous way in which the PMAs have pursued their project. Nor does claiming that Britain's subjugation to the EU represents an old-fashioned foreign takeover, correspond to most people' s understanding of the issue. Since our own political class has been complicit in the undemocratic transfer of power the post-modern revolution needs to be portrayed rather in terms of a political 'cartel' , as Laughland (2002) has analysed it. Thus, this issue is at root a *class* rather than a national conflict; the various peoples of Europe against the elite.

The second task is to explain precisely why it is that nation-states offer the only possible foundation for democratic accountability and politically stable societies. There must be a response to the 'culture war' that has been unleashed by the transnationalists which has dishonestly sought to associate political expressions of national identity with racism. National-modernists need to turn the tables and establish that the agenda of reviving the nation-state has moral force behind it and that it is the superficially more progressive transnational alternative that is leading us towards a highly reactionary destination.

The Post-Modernist Revolution

The hegemony that PMA enjoys is not the result of an honest war of ideas with the case for a supranational government triumphing over that of the nation-state. There has been no spontaneous popular uprising demanding the international centralisation of political power. The relatively honest, traditional advocates of Pan-European and world federalism are now very few in number and have been replaced by a more disingenuous post-modernist political current. The latter have advanced their cause, in contrast, by a campaign of simultaneously undermining the nation-state together with an attempt to obscure the true nature of the system they are working towards.

Hence, in the context of the issue of Europe, the PMAs seek to call into question the assertion of made by defenders of the nation-state that transfers of power to Brussels are leading to the creation of an alternative Pan-European government or state. The supporters of political union typically deny that full federalism is still on the agenda; this was an aspiration in the period of Jacques Delors' presidency of the Commission but which has now been abandoned, they say. Again, a third option is possible, allegedly. It is claimed that we can be at one and the same time citizens of a locality, a region, a country, a continent and, indeed, the world.[7]

The nation-state is obsolete but this doesn' t mean that the polar opposite is a European federal state or World government, the PMAs insist. Political power can be located in a multiplicity of decision-making centres. Martin Wight (2007), in his essay, *Why Is There No International Theory?*, writes that we have been led to believe that '...only within the secure borders of territorial states is it possible to engage in a serious politics, a politics that aspires to some kind of moral status on the basis of some kind of community... Politics, real politics, they suggest, can occur only as long as we are prepared – or able to – live in boxes.' He wants us instead to open ourselves up to the possibility of a new transnational politics where boundaries are less clear and power-relations between nations, between governments and their citizens and between states and supranational entities, are shifting and less defined.

Anthony Giddens in The Third Way and the Renewal of Social Democracy echoes this theme when he says that nations must be forced to immerse themselves in a system of 'cosmopolitan democracy' in which the physical and legal borders between them will be 'fuzzy' , as he evocatively and revealingly puts it. Giddens (1998) argues that the EU is 'pioneering forms of governance that do not fit any traditional mould' and that it is a model that should be replicated globally. The International

---

7   Bill Rammell MP, quoted at public debate on Lisbon Treaty, 28 February 2008, Harlow.

Criminal Court' s jurisdiction 'should extend widely over relations between states and their citizens.'

In a rare and commendable moment of candour, Mark Leonard (2005) of the EU-funded Centre for European Reform, explains the success of the post-modernist strategy:

> Europe' s power is easy to miss. Like an 'invisible hand' , it operates through the shell traditional structures. The British House of Commons, the law courts... are still here, but they have all become agents of the European Union implementing European law. This is no accident. By creating common standards that are implemented national institutions, Europe can take over countries without necessarily becoming a target for hostility... Europe' s invisibility allows it to spread its influence... Europe lacks one leader, being a network of centres of power that are united by common policies and goals.

Thus, the main intention of the PMAs has been, of course, to obscure the incremental diminution of national democracy and its replacement by a new, elitist system of political power. The peoples of Europe must not be alerted to what is happening to their respective democracies and so this climate of intellectual fuzziness is deliberately promoted by the transnationalists. But the Law of Contradiction — the cornerstone of western logic — does require that we choose where we are ultimately governed from and by whom. Supreme end-of-the-line power cannot simultaneously exist in two separate places at the same time within the same jurisdiction.[8]

Traces of post-modernism can also be seen in the way those working for Pan-European government effortlessly brush away inconvenient opposition to their project. There are echoes of this approach in the way the inconvenient referendum results in France, Holland and Ireland over the European Constitution/Lisbon treaty were dismissed by the Brussels elite. The first reaction of many supporters of the losing side after these contests was to question as to whether those voting 'no' were really signifying a rejection of the actual treaties placed before them. Conveniently, the conclusion drawn was that these were not real defeats for the idea of closer European union. Margot Wallstrom[9], vice president of the Commission, commented on her blog that the Constitution was a 'complex issue to vote on" and this had resulted in many citizens using "a referendum to answer a question that was not put to them.'

8   Brian Denny, quoted at press conference, No2EU: Yes to Democracy, House of Commons, 21 April 2009.
9   Quoted in Frank Furedi, From Europe to America: the populist moment has arrived, spiked-online.com, 13 June 2005.

There is also something post-structuralist in the way the Commission and the European Court of Justice (ECJ) circumnavigate occasional challenges by national governments to the right of the EU to legislate in certain areas. Intellectually gymnastic re-interpretations of other articles to be found in the treaty enable the ECJ to then assert that the parties to the treaty did in fact give their consent to the EU being able to legislate in exactly the way it wishes to. The often cited example of 'subsidiarity' , with its vague implication and promise of decentralisation, demonstrates that anything can indeed mean whatever it is the ruling interests want it to mean: ...a rich and prime example of gobbledygook' was how a former president of the ECJ, Lord MacKenzie Stuart,[10] accurately described this concept. In Brussels, it is always a case of 'heads we win, tails you lose' , and this is why the rule of law does not apply there.

The first key task facing defenders of the nation-state, then, is to strip bare the post-modernist strategy we have been subjected to and the nature of the system of governance in the process of creation. As a starting point, we need to draw a distinction between, on the one hand, the concept of government, the physical institutions of the state, including the most visible pinnacle of the system, a publicly accountable executive, and, on the other, that of governance, the activity of making political decisions and laws. We must explain that transnational politics in the post-modern era is about separating the two, obscuring where and how the latter takes place, whilst leaving the traditional, national institutions of state still in place (albeit hollowed out). A shadow, parallel, system of executive power is thus being created that remains largely hidden from view. There needs to be an exposing of the precise process by which national self-government is being dismantled if we are to stand any chance of mobilising popular opposition to it.

States Need Nations

The ultimate objective of PMA is to disconnect the political system from its cultural underpinning, namely 'the people' ; a national community that owes allegiance to a particular state. The new international political class appreciates that a system of governance cut free from a distinct, self-conscious electorate with a common identity will be unaccountable to those they rule over.

---

10   Quoted in Aiming for the Heart of Europe: A Misguided Venture, Bruges group Paper No.33. 2003.

This is not just because supranational institutions are typically undemocratic and non-transparent, but also because enormous imperial-like structures are too diverse linguistically and culturally for there to be the intensity of focus required for proper accountability. There is a fragmented media and oppositional political movements are divided by national origin. The costs of organising politically are made much, much higher in a transnational setting because of the vast territorial area and population involved. There are huge financial disparities between the interests supporting the new order and those opposing it.

The elitist model of governance in Brussels has traditionally been highly attractive to the continental centre-right, in part, because it has offered business lobbying access to one set of centralised decision-takers in the Commission and the opportunity to get measures implemented that would be difficult to get past social democratic leaning electorates in their own member states. The total lack of transparency concerning lobbying activities has thus been seen as a major advantage of the system. The European Round Table of Industrialists set up in 1983 has been a very effective mechanism for communicating the policy demands of big business within the EU, as Currid (2009) has shown. As the Labour party and the European centre-left has gravitated towards the politics of the Third Way it too has become more comfortable with this type of policy formulation and the huge influence big multinational corporations have in Brussels.

Chandler (2007) has argued that elements of the once radical, outsider, left that had its point of origin in the counter-cultural movements of the 1960s, have also gravitated towards their own elitist form of political engagement. The new left of the late 1960s rejected the idea of working through conventional parliamentary structures and political parties based on the mass mobilisation of the electorate, and was instinctively anti-national. But whereas classical Marxists envisaged an international workers movement, led by disciplined parties with clear socialist programmes, the new left came to posit instead the far less defined idea of a global 'civil society' and favoured an anarchic approach to campaigning based on direct action and spasmodic acts of violence. In more recent and less febrile times this tendency has gravitated towards building a transnational network of NGOs, new social movements and campaigns based around a series of single-issue causes rather than a cohesive ideological framework.

Transnationalism therefore needs to be understood in terms of the class interest of professional politicians, senior civil servants, and numerous client groups including big multinational corporations, powerful NGOs and, in most European countries, the media establishment. PMA today is the coming into being of the technocratic, post-ideological elitism James Burnham and George Orwell so accurately predicted seventy or so years ago. A new class characterised by its ownership of the political system rather than industry or land; a grouping devoid of any meaningful political beliefs beyond the desire to retain power and the advantages in terms of status and wealth that derive from it (Orwell, 1946).

Further to undermining the concept of the nation state as a decision making entity, the second key objective of the PMAs has been to taint and proscribe the notion of national allegiance; to inhibit the free expression of a national 'we' , of a shared collective adherence to a particular state. Hence, the attempt to portray any manifestation of national identity as being, by definition racist and leading potentially to bloody conflict. The PMAs have been waging a culture-war intended to encourage an irrational association between the advocacy of national independence with fascistic imagery (conveniently ignoring, in the process, the close historical associations between the Pan-European ideal and extreme authoritarian movements going back to the 1930s) (Laughland, 2000).

Hence, those seeking to defend the political heritage of modernism need to urgently articulate the positive case for national communities and identities. This must be done by evoking an existential patriotism that is not based on the discredited notion of a common, genetic essence or 'spirit' , but on the idea of shared communal allegiance. A common identity forged by contingent factors such as shared historical experiences and cultural traits, geography, and commitment to certain broad political values.

Nation-states, it must be argued, are the only forms of government compatible with a fundamental respect for human agency. It is those in the national-modernist tradition, unlike the PMAs, who are in tune with the liberal and humanitarian values of the Enlightenment. The Age of Reason gave rise to a recognition that since human beings had the capacity to make choices and were not ahistorical beings devoid of memory, then communal political arrangements should be a reflection of the aspirations of *actual* groups of people. The capacity to express *difference* is a key human characteristic and in the collective political sphere respecting this reality means accepting that the world is divided into separate and autonomous political units.

The artificial and imposed unity the PMAs favour is, in contrast, in the sinister tradition of European thought that refuses to acknowledge the full reality of human existence, its capacity for spontaneous evolution and diversity. This alternative mindset assumes that ultimately humanity can be moulded and directed from above as if it were an inanimate object. With time, the PMAs believe, a new and compliant transnational consciousness will be achieved through central imposition.

The great advantage for the PMAs of the evoking of a universal humanity is that, in reality, of course, it does not actually exist or have the means to inconveniently declare its political desires to the political class. At the transnational 'fantasy-politics' level the elite can assert it is acting for the 'international community' in the safe knowledge that there is no such community to contradict it. The citizens of diverse countries have never consciously declared their desire to be merged into a continental or World authority. In the top-down system of transnational politics the laws of political gravity therefore do not appear to apply. The material forces that once underpinned and constrained the modern-era democratic states have been written out of the script through the simple expedient of denying them the means of democratic self-expression.

However, in the rational world actually-existing forces cannot be simply wished away and will find ways to reassert themselves. Political systems make demands of citizens and if the rulers do not have the consent of the governed then serious instability will follow. The sense of social solidarity that any harmonious political system requires in order that large scale transfers of wealth can take place between citizens – such as those required to maintain a single currency system in the long-term—can *only* take place in the context of a single, bounded political community.

Europe has begun to see disturbing indications of what may become commonplace with riots in recent times in Hungary and Greece because of single currency-related financial strictures. The rise of fascistic parties across the EU member states, as seen in the elections to the European Parliament in 2009, in part, because immigration is no longer an issue that is subject to democratic debate and national law, as well as associated conflicts arising from employment policy, are another indication of what can happen when citizens have been disconnected from the levers of power and feel no allegiance to those who rule over them. As Labour MP Gisela Stuart[11] has correctly warned: 'When electorates sense that the people and institutions they elect are increasingly unaccountable and that the political institutions that define the nation are undermined, nationalism will find expressions in other ways: colour, religion or ethnic origin.'

11   Speech, *The EU Constitution: Where Next?*, *Bruges Group*, 19 May, 2004.

Conclusion

If support for the idea of a Europe and wider World of self-governing and voluntarily co-operating nations is to grow there will need to be a turning of the tables on PMA. National Modernists will have to counter the impression that by resisting the drift towards transnational governance we are motivated by a primordial racism and seek a return to an out-dated state of affairs, the Europe of the treaty of Westphalia, as is so often alleged by transnationalist academics.

We must demonstrate that it is the PMAs who are now bringing about a new *Counter-Enlightenment* in which the idea of sovereignty residing collectively with 'the people' is being rendered redundant. However, whereas the religiously motivated conservatives who defended the principle also enshrined at Westphalia that supreme power should reside with individual monarchs ordained by God, the new absolutism of today is based on a politically disconnected new elite class and the numerous client interests beholden to it. And, while the traditionalist opponents of democracy were honest in articulating mystical justifications for the regimes they wanted to defend against the tide of rationalism that was just beginning to gather momentum in Europe in the Seventeenth-Century, their counterparts of today employ liberal sounding rhetoric to hide the reality of the system they are creating and the class-based interests that lay behind it.

While the atmospherics of the period we are experiencing may not convey a sinister authoritarianism, the ideal of democracy — the idea that human beings should collectively be able to express political agency — is under very great threat. The apparently progressive way in which this is being achieved makes this offensive all the more potent. Its analysis and exposure is a first step towards a liberal democratic new Enlightenment in Europe.

Ian Milne

Options for British Foreign Policy

Introduction

This chapter, firstly, examines the history of British foreign policy since its participation in the European project, focusing upon the three principles that are supposed to have governed the foreign policy establishment's mentality in the last thirty or so years. These are 'the bridge principle', the 'EU integration works' principle and the 'British ideas are prevailing in the EU' principle. However, from analysing these principles it is clear that no European country needs Britain to be a bridge between it and the United States and neither does the US think of Britain in those terms. Moreover, EU integration has not actually been successful even on its own terms and has given nothing to Britain, who would be a far more influential player outside it; whilst in some unfathomable way British ideas, never clearly enunciated by the Foreign Office, are prevailing in the EU.

Secondly, the chapter examines various ideas of foreign policy that Britain could adopt on her exit from the harmful and unnecessary European Union. Close relations with the US will always be of importance, but additionally Britain should seek to revive her activity in a number of international organisations, especially the Commonwealth, an organisation that could play an important part in the post-EU world.

Lost Illusions: The Past

For the last sixty years British foreign policy has been conducted mainly through the UN, NATO and the EU. Those bodies have recently come under unprecedented strain. Sharp divisions over Iraq and Afghanistan, far from being the cause, are merely the symptoms of a much deeper malaise. Personality clashes may have exacerbated the discord; but the real failure has been institutional. The UN, NATO and EU structures are not capable of accommodating opposing national interests and philosophies. Recent failures in this respect highlight the collapse of three of the four principles or postulates on which British foreign policy has been based for the last fifty years, namely:

1.   The 'bridge' principle
2.   The 'EU integration works' principle
3.   The 'British ideas are prevailing in the EU' principle
4.   The primacy of the Anglo-American relationship

The bridge principle

The argument goes that the UK is a 'bridge' between the EU and the USA, and that the stronger British influence is in Paris or Berlin the stronger it is in Washington, and vice-versa. The rationale behind the Bridge Principle is patronising, condescending and arrogant, and seen as exactly that in Paris and Berlin, who tend to view the UK not as a bridge but as an American Trojan Horse. The assumption is that if, say, Berlin needs to talk to Washington, then going through the British 'honest broker' works better than Berlin picking up the 'phone or telling its embassy in Washington to put the German case to the White House or the State Department. However, the Bridge Principle has no foundation in reality: and the Germans and French in particular have always regarded this peculiarly British illusion with the wry amusement, not to say contempt, it deserves (Baldwin, 2007).

Interestingly, in some Whitehall quarters, a parallel Bridge Principle, called the Gateway Principle, is held to operate in the economic field. This postulates that Inward Investment comes to the UK because, it being a member of the EU, the foreign investor 'gets access' to other EU countries' markets. Hence, the UK, according to this theory, is merely a 'gateway' to other EU countries. To the overwhelming majority of businessmen and investors the Gateway Principle is of course fantasy. If an American company really wants to get access to, say, the German market, it buys a company or builds a plant in Germany, not the UK.

Proponents of the Bridge Principle assume, wrongly, that influence is synonymous with agreement. However, Britain has enjoyed most infuence, on both sides of the Atlantic, when it went against the political trend of Continental Europe. Thus, the incoherence of Foreign Office thinking is obvious the moment the Bridge Principle is articulated. In persisting with the European project the UK is embarked on a process which by definition can only end in diplomatic self-emasculation, and thus fatally weaken one of the buttresses on which the purported 'bridge' rests. In the absence of a strong contrarian British voice, the EU will be even less inhibited in pursuing its self-proclaimed mission of challenging and rivalling the United States.

The 'EU integration works' principle

The argument is that more than 30 years of intensely close intra-EU cooperation at all levels has ensured harmonious, productive and mutually-beneficial outcomes. Nevertheless, British ministers, who spend a large part of their working life travelling to or in meetings with EU counterparts, badly misread intentions over Iraq, the draft Constitution which emerged from the Convention and of all their EU 'partners' over the EU Financial Perspective 2007-2013. All this happened despite the fact that most British civil servants and diplomats do little else nowadays but interact with their EU counterparts. That of course is the problem: by spending so much time with their EU opposite numbers discussing the esoteric navel-gazing rituals of 'process' they cut themselves off from what is really going on in the wider world.

This prompts the question: does 'Integration' work? On the evidence, no. The focus on process rather than outcomes, having to intermediate every word, phrase and comma through the EU, palpably subtracts value. Direct negotiations between sovereign independent nation-states, that is to say, inter-governmentalism, would work quicker, and almost certainly better.

To understand why EU integration does not 'work', consider just one EU integrationist policy: trade. The UK ceased to have its own trade policy on accession in 1973, when it joined the EU Customs Union and ceded to Brussels its seat and vote at the World Trade Organisation (the WTO). However, given that the structure and pattern of UK global trade is quite different from that of its EU partners, there is no a priori reason to suppose that, on balance, British interests and those of its EU partners coincide more often than they diverge.

The unhappy experience of the UK in trade matters as a result of EU integrationist policy is replicated in other areas of EU policy, from fishing to agriculture to justice and home affairs, where British interests coincide only occasionally or accidentally with those of its EU partners. If the UK really believed in 'integration', it would be busily giving up its sovereignty in other international institutions. But that is simply not happening. At the United Nations, the World Bank, the International Monetary Fund and NATO the other main global institutions set up after the Second

World War the UK shows no inclination to surrender its votes and seats to functionaries of a regional bloc. The conclusion must be that in the conduct of British policy there exists an inconsistency. That inconsistency is obvious to friends of the UK, who are no longer sure whether, in any particular policy area, their first port of call should be Brussels or London. It is also, needless to say, obvious to countries whose intentions towards the UK are less than friendly.

Behind the EU integration principle is its mirror image: the proposition that the age of the nation-state is over which for different reasons that view is shared by the elites of many other Continental EU countries. The strange thing is that the EU project to sideline the nation-state, inherent in the Treaty of Rome and recently embodied in the Constitution/Lisbon Treaty, is a peculiar obsession confined to Continental Europe. Almost everywhere else in the world the nation-state is cherished and aspired to.

Moreover, paradoxically even the 'post-national' EU, in spite of its denigration of the nation-state, behaves like a nation-state. For the last fifty years Brussels has been equipping itself with the symbolic and real trappings of a nation-state: a flag, an anthem, a currency, a central bank, a diplomatic service, an army, a parliament, a supreme court, a constitution. Soon, it will have its own President and Foreign Minister. In short, it conducts itself, externally and internally, as a nation-state, though unlike the traditional Western nation-state, as a deliberately anti-democratic one.

The absence of coherence between the EU's justification of its existence, that 'the age of the nation-state is over', and its own behaviour as a nation-state, is replicated amongst its own member-states whereby 'Europe' is explicitly seen by those countries as a mechanism to project or multiply national power or influence, but behind the *communautaire* official discourse, it is business as usual. Thus, reports of the death of the nation-state have been exaggerated. The independent sovereign nation-state is the only social organisation yet invented which allows its citizens, however imperfectly, the exercise of their democratic rights. The corollary is that the EU, however well-intentioned, is proving to be the major factor in the slow-moving evisceration of British democracy. Over 80 per cent of British law is now made in Brussels and almost all of it is transposed into British law without debate or scrutiny, let alone a vote, in Westminster.

Nation-states, and inter-governmentalism, taking their cue from that über-nation-state, America, will prosper; concomitantly, multilateral and supranational bodies will continue to atrophy. One example is the WTO, in response to whose agonisingly slow procedures the USA, and others, have resorted to striking bilateral government-to-government trade deals.

The 'Britain is winning the argument in the EU' principle

Variations on this are 'The British vision of the EU is now prevailing', or 'Britain is punching above her weight in the EU'. However, these theories are at odds with EU-reality as British diplomacy has failed to create an EU that respects the nooks and crannies of national life, let alone national sovereignty and fundamentally failed on numerous occasions:

- the new Lisbon Treaty is irrefutable proof that British ideas on the future of the EU have, as usual, been ignored
- the 2007–2013 EU Financial Perspective agreed in December 2005, in which, despite giving up £7 billions of the rebate, Mr Blair got no undertaking to reform the CAP. Indeed, France immediately insisted that the CAP had been 'saved' and that there will be no CAP 'reform' before 2014 or even 2020
- the goal of a single market, for many firms and industries a distant prospect, just as it has failed to bring about the dismantling of the Common Agricultural Policy
- to persuade France to accept Turkey as a member-state
- to prevent France blocking progress on the Doha Round of world trade negotiations
- to fill the democratic deficit by narrowing the gap between Europe's elites and its electorates, just as it has failed absolutely to give any substance to the concept of 'subsidiarity', and failed to stem, even to slow down, the prolific outpourings of the Brussels regulatory machine
- to stop the EU Charter of Fundamental Rights being an integral part of the draft Constitution, justiciable at the European Court of Justice, whereby despite the rejection of the Constitution, both the Commission and the European Court of Justice are now explicitly incorporating the Charter's provisions in fresh legislation and in rulings on existing legislation
- to reconcile the opposing geo-political visions of the USA and of France and Germany.

Thus the list of things that British governments said they would do but have not done is very long indeed; in fact, many of the aims noted above are no longer aims at all.

Very occasionally, however, through fragile temporary opt-outs, British diplomacy succeeds in briefly slowing the pace of EU integration. That aside, the only real influence that successive British governments have been able to exert is persuading the Council and Commission to act as accomplices, through deliberate obfuscation, in concealing from the British electorate the nature of what is being created. Thus, after a decade of signing up to the federalising treaties of Maastricht, Amsterdam, Nice and Lisbon the UK still finds itself isolated on everything except the trivial, the insignificant and the irrelevant. Once again, EU-theory has turned out to be at odds with EU-reality. The British assumptions that a vacancy exists at the 'heart of Europe' and that the way to occupy it lies in signing up to everything, have proved to be illusory.

The above analysis illustrates that British policies on the EU, exemplified by the three principles described above, were built on sand. Most damaging of all is the defeatist self-delusion that British influence in Washington is merely a function of British influence in Paris and Berlin. That brings us to what is undoubtedly a success story for British foreign policy: the prosecution of the alliance with the United States.

The Anglo-American relationship

The fourth principle underpinning British foreign policy is to stay close to the Americans. The Foreign Office and successive British governments have rightly viewed this as the bedrock, the pivot around which their policy should be articulated. Over sixty years it has worked pretty well. Post 9/11, instability in the Middle East may have been exacerbated by misguided Anglo-American policies, but the present closeness of the relationship, as distinct from its effectiveness, is not in question — many critics, understandably, argue that it has been too close.

Nevertheless, the so-called special relationship is an uneasy one, given the enormous disproportion in power, which looks set to widen in the next fifty years. In military terms, the US Marine Corps alone is already bigger than the entire British Army, while in economic terms American GDP is six times that of the UK (and bigger than that of Japan, Germany, the UK and France combined). Inevitably, the charge that a British prime minister is a poodle of the Americans carries substance. The special relationship is usually more special to the British than to the Americans. However, the reality is that, if push comes to shove, the Americans can do without the British. That is not meant as a criticism of the Americans. But it is one reason why most post-war British governments have pursued the chimera of 'Europe', since deep down the UK has always known that it can never rely absolutely on the special relationship. If and when it were to be found wanting, the UK could seek comfort in the arms of 'Europe'. So the theory went, anyway.

As noted above, British governments assume that their influence in Washington is proportional to their influence in 'Europe', and vice-versa, although that assumption was never shared in Paris or Berlin or Washington. Instead, London's influence in Washington is, or ought to be, a function of its material leverage (in this case the UK's military, intelligence and diplomatic contribution), coupled with UK negotiating skill.

National Interest as the Guiding Principle

So where now for the UK? On the EU, its policy has ended in profound failure whereby the UK should re-think its fraught entanglement with the EU. Another powerful reason for so doing is that the Continental is in irreversible economic decline, primarily because of its weak demographics. Since scepticism about the 'European project' in France, Germany and elsewhere is growing, a British re-assessment of the European project would not exactly come as a surprise to its EU 'partners'.

However, the British government cannot simultaneously pursue a pro-American and a pro-EU policy. The two are mutually exclusive. As Dr Kissinger has remarked, the EU has got to make up its mind whether it wants to be, in relation to the USA, a 'counterweight', in other words a rival, or an ally. The French and Germans have made their choice: the counterweight. That is the geo-political reality with which British policy must now come to terms whereby the claim that 'Britain's destiny is Europe' is geo-political Malthusianism. Britain's destiny ceased to be European centuries ago when English settlers began their transatlantic odyssey. Within the next fifty years the USA and China between them will account for half of the world economy; quite possibly, India will account for another quarter. According to the EU Commission, Continental Europe, even after enlargement, will be lucky to muster ten per cent. For the next century the world will be dominated by the USA, China and India. Continental Europe will be increasingly irrelevant (Kagan, 2003). That being so, the notion that British interests will be best served by further integration into a failing regional bloc is far from self-evident. It follows that the UK should draw a line under its experiment with European 'integration' and disengage from the European Union, resume its seat and vote at the WTO and re-focus its defence policy on NATO.

Thus, just as, since 1973, British trade policy has been not to have a British trade policy, so, since Maastricht in 1992, British foreign policy has been not to have a British foreign policy with the introduction of the EU's

Common Foreign and Security Policy. Hence, the first step id the repatriation of British foreign policy such that national self interest becomes its
guiding principle. It is no accident that EU member-states accord a different priority to 'national interest' than do states that are not members of the
EU. After all, the national interest and the EU are contradictory notions:
the point of the EU is to make the nation-state redundant, or, more accurately, to transfer the functions of the nation-state from the nations of
which it is composed to the supranational bureaucracy in Brussels.

Although many in Continental Europe have always regarded the UK as
an American Trojan Horse, the fact is that British public opinion is as
sceptical about American foreign policy as it is about UK membership of
the European Union. Given that the American alliance and EU membership are the twin pillars of current British foreign policy, subjecting each
of them to hard questioning is in order. Are the assumptions which
underpin current British policy valid? If not, how should that foreign policy be reconfigured?

The primacy of the American alliance

The military, economic, scientific and diplomatic weight of the USA in the
world (and in space) will continue to grow, in relative and absolute terms,
for the foreseeable future. It follows that Britain should continue to give
primacy to the alliance with America. That alliance will be an unequal
one. As in the past, there will be times when American and British interests will not coincide. There will also be periods, as at present, when British public opinion will be sceptical about America's role in the world and
about the value of the alliance. Notwithstanding, over time, it will be in
Britain's interests to be America's closest ally. However, any illusions
about the relationship being 'special', in the sense that sentiment is
allowed by the British to cloud perceptions of each country's self-interest,
should be cast aside. Both countries need a robustly frank and independent relationship. This does not mean that the UK should strive for closer
institutional links with the USA. In trade matters, for example, having
disentangled itself from the EU, the UK should not apply to join NAFTA
on the rebound. The potential gains from NAFTA membership are marginal, as much for the British as for the Americans.

In theory, Britain could downgrade the Anglo-American alliance and
instead favour alliances with other great powers. The EU is not and never
will be a great power, for the reasons set out earlier. However, China, by
the end (or even by the middle) of the century looks set to be a power to
rival the United States. Russia is still powerful and dangerous, and, until

its population and energy resources both begin their rapid decline (well before 2050) will remain so. However, even if China and Russia were to become genuinely Western-style democracies, another powerful reason argues against Britain prioritising alliances with one or other of those countries over the American alliance. This is the risk that, sooner or later, Britain would find herself on the wrong side of a great-power confrontation between America and China, or America and Russia – a situation, from Britain's point of view, to be avoided, for obvious reasons. In contrast, the EU, especially following UK withdrawal, will not be able to achieve great power status, partly because of its inexorable demographic and economic decline, partly because of irreconcilable differences between its members.

Complementing the American alliance

Though neither hyperpower nor superpower, the UK is a global power with global interests to promote and defend. The alliance with America, though crucial, cannot and should not be exclusive. The UK needs enduring relationships on all continents with friendly countries that share the same values and traditions as herself. The mechanisms and structures for nurturing those enduring relationships already exist. First, outside 'official channels', there are innumerable family and business links, often centuries old, between British residents and their counterparts overseas. Second, there are the hundreds of more formal associations: political, trading, industrial, agricultural, religious, academic, scientific, cultural, sporting and so on. Some are long-standing, others more recent; some are treaty-based, some contract-based; still more operate as ad hoc arrangements. In the political field, examples include the United Nations and its associated bodies; the ever-expanding G8, and a uniquely informal voluntary association, the 54-member Commonwealth. In economics, the best-known examples are the IMF, the World Bank and the OECD. Third come the NGOs whereby millions of British private citizens support national and international humanitarian NGOs. Fourth, interacting with and supporting the work of the various bodies described above is the UK diplomatic service, generally regarded (overseas at least) as the best in the world.

Thus, post EU-withdrawal, a British government's task is not thus to re-invent the wheel of foreign policy, but rather to shift emphasis and realign it on twenty-first century geopolitical realities, away from excessive concentration on 'Europe' towards the Americas and South and East

Asia. There is no need to create new bilateral or multilateral alliances, of which an ample sufficiency already exists.

The Commonwealth is one example of an organisation to which UK governments might devote more attention. It has fifty-four members on all continents (exactly double the number of EU members) with a combined population of two billion (four times that of the EU). The Commonwealth includes the most populous nation in Asia and coming superpower, India; the biggest economy in Africa, South Africa; a NAFTA member, Canada; and the fast-growing economies of Australia and New Zealand (Global Britain, 2005). Its population and GDP are growing rapidly (in stark contrast to Continental EU), and it has already expanded to include Mozambique and Cameroon, countries with no historical links to the UK, with both Middle Eastern and African countries presently considering applying for membership. With encouragement from the UK, India might be persuaded to take on the leadership role in the Commonwealth and further expand the latter's global influence in promoting policies the UK supports such as liberalising trade, reducing poverty and protecting the environment.

Conclusion

British foreign policy, and the British Foreign Office, having cast aside the frame of mind exemplified by the discredited 'Bridge Principle', lurching alternately between deference to 'Europe' and deference to Washington, should elevate British self-reliance to the rank of guiding principle in the conduct of policy. The notion that Britain's destiny is to be a province of some half-baked European federation is grounded neither in history nor in reality. Britain's destiny is to resume its condition as a sovereign democratic independent nation-state, continuing 'to create the history of the world'. The UK should disengage from the EU.

Post EU withdrawal, the UK will continue to trade and have close and friendly relations with EU member-states, just as Switzerland and the US do today, and with whatever European institutions may succeed the present-day EU. The UK should continue to give primacy to staying close to the Americans. The right policy in the past, this will be ever more so in the future, as the military, economic and diplomatic 'weight' of the USA in the world continues to grow, and that of the EU to shrink. Furthermore, the UK should stay in NATO (or whatever successor body replaces it) for so long as the US remains committed to it. The UK should stay in, and resume its sovereign voting status in, the World Trade Organisation. It should participate in the other intergovernmental (and, unlike the EU, not supranational) bodies set up immediately after the Second World War, or their successor bodies, as well as more recent groupings such as the G8.

John Redwood

The EU

An Unloved Institution

Introduction

The UK was sold membership of the European Economic Community on the grounds that it was a trading arrangement. The main political parties lined up in 1975 to persuade the British public in a referendum that their sovereignty was not being given away. They would retain the veto over every policy of the Community. They were promised that there would be more jobs if they entered into a tariff-reducing arrangement with their European partners on the Continent in order to encourage a freer and more open market in industrial products.

From Free Trade to Superstate

This argument was wrong, as it skewed the tariff reductions to those areas where the Germans and French were strong and failed to open markets sufficiently in areas like financial business services where the UK was stronger. Nonetheless, it was one which was popular with the British people who voted strongly in favour of continued membership of the EEC. Indeed, the organisation was called the Common Market during and after the referendum to give people the strong impression that it was merely a trading arrangement. Labour ministers lined up to reassure us that our power of self-government was not being given away. We were reassured that we would still run our own economic policy, set our own interest rates, conduct our own foreign policy and retain our unique common law system of civil and criminal law.

Additionally, there are many features to the European project which are damaging constitutionally. One of the worst is the concept of a 'Europe of the Regions'. Those who are constructing the architecture for a more integrated Europe have understood that there are internal pressures against the nation states. They have seen that there are two Belgiums fighting to get out, that the Basques and the Catalans are not happy in their relationship with the Castilians in Spain, that northern and southern Italy are deeply divided, and, in the case of the United Kingdom, Scotland may well wish to have a much looser arrangement with the UK federation, or may wish to leave altogether. The EU, through its accent on regional government, is attempting to strengthen these regional forces against the member states. It is undoubtedly the case that the European regionalisation project has helped fuel Scottish nationalism, which often parades its European credentials, and is now stoking English nationalism in anger at the way the EU wishes to break England into a series of much unloved 'Euro-regions' and stifle English national identity. Similarly, many freedom loving British people deeply dislike the EU's style of governing where so much has to be written down in law codes of a prescriptive nature. They feel regulated to death, stifled by the stale air of bureaucratic prose and too many rules and regulations. It is the British style to allow people to do anything not banned by law, rather than seeking to write down ever more code setting out what you *are* allowed to do in painstaking and often outdated detail.

We also dislike the lack of democracy in the EU. In the early days it was said the British would make a unique contribution by helping to make the European Parliament a truly democratic institution, which could deal with the otherwise glaring lack of accountability. Nothing could be further from the truth. The European Parliament is a pale imitation of a proper democratic parliament. There are no cross-national parties campaigning as one. The ministers or commissioners are not chosen from amongst the elected body. Mercifully the elected body has no power to tax us, and has no sole power to make laws – indeed, it cannot even propose a new one. Its debates are short, without the intervention and cut-and-thrust which is the common feature of lively democracy in the Westminster parliament. People feel remote from their MEPs and the only time we really see anything in the newspapers is when one of them has misbehaved over their expenses.

1975 is now a very long time ago. The European Economic Community, or Common Market, has morphed into the European Union. Successive treaties have built on what was already apparent in the original Treaty of Rome that our partners on the Continent wish to take more and more power to the centre and create a federal state. That is why the EU now boasts an anthem, a parliament, a flag, a single currency for many of the countries involved, and has aspirations of wide ranging powers in civil and criminal justice, foreign affairs, defence policy and every other major area of governmental activity. That is why the Treaty of Lisbon has as its centrepiece the strengthening of the powers of the EU in foreign policy and defence, and the invention of a more powerful presidency to represent and guide the EU at home and abroad.

It is no wonder that many of the British people who had the benefit of a vote in 1975 feel cheated. I have met many people who voted Yes in 1975, but now tell me they would have voted No had they realised that this is not just about a common market but a proto-European state in the making. There are now, of course, subsequent generations who do not even have the benefit of having voted in 1975 who would welcome the opportunity to express their view on how far the EU has gone already, and the direction of travel it wishes to pursue.

Everyone can see how unhappy the current British electorate is with the European situation. Around a fifth of the electorate like what the European political elite is doing and feels Britain should be a part of the emerging EU. They would still like us to enter the single currency and would be happy to see greater cooperation in foreign policy and defence, and in justice matters. At the other end of the spectrum, maybe a quarter of the public have seen enough to know that, in their view, Britain would be better off out. They deeply resent the growing amount of law and regulation coming from Brussels. They feel that the UK could spend the public's money so much better than the EU does, either directly or indirectly by sending it back to us with strings attached.

The rest of the electorate are those sceptical of the build up of bureaucracy, the growing bills, the evidence of fraud, waste and mismanagement, the growing bossiness from too much regulation, and the pretensions of the EU. They would be prepared to look at a new settlement which allowed us to carry on trading with our European neighbours, and in some kind of relationship with them. It means that 80% of the electorate are frustrated with the attitude of the Labour and Liberal Democrat parties, who have enjoyed jointly a substantial majority in parliament since 1997 and who have conspired together to push through the Nice, Amsterdam, and Lisbon treaties without any reference to the British electorate for a referendum and without public or even parliamentary debate on many of the crucial issues. It is the purpose of this chapter to examine what the options are for political change, and to see how it might be brought about.

Going Along With the Whole of the Current EU Agenda, or Pulling Out Completely

This is self-explanatory. The first is effectively the policy of the current government. It is easy to do at the European level, but it does mean that a government following it becomes increasingly distant and remote from the pulse of the British people, and increasingly unpopular for its pro-European policy. It fails to get a good deal for Britain as we have seen with the British government surrendering some of the rebate Margaret Thatcher had carefully negotiated for the UK to make the financial settlement a little less unfavourable. In return the British government got nothing by way of Common Agricultural Policy reform, which was rightly a top objective of the administration.

Pulling out seems like an easy and swift proposal. Its exponents, I presume, imagine that one day a sufficiently Eurosceptic Parliament will be elected by the British people and will then vote unilaterally to repeal the 1972 European Communities Act, thereby terminating Britain's membership of the EU. However, most sensible commentators and voters can see that this would be a clumsy and difficult way of proceeding. It is quite obvious looking at voting trends over the last 20 years that the British electorate is a million miles away from wishing to elect a group of single minded, single subject MPs whose sole pledge would be the unilateral withdrawal from the EU as soon as possible, without any discussion or negotiation with our partners on the continent. More sensible "Better Off Out" people accept that there would need to be discussion or negotiation with our EU partners on the terms of exit. Britain now has so much tied up and enmeshed with the Continent, thanks to its long years in the EU, that there would need to be discussion over a whole range of subjects on which projects would continue after withdrawal, and what the trading and legal arrangements were going to be following termination of membership.

In practice, any sensible British government would go to Brussels and make it very clear that it wishes to have a series of arrangements and relationship with our European partners, but that it cannot be a full member of the entire EU project. Because successive governments have realised both that the EU does not always work in Britain's interests, and that joining all of the European club is unpopular at home, we have so far muddled our way through with a series of temporary or permanent opt-outs and exclusions from the full rigours of European bureaucracy. John Major successfully negotiated an opt-out from the main feature of the Maastricht Treaty, membership of the single currency. The decision of both the Conservatives and Labour to offer the public a referendum before joining the single currency has saved the pound. John Major's government negotiated an extremely useful and helpful opt-out from all social chapter measures of social and employment legislation. This meant that Britain was still free to legislate to her own high standards in these areas in a way which meant future Parliaments could change these as and when they saw fit. The Labour government's surrender of this opt-out early in its time in office was foolish. It now means that Britain cannot take her own independent view of employment and social matters wherever the EU has legislated. The John Major government also negotiated a very useful opt-out from the Common Borders Policy which the EU had started to pursue. Common borders make little sense for the island of Great Britain, whilst they make considerable sense for the Continental countries where they have long land frontiers with one another. This government has again given away this important opt-out, and made it much more difficult to control and police our borders effectively, and to control the movement of people.

This government has continued with the opt-out from the single currency, and may now find it needs to opt-out from some of the more extreme versions of integration over taxation, foreign policy and defence.

An incoming British government wishing to sort out the European problem should go to Brussels and say that the British people, if asked in a referendum, would not accept the Lisbon Treaty, and would doubtless also disagree with quite a lot in the treaties of Maastricht, Nice and Amsterdam. Indeed, such a government should explain to Brussels that the British people would need a substantial repatriation of powers to be happy with their EU membership.

What do British people want from their association with the European Continent? They want the right to trade freely in services as well as goods, accepting some common rules and standards where this facilitates trade. Increasingly, the position in trade is guaranteed by membership of the World Trade Organisation anyway, hence a future government would be happy to renew and improve the Common Market arrangements which the British people voted for in 1975 and remain the core of the present government's basis for our membership of the EU.

At the other extreme, an incoming British government should make clear to the EU that we have no wish to see Europe meddling with taxation, defence, foreign affairs, criminal and civil justice, immigration and borders. We regard these as crucial areas where we must be sovereign in the British Parliament and capable of responding to the views and wishes of the British people. British politicians should want to put their conduct in these affairs to the British electorate in General Elections. A sensible government would wish to have institutions and facilities to conduct common policies and develop common projects in areas of mutual interest. Obviously there needs to be discussions and frameworks in areas like air transport within European airspace, cross-channel rail and shipping, cross-border financial business services, and other related areas. We need membership of the institutions which facilitate such discussions and progress without drawing us into a heavy and cumbersome bureaucracy or too much law making.

The British government should seek to hammer out a sensible deal with our European partners to whom it should make clear that it wishes to put the resulting package to the popular vote. This should provide an incentive to the EU to grant enough return of power to make it likely that the British people would vote 'yes' to our continued and revised membership. There does not need to be threats or levers. The EU would get the message that if it does not come up with a package suited to the new British government and the temperament of the British people, the whole package will be rejected, which means that Britain will leave altogether. It will not be a British government wishing to leave, but it will be the choice of the British people in light of what was on offer from Brussels.

Conclusion

All these features of the EU, its wish to damage nation states, its lack of legitimacy and its pitiful lack of democracy, are reasons why it remains a much unloved institution in the United Kingdom. The time is right for reform. The growing gap between what the public want and what the political elite are delivering is too glaring and too damaging. It needs a new settlement. A new settlement requires the repatriation of powers. This can best be done by the new government, with a new mandate, going to Brussels and explaining patiently why the British people do not love the current Union, and how democracy, energy and freedom can be restored through repatriation. If the EU really gets it, and offers a sensible package, then both the new British government and the British people will be happy, and will vote accordingly.

Roger Helmer

Options for Sovereignty

Introduction

Let's start with a caveat. 'Sovereignty' is, in political terms, a dangerous word. Like 'Empire', it has a very nineteenth-century feel. As we all know, voters' concerns centre on domestic issues: schools and hospitals, crime, immigration, jobs and taxation, and (especially today) just making ends meet. Esoteric discussions of sovereignty leave them cold. This may not be a good thing, but it is a fact we have to live with.

As we seek to make our case against political union in Europe, we need to frame the debate in terms that connect with the voters. There is no doubt (though it is beyond the scope of this chapter) that EU membership is hurting our economy, and that the costs of regulation greatly exceed any trade benefits of the Single Market. In the EU, voters are less well off than they need to be. And they will increasingly find that they and their government have lost control of day-to-day concerns like immigration that matter to them. These are the issues that persuade.

If we need to turn to the political principles involved, we will find that independence and self-determination, freedom and democracy, resonate far better with voters than the rather old-world concept of sovereignty.

This chapter will look at a range of issues. The way in which control of our daily lives is passing to Brussels. How the EU institutions behave, and why they are not only undemocratic, but are in principle incapable of becoming democratic. Why the pro-EU arguments of influence within a larger entity ring hollow. And finally, what the alternative to EU membership might be, and why it is so much more attractive than the *status quo*.

Dilution of Self-Governance

Everyone likely to be reading this book will, of course, be familiar with the hectic rate at which competences are passing from Westminster to

Brussels (though I continue to be astonished by the lack of public aware-
ness). The British Chambers of Commerce say that 71% of regulations
now originate in Brussels (British Chamber of Commerce, 2008). Commissioner Charlie McCreevy (2008) says that the EU is responsible for 80% of
business regulation and we know that in Westminster, scrutiny of EU legislation is derisory (Open Europe, 2006).

Peter Lilley MP introduced a bill at Westminster calling for the salaries
of MPs to be reduced, commensurate with the reduction of their powers
and responsibilities. It is not expected to succeed, but it was a brave ges-
ture (BBC, 2008).

Since joining the then Common Market in 1973, we have lost control of
our trade policy, our fisheries and our agriculture. By degrees we have
lost, or are losing, control of employment policy where the last sad stages
of our retreat on temporary workers and the Working Time Directive are
just playing out (Financial Times, 2008). Although we have not joined the
euro, our economic policy is constrained by commitments under the EMS.

We have largely lost control of immigration, at least from EU member-states, and under the Lisbon Treaty we will further pass control to
Brussels. European Border Guards and an EU Gendarmerie, with rights
to make arrests in the UK, are also on the Brussels agenda. Justice and
Home Affairs are being subsumed under the Brussels banner. The European Arrest Warrant allows a British citizen to be arrested in the UK and
deported to any EU member-state on a warrant issued by a foreign magis-
trate. British judges increasingly refer to European law and precedent and
the Charter of Fundamental Rights in their decisions. The basic freedoms
of our citizens are under threat as never before.

The Lisbon Treaty also brings energy under the control of Brussels. In
1973 the EU took control of our North Sea fisheries and effectively
destroyed them. Now we seem set to send our remaining North Sea oil the
same way.

The EU diplomatic service foreseen by Lisbon is already in development ahead of the Treaty's ratification, and as EU Embassies are set up,
we will inevitably see the progressive closure of British Embassies, starting in small countries but progressing until only a handful, if any, remain.
While on the one hand EU leaders insist that the idea of an EU super-state
has been abandoned (so very last-century, you know) on the other hand
they are busy building the very super-state they deny.

Even those policy areas we traditionally think of as wholly national (i.e.
taxation, health, education, regional policy) are increasingly influenced
from Brussels. The direction of travel is clear, as is the momentum. With-

out decisive action, our future status is settled, as a remote off-shore province in a country called Europe.

Democracy in the EU

But there are those who say that if the new country of Europe is prosperous, powerful, democratic and peaceful, then perhaps we should welcome the development. After all, EU leaders speak *ad nauseam* of 'A
Europe of values based on democracy and the rule of law'.

To understand how democracy works, or fails to work, in the EU, we
need a quick tour of the institutions. We have the Commission, appointed
by member-states, with the sole right of initiating legislation. We have the
Parliament, elected from 27 member-states, tasked with amending legislation and scrutinising the work of the Commission. And we have the
Council, also appointed by member-states and representing their interests. There is also a long tail of smaller institutions: the ECB, the ECJ, and
so on.

Only the Parliament is elected, although it has abysmal standards of
accountability and fails to reflect the views of citizens, most notably on
the question of integration and the European project. For example, while
French and Dutch voters resoundingly rejected the EU Constitution in
2005, something like 90% of their MEPs voted in favour of it.

To understand why this should be, it is worth recalling how MEPs are
selected. With very few exceptions, the first step comes when they put up
their hand and say 'I should like to be considered as a Euro-candidate for
my party'. What sort of people will do a thing like that? A very few (like
myself) did so because we were appalled by the way the EU project was
going, and wanted to do our bit to oppose it. But the great majority did so
because they were enthusiasts for the project and determined to drive it
forward.

The MEPs of all three major UK political parties are on balance far more
enthusiastic (with a few honourable exceptions amongst the Conservatives) about the EU than are their parties at home.

I well recall a vote in the Unemployment Committee (on which I sit)
where we voted through the Working Time Directive. I was so exasperated that I accosted several socialist MEPs. I pointed out that the measure
would reduce labour market flexibility, cost jobs and damage competitiveness. They didn't try to argue about the damage. Instead, they replied
'Yes, but it's EU legislation. It's building the European house. It's taking
forward the European project'. To them, 'building Europe' was much
more important than their constituents' jobs.

I rarely agree with Tony Benn, but I wholeheartedly agree with his test of democracy. He says that the defining feature of a democracy is that we can fire the people who make our laws. That's the case in the UK. And in the US, where a change of President can mean thousands of jobs changing hands, and quite literally a new Administration.

But it is not true in Brussels. The Parliament has eight political groups, many with incomprehensible names like 'The European People's Party', and well over a hundred national delegations. So the voters can make marginal changes in the shifting coalitions and alliances within the Parliament, but the juggernaut rolls on. The jobs-for-life officials and their policies stay in place regardless of the people.

The voters are not stupid. They've worked out that their votes in euro-elections make little difference, which is why all euro-elections are now won by the stay-at-home party.[1] And in any case, only one of the three major EU institutions is elected to start with. Frequently the voters use the euro-elections register a protest on domestic issues and concerns, which is a rational tactic, since they can make no difference in Brussels.

Some Europhiles recognise that the Council and Commission are unelected, and they see a solution: just agree to elect those bodies, elect the EU President, and all will be well. But democracy is about more than counting votes. Counting votes is merely arithmetic. Enoch Powell put it best when he said that true democracy requires a demos, that is a people 'who share enough in common, in terms of history, culture, language and economic interests, that they are prepared to accept governance at each others' hands'.

In other words, for democracy to be legitimate it must be conducted amongst a group of people who regard themselves in some sense as 'all in the same boat'. This generally applies within the nation state. It clearly cannot apply in the EU. There is no reason why an Austrian voter (say) should respect a majority decision made by Iberians, Scandinavians and East Europeans.

Alternatives to EU Membership

Political structures have to reflect the identity and aspirations of the people, or they are meaningless and lack legitimacy. This is why in the UK,

---

1   Voter turnout in European elections has followed a downward trend since 1979. This represents a participation figure of 45.5 per cent for the EU as a whole, with participation 7.1 per cent per cent in the EU-15 and of 26.4 per cent of eligible voters in the new Member States. In 2004, only 38.9% of eligible voters in the UK went to the polls. See: http://www.europarl.europa.eu/elections2004/ep-election/sites/en/results1306/turnout_ep/index.html

county-based local government makes sense, while the so-called 'regions' do not. It is perfectly possible to have a democratic Europe, but it must be a Europe of democratic nations trading and cooperating together, not a trans-national union. It must be intergovernmental rather than supranational. Yet the Lisbon Treaty abandons the intergovernmental approach.

The EU's total denial of democracy, and of its own principles, is nowhere better shown than in its response to the rejection of the Constitution by France and Holland in 2005. Rather than accept the people's verdict, it chose to repackage the entire content of the Constitution as the 'Lisbon Treaty', and then force it through without consulting the people (with the sole exception of Ireland).

In a spectacular demonstration of hypocrisy and deceit, Angela Merkel, then President-in-Office of the Council, wrote to heads of government proposing 'cosmetic changes and terminological differences *but with the same legal effect*' (my emphasis). Their contempt for democracy and the rule of law, and for the people, is breathtaking.

There are few remaining plausible arguments for British membership of the EU, now that the 'trade, jobs and prosperity' case is holed below the waterline. Apologists tend to speak of influence within a larger entity, and contrast it with a Britain 'isolated and marginalised' outside the EU. We see a world of trading blocs, they argue. The EU, NAFTA, ASEAN. Or great countries like China and India. How would our small voice be heard in such a world, without the EU? It is sufficient to ask the question to see its absurdity.

First, there are excellent counter-examples. Far smaller countries than the UK, like Switzerland and Singapore (where I lived for some time in the 1990s), are highly successful, prosperous and peaceful countries. Admittedly Singapore is within ASEAN, but ASEAN is a very loose-knit association compared to the EU. It is absurd to suggest that Britain is too small to prosper outside the EU.

Secondly, Britain remains a major economy. We are around the fifth largest economy in the world, and likely to remain in the top ten even as China and India forge ahead. Again, size (or lack of it) is not an issue.

Third, in the EU we frequently add our voice and our weight to the wrong side of the argument. Most notably I recall British Trade Commissioner Peter Mandelson in Hong Kong in 2006 arguing a protectionist case for the EU which was clearly against Britain's interests. In order to protect inefficient companies in Southern Europe, he was obliged to argue a case which was bad for world trade, bad for the EU, bad for Britain, and above all a disaster for the developing world. So much for influence! There is only a benefit in joining a larger club if we agree with its objectives, with no point in an Anglo-Saxon free-market economy joining a Union based on the Continental model, and hoping to 'win the arguments in Europe'. We need to get real. Either we go where the EU is going.

Fourth, if we leave the EU, it will not leave us without allies, far from it. EU apologists seem to assume that the EU is the only game in town. But Britain is also a permanent member of the UN Security Council. A member of the OECD, the G8, the World Bank, NATO, the Commonwealth and a host of other international organisations. Outside the EU, we could take back our seat at the WTO. The idea that we will be isolated unless we agree to be governed by Brussels is both offensive and absurd.

Conclusion

As Lord Palmerston famously said, Britain has no permanent allies, only permanent interests. We should choose our allies issue by issue as they serve those interests. But in the EU we have the reverse approach: we have chosen to link ourselves, exclusively or at least preferentially, to a particular group of countries, with some of whom we have no particular affinity, and regardless of whether or not particular British interests are served by those links.

Put that way, the solution is obvious. First, we need to be out of the EU. We need a new relationship with Europe based solely on free trade and inter-governmental cooperation. If it comforts the Foreign Office, we may well choose to call it 'Associate Membership'. I don't mind what we call it, so long as we deliver the substance, and extract ourselves from the dead hand of political union.

Clearly we need to negotiate free trade terms with our neighbours, a project that will be facilitated by the fact that we are a major net customer of the Continent. And we must be prepared to buy-in on a case-by-case basis to European projects and policies where we believe that these are in our national interest. Why should the EU negotiate at all with us on that basis? Because they want to see their policies adopted as widely as possible. But now they will have to persuade us rather than instruct us.

We must restore the competitiveness of our labour markets and our industry and free them from the deadweight of Brussels regulation, together with our place as a great global trading nation. We must refocus our myopic vision away from the Western butt-end of the Eurasian land-mass, and realise that there is a whole world out there. Already, for reasons of history, culture and language, more of our trade is with the

Anglosphere than is the case for continental economies. We must exploit the opportunities that the world and the English language offer us.

I do not see the Commonwealth through rose-tinted spectacles, and I absolutely do not want to turn it into a pale shadow of the EU. But I believe it offers great potential for the UK, potential which we have missed as we have focused too closely on Europe. With the EU growing at 2% and India growing at 8%, where is the greater potential?

Many politicians in Brussels are exasperated with Britain in its traditional EU role as 'the slowest ship in the convoy'. But others would hate to lose us: they need our trade, and our budget contributions. The more far-sighted, though, would be terrified that our example, as an independent, high-growth, flexible, competitive economy just off the EU mainland would show up the EU system for what it is: low-growth, uncompetitive, rigid, over-taxed and over-regulated.

But that would be a problem for the EU, not for us. We would be able to say, with the Younger Pitt, that we had saved England by our exertions, and saved Europe by our example.

Andrew Mullen

Reclaiming Sovereignty

The Progressive Case

Introduction

This chapter addresses the issue of sovereignty, both economic and political, from a left-progressive perspective. The second section tackles the
thorny question as to what is sovereignty, arguing that any serious discussion needs to attend to both the political and economic dimension of
the concept if it is to be meaningful. The third and fourth sections detail
the plans put forward in the past to reclaim sovereignty from Europe in
terms of intergovernmental and Keynesian-socialist alternatives, together
with some left-progressive options for reasserting sovereignty. However,
the sixth section reminds left-progressive forces that implementing such a
project would be far from easy; the restoration of economic and political
sovereignty in a meaningful way would transform Britain and its place in
the global economy and the world order.

What is Sovereignty?

Sovereignty has been defined as the possession of 'absolute and unlim-
ited power' (Heywood, 1999, p. 90). Such a simple definition, however, is
misleading; sovereignty is an essentially contested concept and there are
a number of important and long-standing debates as to what it is and
what is should be. One debate concerns who *does* and who *should* exercise
sovereignty? For anarchists and other libertarians, sovereignty rests with
the individual; for fascists it resides in the all-powerful leader; for liberals
it is wielded by elected and representative assemblies; while for monar-
chists it is manifest in the 'divine right of kings'.

Another debate relates to the distinction between *legal* and *political* sovereignty or, put another way, between authority and power. Given that sovereignty is commonly associated with the modern nation-state, following the 1648 Peace of Westphalia and the 1789 French Revolution, Heywood (1999, p.91) explained that:

> Legal sovereignty is based upon the belief that ultimate and final authority resides in the law of the state ... By contrast, political sovereignty is not in any way based upon a claim to legal authority but is concerned simply about the actual distribution of power, that is, de facto sovereignty.

A further debate focuses upon the difference between *internal* and *external* sovereignty. The former refers to the distribution of power within the nation-state i.e. 'the need for supreme power and its location within the political system' (Heywood, 1999, p. 90). An internal sovereign 'is therefore a political body that possesses ultimate, final and independent authority; one whose decisions are binding upon all citizens, groups and institutions in society' (Heywood, 1999, p. 92). The latter pertains to the nation-state's place in the international order and its relationship with other nation-states. Importantly, a nation-state 'can be considered sovereign over its people and territory despite the fact that no sovereign figures in its internal structure of government. External sovereignty can thus be respected even though internal sovereignty may be a matter of dispute or confusion' (Heywood, 1999, p. 95).

It is clear from contemporary debates that the modern nation-state is, deservedly, central to any discussion of sovereignty. Indeed, such a formation is commonly viewed as the optimal unit of political rule and, in practice, has provided the foundation for the post-war system of international law, manifest in the 1945 United Nations Charter, and the world order more generally. Nevertheless, since the end of the Second World War the sovereignty of nation-states has been increasingly challenged by new international and supranational political forms, such as the EU.

Thus far, the discussion has focused upon the *political* aspect of sovereignty. Critically, however, there is an equally important dimension to the concept, *economic* sovereignty, which is lamentably missing from much of the empirical and theoretical literature on the subject.

Over the last two centuries a new economic entity has emerged which has challenged, if not eclipsed, the nation-state: the corporation. Bakan (2005, p. 5) observed that such an organization had 'risen from relative obscurity to become the world's dominant economic institution.' Until the creation of the first corporations in the late 16th century, partnerships (composed of wealthy individuals who pooled their resources) were the principal economic model. Indeed, many businesspeople and politicians were hostile towards the joint stock company (i.e. the corporation) and it was banned in England by an Act of Parliament in 1720. Nevertheless, capitalism, imperialist expansion and the industrial revolution – with their associated economic opportunities – necessitated a substantial increase in capital investment which partnerships could rarely deliver. Consequently, pressure mounted for the legalization of the corporation and the Act was repealed in 1825. The subsequent proliferation of corporations was further encouraged by the introduction of limited liability in 1856. Investors, who had previously been personally liable for company debts, were thereafter granted clearly defined limits on their liability.

The corporation underwent a further transformation in the early 20th century when two states in the United States (US) 'repealed the rules that required businesses to incorporate only for narrow purposes, to exist only for limited durations, and to operate only in particular locations.' They also 'loosened controls on mergers and acquisitions' and 'abolished the rule that one company could not own stock in another' (Bakan, 2005, p. 13–14). The ultimate dominance of the new economic model was secured in 1886 when the US Supreme Court ruled that the corporation should be treated as a 'person', whose rights should be protected by the US Constitution. The success of the corporate revolution was such that, by 2006, there were 78,000 transnational corporations (TNCs) in existence and 58,000 of these were based in the 'triad' of Europe, Japan and North America. These TNCs increasingly dominate the global economy, in terms of international finance, production and 'trade', and their wealth is highly concentrated.

There is an ongoing debate about whether the nation-state has been rendered obsolete by the growing power of the corporate sector, particularly TNCs – put simply, whether economic power has trumped political sovereignty. Morrell (1988), Barratt Brown (1991) and Radice (1984, 1996, 1999), for example, insisted that globalization had undermined the nation-state, while Helleiner (1995), Kitson and Michie (1998), Elliott and Atkinson (1998, 2008), Weiss (1998, 2003) and Hirst and Thompson (1999) maintained that the 'powerless state' thesis was exaggerated. Protagonists within this debate, however, often neglect the crucial question: is it possible to legitimately talk about sovereignty, whether political or economic, when vast swathes of the economy and wider society are dominated by corporate (essentially private) power? Furthermore, with the exception of the (marginalized) Marxist-radical tradition, the discipline of political science has also avoided this question; in short, it has evaded the implications of growing economic power for political sovereignty and the wider issue of economic sovereignty itself.

A number of critical scholars highlighted the threat posed by the corporate sector to the democratic system, and therefore internal political sovereignty, and laid bare the radical implications of attempting to exercise economic sovereignty (Brady, 1943; Miliband, 1973; Chomsky, 2005). Thus it is clear that sovereignty, when considered in a holistic way that embraces both the political and the economic, is thus a potentially revolutionary concept. Indeed, the Marxist-radical critique of the conservative-liberal conception of sovereignty is a powerful one for conservatives and (modern) liberals who have little, if anything, to say about the threat posed by private economic power to political sovereignty, or about economic sovereignty. Those on the centre and the right of the political spectrum have consistently focused upon political sovereignty, but have ignored the issue of economic sovereignty. The case of the Conservative Party and the North American Free Trade Agreement (NAFTA) illustrates the point.

The then leader of the Conservative Party, William Hague, was interviewed by the *International Herald Tribune* in January 2000 (cited in Helmer, 2000) during which he argued that NAFTA, unlike Europe, posed no threat to Britain's sovereignty. Instead, NAFTA was presented as a mere 'free trade' area. However, this was false on three counts. Firstly, NAFTA opened the way for corporations to challenge the legal sovereignty of member states because signatories 'are obliged to offer foreign corporations precisely the same terms as domestic ones ... [and because] NAFTA empowers companies to sue governments for the removal of regulations which might affect their profits. [Accordingly] US corporations have begun suits against environmental protection laws in both Canada and Mexico' (Monbiot, 2000). Secondly, the framers of NAFTA explicitly aimed to embed neo-liberal policies. As the chairperson of Eastman Kodak stated, the intention was that NAFTA would 'lock in the opening of Mexico's economy so that it cannot return to its protectionist ways' (cited in Chomsky, 1994, p.163), thus violating the principle of political sovereignty. Thirdly, NAFTA seriously eroded the economic sovereignty of member states as it bolstered the power of TNCs, through mergers and acquisitions, the relocation of production to areas where labour was cheaper and where regulations were more lax, the demand for lower corporate taxation, etc. all of which are features associated with a 'free trade' area. Studies evaluating NAFTA and its effects found that this was exactly what happened (Labour Advisory Committee, 1992; Office of Technology Assessment, 1992; MacArthur, 2000; Public Citizen, 2003). In short, as observed by Monbiot (2000), 'big companies, most of them from the US, expanded their markets at the expense of everyone else.' In the event a US Senate Committee which was tasked with investigating the possibility of Britain joining NAFTA rejected the plan. Nevertheless, the Conservative Party subsequently maintained its opposition to further European integration, citing the need to protect Britain's sovereignty, while joining Gordon Brown, as Chancellor and then Prime Minister, in calling for a transatlantic marketplace consisting of a free trade area encompassing Europe and NAFTA.

By contrast, those on the left of the political spectrum have a long history of concern for the issue of economic sovereignty, manifest in the debates around, and policy proposals for, collectivization, consumer and producer co-operatives, economic planning, nationalization, workers' control, etc. In short, only the left has addressed the issue of sovereignty in a holistic and meaningful way, recognizing that real sovereignty requires both political *and* economic control.

Historical Attempts to Reclaim Sovereignty

Several intergovernmental alternatives to Europe were advanced by Britain in the 1950s and 1960s. For example, the plan for a free-trade area (FTA) in manufactured goods was presented to the Cabinet by Macmillan in September 1956 was one of seven options devised by the Treasury in anticipation of the 1955 Messina Conference. It envisaged the creation of a 17-member FTA in which the Six would constitute the core of a wider membership. In an effort to reinstate the intergovernmental principle, and thus supplant the Six, the British recommended the integration of the FTA within the Organisation for European Economic Co-operation. France and the US, however, rejected the proposal. Britain persevered and, along with Austria, Denmark, Norway, Portugal, Sweden and Switzerland, established the European Free Trade Association (EFTA) in November 1959. A cross-party organization, the Forward Britain Movement, extended the EFTA idea and recommended a British Commonwealth-EFTA association, which would have been global in its reach.

France under President Charles de Gaulle, elected in December 1958, also put forward an intergovernmental alternative when following the Bonn Summit in July 1961 the Six established a committee to consider proposals for political union, as envisaged in the Treaties of Rome. The French plan was submitted by the Ambassador to Denmark, Christian

Fouchet and advocated a union of states which would co-exist with some of the European institutions, which would be administered in an inter-governmental manner and which would be independent of the US. Many of its recommendations, however, were deemed unacceptable to other member states and the plan, rejected outright by the US, was abandoned. A further attempt by de Gaulle to curtail the supranational ambitions of the Six led to the so-called 'empty chair' crisis of July 1965, when France withdrew its representatives from the European institutions. It was resolved by the 'Luxembourg compromise' of January 1966 which created a national veto within the Council of Ministers.

A number of Keynesian and socialist alternatives to the EU were pro-posed in the 1980s and 1990s. Exchange rate instability, global recession and declining international competitiveness all contributed to a state of malaise in European politics in the 1970s. This precipitated the election of Francois Mitterrand as French President in May 1981 and the formation of the Socialist-Communist Government, with its Common Programme, in June. Critically, 'before it took office, the French Left had assessed the pit-falls of a policy of reflation. And to avoid them it had, either implicitly or explicitly, accepted the need to consider trade protection and currency devaluation' (Halimi et al. 1994, p.101). Devaluation and protectionism, however, were at odds with both the Treaties of Rome and ERM member-ship. By defending its *franc fort* policy of shadowing the deutschmark within the ERM, the French Government's room for manoeuvre was severely curtailed and by 1982 the 'Mitterrand experiment' had collapsed. Faced with the choice between pursuing its programme and maintaining its European policy, the French Left chose the latter.

From a broader perspective, the full implementation of the Common Programme and other socialist plans, such as the British Left's Alternative Economic Strategy, may have precipitated conflict with the EU as these programmes envisaged the co-ordinated reflation of European econo-mies via Keynesian and socialist measures that would have violated the four freedoms regarding the movement of goods, services, capital and people. One of the possible outcomes of such a clash may have been the renegotiation of member states' terms of membership and a new inter-governmental direction for the EU. Indeed, this was anticipated by the Out of Crisis project established in 1981, coordinated by the former Labour MP, Stuart Holland, and sponsored by key members of the French Government and many of Europe's left-wing politicians and trade union-ists (Holland, 1983).

In the 1990s the austerity associated with the deflationary Maastricht Convergence Criteria exacerbated the already high unemployment rates across Europe, prompting several member states to introduce extensive privatization programmes, in addition to welfare cuts, in an attempt to reduce government deficits and public debt. Such measures provoked a series of mass demonstrations and strikes in several countries. Meanwhile, Euro-Keynesian alternatives were actively promoted by the French Prime Minister, Lionel Jospin, by the German Finance Minister, Oskar Lafontaine, and by Our Europe, the think tank established by Jacques Delors. Their objectives included full employment as a European treaty commitment, an expanded European budget (to facilitate intra-European transfers), new borrowing instruments (European bonds), greater funding for the European Investment Bank, plus the development of a social Europe via the Social Chapter and the Social Dialogue procedure. The response of the June 1997 European Council, however, was to implement the Stability and Growth Pact, the primary objective of which was to safeguard member states' commitment to the MCC. Neither the intergovernmental nor the Keynesian and socialist alternatives to Europe have managed, thus far, to garner sufficient support to pose a serious challenge.

Future Options to Reclaim Sovereignty

Reasserting Britain's economic and political sovereignty is an urgent task and there are a number of available options. Many of these have been promoted, in one form or another, by left-progressive forces over the past few decades.

Socialism-in-one-country model

Britain could withdraw from Europe, having voted for a party committed to such a policy or having voted for such a move in a referendum, and could re-establish Parliament as the politically sovereign body. It could then begin to achieve economic sovereignty by introducing capital, exchange, import/export and price controls, nationalizing key sectors of the economy, negotiating planning agreements with the private sector, expanding public spending to meet social needs and promoting workers' control of industry. Indeed, this was the policy of the Labour Party and much of the trade union movement in the 1970s and 1980s. Then, more radically, Britain could move towards creating a society based upon federations of consumer and producer co-operatives. Britain's mixed economy could then be transformed into a fully socialized one.

Commonwealth of Europe model

Tony Benn presented his Commonwealth of Europe Bill in the House of Commons in June 1992 as an alternative to the Europe envisaged in the Maastricht Treaty. He insisted that:

The concept of a Commonwealth of Europe is quite distinct from a Union or a fully-fledged American-style federation because it seeks to harmonize the policies of the continent on the basis of consent, at a pace chosen by each country adhering to the Commonwealth, of which there would be over fifty. (Benn and Hood, 1993, p. 114)

Such an intergovernmental formation would include an assembly, council of ministers, court of justice, human rights commission and a secretariat, 'but they would have no power to take action that would prejudice the democratic decisions of the member states' (Benn and Hood, 1993, p.114). It is 'intended to achieve co-operation built upon the democratic traditions of the member states' (Benn and Hood, 1993, p.117).

Europe of the Regions model

The Europe of Regions model, promoted by the Green Party, would

> ...replace the unsustainable economics of free trade and growth with the ecological alternative of local self reliance and resource conservation, within a context of wider diversity. To achieve the Green vision, Europe will need very different structures from those currently in existence. Europe should be made up of overlapping, co-operative, democratic, decentralized groupings of nations and regions. The Green Party seeks a Europe of co-operation and diversity where regions are sustainable and self reliant. Power would rest with local communities and regions, rather than the reality of 'subsidiarity' in Europe at present, a top down distribution of a fraction of the power accumulated at the centre. (Green Party, 2005)

Theirs was a strategy of localization, which would involve the development of a decentralized industrial policy, the reintroduction of local currencies, capital controls, quotas, tariffs and the reform of aid and trade regimes. The main problem with all of these options is the lack of support from left-progressive forces which, as noted, continue to be divided on Europe (Mullen, 2007).

World Order and Sovereignty

However, potentially the largest problem facing any country wishing to assert its sovereignty is an external one: the world order. Over the last three centuries, imperialist powers such as Britain and the US have effectively constructed and maintained an international economic and political system that serves their interests. The primary objectives of post-war US foreign policy, for example, were access to strategic resources and an 'open door' policy in international investment and trade.

Firstly, in terms of the 'open door' policy, state planners declared that the US was opposed to 'barriers or onerous restrictions imposed by governments on the investment and withdrawal of foreign capital' (State Department, 1948). Indeed, the US insisted upon an 'open door' policy on the basis that US-based corporations could, in any competition, exploit their size and utilize a variety of economic mechanisms to outmatch their rivals and thus dominate foreign markets. Britain also adopted a free trade policy during its hegemonic period (Bairoch and Kozul-Wright, 1996; Shafaeddin, 1998; Lobell, 1999; O'Rourke, 2000).

Secondly, the principal threats to US foreign policy objectives during the Cold War were economic nationalism (independent development) and ultra-nationalism (delinking from the capitalist global economy). Hence, economic nationalism and ultra-nationalism were perceived as contagious, in the sense that they threatened to set an example to other countries, the so-called 'domino effect'. The US (and Britain) conducted scores of covert and military interventions against nationalist regimes during the Cold War in order to secure their objectives (Curtis, 1995, 1998, 2003, 2004; Blum, 2000, 2003). Importantly, the primary objectives of US foreign policy in the post-Cold War period remain as before, as stated in official documents (National Security Council, 1990; US Department of Defence, 2000, 2006) and manifest in the attempted coup in Venezuela in 2002.

The essential point is that any country that attempts to assert its independence (i.e. its economic and political sovereignty), in a way that threatens the interests of the corporate sector and its political allies, is dealt with harshly. Britain would be no different and this is the reality that left-progressive forces must face and prepare for.

Conclusion

There are a number of notable features about Britain's relationship with Europe. Firstly, there is a clear tendency towards obfuscation, if not deceit, on the part of the political elite about the nature of Europe and what participation means for British sovereignty. As the pro-European Labour Member of Parliament (MP), Roy Hattersley, conceded, 'joining the European Community involved loss of significant sovereignty, but by telling the British people that was not involved, I think the ... argument was prejudiced for the next 30 years' (cited in Broad, 2001, p. 108). Secondly, there has been a considerable amount of conflict within the British State, the main political parties and the trade unions about Europe and Britain's engagement with it. This is particularly true for the left (Mullen, 2007). Thirdly, anti- and pro-European forces have repeatedly deployed propaganda at critical junctures in the developing relationship between Britain and Europe, in an attempt to both influence public opinion and to shape policy. The issue of sovereignty was a potent one in these campaigns (Mullen, 2009).

This chapter argued that sovereignty, understood in a holistic way that encompasses both the political and the economic, is a potentially revolutionary concept. It showed how Britain's membership of the EU has seriously eroded its capacity for self-government. It recounted how opposition forces have unsuccessfully attempted to construct intergovernmental, Keynesian and socialist alternatives to Europe. It put forward a number of options for reasserting sovereignty, while reminding left-progressive forces that such a policy would be vigorously opposed. The issue of sovereignty, and how to exercise it, is thus far from a simple one.

Brian Burkitt, Mark Baimbridge, Philip B. Whyman

The Importance of British Self-Governance

Introduction

Federalists are trying to build a United States of Europe from the top down, whereby institutions to manage monetary union have now been constructed and political institutions to manage these monetary union institutions are being designed. Such a process of building a federal union is the opposite of how every other nation has been created. It will be disastrous, because it will deploy exchange and interest rates as weapons of nation building; converting economic institutions into political ones to build an ever-more integrated EU, thus distorting their real purpose and function. Moreover, this will lead to calls for further harmonisation of laws and customs, culminating in a single fiscal policy, which will diminish still more Britain's ability to take fundamental decisions in its own interests.

Hence, the chapter outlines the importance of British parliamentary democracy based upon the sovereignty of the people, who by exercising their vote lend their sovereign powers to Members of Parliament, which are then returned to the electorate, to return again to the Members of Parliament they elect at each subsequent General Election. Moreover, the EU's integrationalist trend implies a major change in the operation of the UK constitution carries profound implications for the exercise of national sovereignty. However, the concept of 'sovereignty' has been much disputed in recent debates, particularly with respect to the relationship between Britain and the EU; therefore the chapter also analyses this concept in detail.

Democracy

The parliamentary democracy developed and established in Britain is based upon the sovereignty of the people, who by exercising their vote lend their sovereign powers to Members of Parliament, to use on their behalf for the duration of a single parliament; these powers are returned intact to the electorate to whom they belong, to return again to the Members of Parliament they elect at each subsequent General Election. Five basic democratic rights emerge from this process, each of which is fundamentally diminished by British membership of the EU.

Firstly, parliamentary democracy means that every person over 18 is entitled to vote to elect his or her Member of Parliament to serve in the House of Commons. The consent of the House of Commons is necessary before Parliament can pass any Act laying down new laws or imposing new taxation upon the people. British membership of the EU subjects all its citizens to laws and taxes, which their Members of Parliament do not enact. Such laws and taxes are implemented by EU institutions that they do not directly elect, and cannot dismiss, through the ballot box.

Secondly, parliamentary democracy means that Members of Parliament, who derive their power directly from the British people, can change any law and any tax by majority vote. British membership of the Union prevents EU laws and taxes from being changed or repealed by the British Parliament. They can only be altered or abolished by EU bodies not directly elected by the British people.

Thirdly, parliamentary democracy requires that British courts and judges must uphold all laws passed by Parliament. If Parliament changes any law, the courts must enforce the new law because it has been passed by Parliament, which is directly elected by the people. British membership of the EU forces British courts to uphold and enforce EU laws, which have not been passed by Parliament. Nor can Parliament amend or repeal them, even when they conflict with laws passed by Parliament, since EU law overrides British law.

Fourthly, parliamentary democracy means that all British governments, ministers and civil servants under their control can only act within the Laws of Britain. They are accountable to Parliament for all their public actions and, through Parliament, to the electorate as a whole. British membership of the EU imposes duties and constraints upon British governments not deriving from the British parliament. Therefore, in discharging these duties, Ministers are not accountable to Parliament or to the British citizens who elect them.

Finally, parliamentary democracy is vital because it entrenches the right of the people to elect and dismiss Members of Parliament, secures their continuing accountability to the electorate, obliging them to listen to the views of British citizens between as well as during General Elections. It thus offers the possibility of peaceful change through Parliament to meet the voters' needs. British membership of the EU, by permanently transferring financial and legislative powers to EU institutions not directly elected by the British people, insulates those institutions from the control of British voters who cannot dismiss them and whose opinions, therefore, need carry no weight with them and whose grievances they cannot be compelled to remedy.

These five rights have protected British citizens from the worst abuses of power by the state, safeguarded them against the excesses of bureaucracy, defended their basic liberties, offered them an opportunity for peaceful change, reduced the risk of civil strife and created a national framework of consent for the law-making process. However, the powers of the British electorate, through their direct representatives in Parliament, to levy taxes, to make laws which the courts must uphold and to control the conduct of public affairs, has been substantially ceded to the EU, whose Commission and Council of Ministers are neither collectively elected nor collectively dismissed by the British people, or by the peoples of the EU countries put together.

Hence, the EU, through the fundamental character of its institutions and their behaviour, severely curtails the operation of British Parliamentary democracy. This process, undermining the rights of the British people, will be accelerated by further economic integration.

Sovereignty

Such a major change in the operation of the UK constitution carries profound implications for the exercise of national sovereignty. The concept of 'sovereignty' has been much disputed in recent debates, particularly with respect to the relationship between Britain and the EU. Therefore it is appropriate to analyse its essentials in detail.

Malcolm (1996) defined sovereignty as constitutional independence, i.e. the exercise of plenary and exclusive political authority in a legal order. A sovereign state possesses independent authority, e.g. a small country may be dwarfed by a powerful nation, but so long as it is not legally subordinate to that neighbour, it remains sovereign. Sovereignty rests upon authority rather than power; in a famous opinion on the Austria-German customs union in 1931 Judge Anzilotti declared, 'sovereignty means that the state has over it no other authority than that of international law'. An independent state must possess full competence to act internationally; it acts under its own authority not requiring authorisation from any superior state. If a state is constitutionally independent, it is sovereign; if it is not, it is not. There are no intermediate stages of sovereignty.

The idea that sovereignty (constitutional independence) can be 'pooled' is an evident absurdity. Power can be pooled, but authority cannot. 'Pooling' is a dangerous concept, because it falsely implies that authority can both be retained and given away simultaneously. If the sovereign authority of the UK is pooled within the EU, that sovereign authority will cease to exist, because British laws would become subject to a higher authority. So far this has not happened; to date, the UK has delegated a part of its sovereign authority to some EU bodies on which it is represented. It has also delegated the exercise of important elements of administrative, jurisdictional and legislative authority by treaties and by statutes. The latter were expressions of the UK's authority. The UK remains sovereign so long as it retains the ability to renounce the treaties and repeal the statutes.

However, the character of delegations to the EU is different from that involved in any previous treaty signed by Britain. The EU Council of Ministers is a law-creating body, whose laws possess 'direct effect' in Britain, overriding British laws. With uniformity the whole procedure can (in theory) be accommodated within the UK's exercise of its own authority. Majority voting, significantly advanced by the 1997 Amsterdam Treaty, destroys the illusion; whenever the UK is in a minority, it becomes obvious that is has given away the exercise of legislative authority to a body it cannot control. Article 100 of the Single European Act allows majority voting on measures 'which have as their object the establishment and functioning of the internal market'. If the clause focused solely upon establishment, majority voting would be designed only for achieving a single task. Unfortunately, the inclusion of 'and functioning' ensures that a potentially large sphere of legislative authority has been delegated in a totally open-ended way.

If most (or crucial) areas of jurisdictional and legislative authority become subject to long-term delegation, a situation will arise where the UK would cease to resemble a sovereign state. Each time Britain delegates the exercise of its authority to the EU, it does not automatically lose sovereignty, but becomes more likely to do so. Therefore, it comes closer to the moment when its constitution will be remodelled into a subordinate part of a federal EU.

In a federal EU, sovereignty is not abolished; it transfers to the new EU constitution. If such a federal framework is to be constructed, it requires the underpinning of political authority. It must be at least possible to make citizens think that the federal authority is entitled to rule them; if enough citizens do think so, it will be. To achieve the objective, representative politics on an EU-wide scale is required, i.e. European parties functioning as a single entity across the EU as the Democratic and Republican parties do in the USA. Such a system operates effectively in an established political democracy, where people share the same customs, language and traditions. Could this kind of politics operate in the EU? Without a genuine political community, any European constitution will remain an artificial construction. Its political role will not derive from any sense of participation, but from wishful thinking and indifference. Of course, over time people may come to feel part of a genuine EU-wide political community. It could happen, but it would take many generations and involve substantial changes to many aspects of our lives. Therefore, UK membership of the EU depends upon whether the British people will accept heartily and willingly the voice of the people of the whole EU as binding upon them, at first in some, then in more and ultimately in all matters of economic, political and social determination. Closer EU integration cannot be effective in the long-run without creating one electorate, one constituency and one federal EU-wide nation. All supporters of such integration need to answer why such an enormously artificial, disruptive and risky project should be embarked on.

It is frequently claimed that national sovereignty is undermined by globalisation. To a large extent the claim is based upon a confusion between sovereignty (resting on a constitutional independence) and power. However, even within its own terms of reference, the claim is grossly exaggerated. Since 1945 increasingly freer trade, the emergence of transnational corporations and the hugely expanded volume of international capital movements have made the task of national economic management in reconciling full employment, stable prices and rapid growth harder to achieve. These difficulties created political problems, as electorates became frustrated with governments of all persuasions failing to meet their demands. Nevertheless, it remains hard to understand why these developments suggest the need for a closer association between the UK and other members of the EU specifically; rather they pose the imperative for worldwide co-operation. The inability of both national governments and regional blocs to control currency realignments led to the G8 meetings (and if Britain devoted the ministerial and civil service time to the G8 that it spends upon the EU, both it and the world would be more prosperous). Hence, only an international forum can generate effective ecological policy responses. Therefore, those problems that cannot be completely solved at national level require a broader policy implementation framework than the EU provides.

Moreover, acceptance of the limitations of national strategy often obscures the numerous spheres where it remains effective. Voluntary abandonment of its authority in these spheres is detrimental to the exercise of democratic citizenship rights and to living standards. Those who believe that national economic sovereignty is valueless in the modern world need to explain recent British experience. In the months before September 1992, the requirement to maintain interest rates at the level needed to defend sterling's ERM parity resulted in unemployment rising to three million simultaneously with record levels of bankruptcies and home repossessions. The months afterwards, with four percentage point cuts in base rates and when the pound was devalued by 15% saw immediate economic recovery. By contrast, France's determination to achieve exchange rate stability with the deutschmark created stagnation, with unemployment rising to 12 per cent alongside an alarming increase in xenophobia. National economic sovereignty still exists in substantial measure; all that matters is the will to use it.

Thus the UK can still enjoy the advantage of sovereignty, i.e. constitutional independence, if it resists the embrace of continental integration. British strategy should concentrate upon developing fully national policy instruments, whilst co-operating on a global, rather than a regional, basis on issues beyond national control.

Conclusion

The accelerating path of EU economic integration is solely based upon a deflationary single currency, whereby the project was designed to unleash economic demands that would lead to political union. Indeed, the economic-political imbalance is clear; the EU will possess a single currency, whilst levying a proportionally smaller EU-wide budget than Boadicea did over pre-Roman Britain! Acceptance of such an absurdity prevents ruling parties from following an independent economic policy. Therefore it is essential that the UK retains its freedom of manoeuvre to develop discretionary policies. Outside the EU straightjacket of continent-wide outdated deflation, national governments retain the capacity to launch independent policies of wealth creation, employment generation and welfare improvement. If artificial federalist rules frustrate this capacity, extremist movements will fill the unnecessary vacuum.

A United States of Europe would be economically disastrous and politically undesirable. It is a tragic error of historic proportions for the EU to try to bond member countries into one ever-more closely integrated entity. Britain needs to uncouple itself from damaging integrationist trends and seize the tremendous opportunities open to it as an internationally co-operative yet independent country in an interdependent world, which requires effective international and national policy responses (as opposed to regional ones). Such a major change in the direction of UK strategy, away from current drifting with EU tides, requires determination and far-sighted thinking. The prize, however, is great: no less than the survival of a Britain as a worldwide responsive partner yet an independent, economically prosperous, democratically self-governing nation.

David Howell

Time for New Partners

Introduction

We might as well face it. British foreign policy is now in limbo. There it will remain until President Obama somehow constructs a recovery strategy in America's Middle East policy and until the 'renaissance of re-thinking' about Britain's own position gets under way.

The original idea, it will be recalled, was for Britain to be a bridge, (or was it a pivot?) between America and Europe. But the bridge, if it ever stood up for a moment, is now a crumbling heap of concrete on the riverbed. On paper it looked good, like so many Blair designs. Britain would be a fully signed up member of the EU's Common Foreign and Security Policy (CFSP) and at the same time *numero uno* in Washington, the unswerving friend from across the Atlantic. The bridge structure would wonderfully link the two.

A Bridge Over Troubled Water?

The design was never going to work because the anchor points either side would never have supported it. On the US side, for all the protestations that Britain was, or is, America's trusted and equal partner that was never the Bush team's view. It was nice to have Britain on side and Blair was a great guy, and so on. But the Americans needed no middleman to interpret Europe to them. They could see for themselves the virulent anti-Americanism in 'old Europe' and they anyway believed (wrongly, as it turns out) they could manage alone.

On the European side there was, and remains, disunity. The rhetoric is plentiful but the reality is slim. The CFSP, which leading EU Ministers continue to describe daily as being essential to secure Europe's influence on the world stage and which our own Foreign and Commonwealth Office still regard as their foreign policy priority ('working through our

European partners', etc.), is a feeble instrument and little interested in protecting and promoting Britain's real interests, or enabling Britain to make its most effective contribution to global peace, stability and development. Quite simply, while effective foreign policy needs partners and allies – more so than ever in this network age – our main European neighbours are the wrong partners and the CFSP ties us into the wrong partnership. Britain should stay as clear as it can.

The most obvious reason for this is that on most of the key international issues no coherent common EU position exists. With 27 marvellously diverse nations, and 27 different perspectives on the world, anything pushed through the CFSP filter is bound to be muffled, fuzzy and a fertile source of misunderstanding. This is so whether the issue is Iraq or Iran or Israel–Palestine or Lebanon, or Russia and how to handle Mr Putin, or China and weapons, or Turkey and enlargement, or the UN, or above all, how to talk to the Americans.

Transatlantic relations have now fallen to their lowest point for decades. Far from the EU calming and clarifying transatlantic disputes by speaking with one clear voice, it seems to be amplifying them so that what were once containable second class differences are being elevated into damaging first class rows. Despite Peter Mandelson's protestations, and no doubt sincere efforts, the Doha round was sunk by the very existence of what the *Financial Times* described as '*thirteen or fourteen EU Member States, periodically orchestrated by France.*' None of this was, or is, at all in Britain's interest.

But there is a deeper reason for looking for something better than CFSP as a foreign policy vehicle. For all its armed might, America desperately needs real and trusted friends, not just to fulfil its awesome world responsibilities but to deliver security to its own citizens. Even the go-it-alone warriors in Washington are now coming to recognise this. Less easy to swallow in Washington is the fact that true friendship and support mean more than tick-the-box compliance. True friendship means frankness, candour, criticism when appropriate (as long as it is basically constructive and not just born of ill will), complete mutual trust and respect and, even if occasionally, a restraining hand.

The EU does not get to Square One in any of these roles. The rhetoric of EU–US partnership may continue, but even if Javier Solana, could articulate a common European policy towards the Americans, which he cannot, why should he get more than a cold nod from the Administration? Why should Washington give a respectful hearing to an entity which it sees – not without justification – as basically anti-American, sounding less and less like a friend and partner and increasingly like a constantly hostile bloc – a transatlantic neighbour from hell, picking a quarrel on every issue, large or small. 60 years ago Britain fulfilled the steadying partner and friend role – at least up to a point. Then there was Kennedy's twin pillars idea in the Cold War context, although it was never a phrase that could stand too much analysis. NATO, too, was going to be the binding link of equals. But now all that is history and the question to be answered is where we look for the platform on which to gather a partnership or grouping which the American giant really will listen to and work with, and from which the world, and especially Britain, would so obviously benefit. The starting point is to identify the countries which really are America's best friends, who are not all screwed up with anti-American resentments, and who would be comfortable with a solid two-way strategic relationship with the great superpower, not in a poodle capacity but at an equal and full-trust level.

A structure is to hand which could at least form the underpinning for such a platform. This structure, or network, is the 54 nation Commonwealth, which far from being a marginal institution, full of good works and nostalgia, is now emerging as the ideal model for international relations in the new conditions the world faces. Today's Commonwealth now contains thirteen of the world's fastest growing economies, including the most potent emerging markets. Outside the USA and Japan, the key cutting-edge countries in information technology and e-commerce are all Commonwealth members. The new 'jewel in the Commonwealth Crown' turns out to be the old jewel, dramatically repolished and re-set, namely booming India, the world's largest democracy with a population set to exceed China's. This presents a picture so far removed from the old image of the Commonwealth, bogged down in demands for more aid and arguments about South Africa (or latterly Zimbabwe) that many sleepy policy makers find it simply too difficult to absorb. The unloved ugly duckling organisation has grown almost overnight into a true swan. Or to use a different metaphor the Commonwealth of today and tomorrow has been described as 'The Neglected Colossus'. It should be neglected no longer.

A Wider Role than Trade

The new story should not just be about bread and butter matters and new economic opportunities staring us in the face. The Commonwealth needs to be re-assessed in terms of its real weight in securing world stability, in balancing the dialogue with the US giant, in linking rising Asia and the West, in helping to handle the prickliest of issues such as the Middle East and Iran, in promoting better development links, in bringing small and larger nations, poorer and richer, together on mutually respectful and truly friendly terms and in bridging the faith divides which others seek to exploit and widen.

But, it will inevitably be asked, how can such a disparate and scattered grouping possibly be a force and a weight in these dangerous and contentious areas? Who will take the lead? Where is central control going to be? To understand the answer to these questions requires the biggest shift of all between the 20th Century and the 21st Century mindset over foreign policy matters; a shift, which many still find impossible to make. In the 20th Century the solution had to be in terms of blocs, consolidated organisations, centrally controlled in the name of efficiency, organisational pyramids, perhaps with some delegation, but basically radiating down from a superior and central point. If the nation state would no longer do, then a larger structure, a nation state writ large, should replace it.

All this has now been invalidated, not only in business but in governmental affairs and in relations between countries and societies. Thanks to the extraordinary power and pervasiveness of the information revolution, we live in an era now not of blocs and pyramid tiers of power and management but of networks and meshes, both formal and informal. By accident as much as design the Commonwealth emerges from a controversial past to take a perfect place in this new order of thinking and acting. The fact that the Commonwealth now has no dominant Member State, or even a coterie of such states, far from being a weakness is now a strength. Because the Commonwealth is founded on respect for nation states, each following its own path, yet recognising the imperative of interdependence, constant adjustment can take pace to new challenges, with a web of partnerships and coalitions being swiftly tailored to each new scene. This answers three dilemmas which Britain faces.

The first is that people want more than ever in an age of remote globalisation, to develop their own identities, to have countries and localities to love and defend and take pride in. They recognise the fact of interdependence but they long equally for ownership and a degree of independence. Superior ideas of supra-national government and super-states, along with sweeping dismissals of the relevance of the nation state, can play no part in resolving these deep and competing needs, and indeed utterly fail to do so when imposed by well-intentioned integrationists, as in the case of the EU. Second, rigid bloc alliances cannot keep up with the kaleidoscope of change. The more that the European Union tries to draw its members into a rigid and unified political and military bloc the less effective it becomes. The more that the world is seen as clinging to a structure of blocs established in rivalry to each other the more the real criss-cross network of bilateral linkages between nations is neglected. Yet it is just this new and more flexible pattern, which provides by far the best guarantee of stability and security. Third, the new texture of international relations is made up not just of intergovernmental and official contacts but of a mosaic of non-governmental and suboffical agencies and organisations. This takes time to grow, but grow it has under the Commonwealth canopy into an amazing web of organisations and alliances between the professions, the academic and scholastic worlds, the medical, educational, scientific and legal communities and a host of other interest groups linked together across the 54 nation Commonwealth Group.

Filling a Dangerous Vacuum

The tragic decline of America's 'soft power', reputation and influence almost across the entire globe is leaving a dangerous vacuum. Into this vacuum, cautiously, subtly, but steadily are moving not the Europeans, with their slow growth and their inward-looking mentality, but the Chinese — with cash, with investment projects, with trade deals, secured access to oil and gas supplies in an energy hungry world, with military and policing support and with technology. A replay in reverse of the 14th Century is unfolding, when China retreated in on itself and Europe reached outwards to every corner of the planet. Now it is exactly the other way round. The vacuum is one which ought to be filled not by the Chinese dictatorship but by the free democracies of the Commonwealth, from both North and South, banded together by a commitment to freedom under the rule of law and ready to make real and common sacrifices in the interests of a peaceful and stable world and the spread of democratic governance in many different forms.

The Commonwealth possesses the vital attributes for dealing with this new world, which the old 20th Century institutions so conspicuously lack. It stretches across the faiths, with half a billion Muslim members; it stretches across all the continents, thus by its very existence nullifying the dark analysis of a coming clash of civilisations. Better still if a more confident Commonwealth now reaches out and makes friendly associations with other like-minded nations, both in Europe and Asia. Japan, with some 12 per cent of the entire world's GNP, and with its confidence and dynamism now restored, is ready to make links with the Commonwealth, especially with India and Britain together. Poland and some other Central

European nations long to have association with a grouping less parochial than their own local European Union. Even Russia, despite its prickly inward-looking mood and latent nationalist sentiments, could yet emerge a good democratic partner of like-minded nations inside the Commonwealth club.

To do this, the Commonwealth Secretariat should be encouraged to develop its external wing in a much more powerful way than hitherto and perhaps have a nominated high official to work with the Secretary General and act as the Commonwealth's High Representative. Make such an emboldened Commonwealth the central platform of the international future and there will then be an enlightened and responsible grouping on the planet, ready to be America's candid friend, but not its lapdog—a serious and respected force, both in economic and trading terms and in terms of upholding security and peace-keeping.

An enhanced Commonwealth should also spread its wings on energy issues. At present there is no global forum in which a variety of free nations, rich and poor, but all faced with the same problems of staggeringly high oil prices, all faced with energy security challenges and all faced with the much longer term need to curb carbon emissions and create a greener and cleaner long term environment, can meet together, exchange views and technologies, and develop some common clout in face of OPEC and the other giant producers. The Commonwealth should fill that gap, too. A Key UK Priority This is the body, the strengthening of which our own UK should now make its key foreign policy priority and together with which it should re-build its own foreign policy priorities. It should do so because this route offers by far the best way both for a nation such as ours, with our history and our experience and skills, to make a maximum contribution to meeting the world's many ills and, even more, because it is the best way to promote and protect our own interests worldwide. In particular the UK should consider transferring the administration of that part of its overseas development effort, which at present goes through the EU from that unhappy channel to the Commonwealth system, and encourage both other Commonwealth members to do likewise and the Secretariat to develop the full capacity to handle this role. This single move would give the Commonwealth huge new prestige and resources, direct our aid efforts far more effectively to poorer Commonwealth Member States, who are our closest friends and to whom we owe the strongest duty, and greatly strengthen the UK's own prestige and effectiveness in the global development process.

Conclusion

Of course we must always be the best possible local members of our European neighbourhood — as, incidentally we nearly always have been, although some people forget this. But Europe is no longer the world's most prosperous region. It is our duty to build up our links, many of which were so strong in the distant past, with what are becoming the world's most prosperous and dynamic areas of the world, but also with the smaller nations as well as the large ones, the struggling poor ones as well as the rapidly industrialising and increasingly high-tech ones. This is what an enlarged Commonwealth can do for us in a way that the European Union can never do and for which it lacks the reach and the right basic policy structure. That is why Britain's external relations priorities need major re-alignment. And that is why a symbolic re-christening should now take place. The home of our able and experienced diplomats should be relabelled the Commonwealth and Foreign Office — the CFO not the FCO. Small changes can signify a lot.

Mark Baimbridge, Brian Burkitt and Philip B. Whyman

Options for Looser EU Ties

Introduction

The relationship between the UK and the European Union (EU) has always proved to be difficult, juxtaposed between periodic elite-level enthusiasm for closer European economic (if not political) integration and a general lack of enthusiasm for such measures on behalf of a majority of the electorate, as indicated by successive opinion polls. This trend has been marked, and consistent, since Britain left the European Exchange Rate Mechanism in September 1992. Although successive governments have avoided producing an official cost-benefit analysis of EU member-ship, a number of independent studies (Burkitt *et al.*, 1996; Hindley and Howe, 1996; Deva, 2002; Pain and Young, 2004; Milne, 2004; Minford *et al.*, 2005) generated sufficient evidence for policy conclusions to be reached relating to EU membership.

However, the UK political elite continue to assert that no viable alterna-tives exist to the transition towards further European integration. This is a perverse response to the available evidence and it makes little sense to allow a nation's democratic self-determination to be undermined through participation in further initiatives leading towards deeper economic and political integration without first considering a range of alternatives that exist for the UK. Consequently, this chapter seeks to outline a number of these options.

The Status Quo Position

It constitutes the obvious short-term position, whereby the UK retains EU membership, but relies upon its opt-out from EMU and refuses to partici-pate in further economic and political integration. There are a number of precedents where individual member states have pursued their national interests even if this threatened to hamper the effectiveness of the EU institutions. Although the extension of QMV has weakened the potency of this tactic, a determined effort to resist Britain being pulled deeper into economic and political integration might win both support from other member states (e.g. Czech Republic, Denmark, Poland, and Sweden), and compromises. The key question to be resolved, if adopting this approach, is to determine whether the ultimate goal involves non-compliance with future integrationist initiatives, or an attempt to roll-back the tide sweeping the EU towards a United States of Europe.

A second issue relates to Britain's ability to establish a bilateral trade agreement with a third party, as it would appear that such actions are compatible with current EU rules. Although Denmark possessed an agreement with fellow Nordic states, this precedent may not apply to the establishment of new unilateral trade agreements after EU membership. Consequently, the benefits arising from closer co-operation with other trade blocs might cause difficulties within the constraints of EU membership.

The status quo strategy generates a number of, albeit limited, advantages. The most significant of these relates the fact that Britain retains access to the SIM and is able to determine, jointly, harmonisation definitions and other trade-related rules. Additionally, it avoids further costs associated with adopting the single currency, negates future initiatives to move towards a common defence and foreign policy, and avoids the further extension of QMV.

The strategy is, however, problematic. Although further integration measures can be vetoed Britain remains committed to those that already exist. Apart from the obvious direct costs of budgetary contributions, agricultural protectionism and a long-term trade deficit with other EU member states, disadvantages also include the fact that, whilst the UK has an opt-out only from the final stage of EMU, it remains committed to the requirement to meet the convergence criteria established in the Treaty on European Union.

Renegotiation of EU Membership Obligations

A second option available to the UK is to press for renegotiation of the obligations posed by EU membership. It would involve withdrawal from some or all of the EU's burdens upon the British economy, whilst remaining within the organisation. Thus targets for renegotiation could include the reconstitution of the CAP and the CFP, appraisal of the UK's budgetary contribution, together with opt-outs from specific policy initiatives (e.g. the single currency, European foreign and defence policy, any EU-wide judicial system etc).

Such a strategy enjoys a number of precedents, including negotiation of an opt-out from the final stage of EMU, together with the budget rebate in 1984. One obvious source of negotiating strength derives from the fact that the UK is a net budget contributor and would probably remain so even after further contribution rebates and/or opt-outs, whilst the other member states enjoy the benefit of a large trade surplus with the UK.

This strategy would not necessarily isolate Britain from all other member states where a dropping of the ceaseless pursuit of increasing integration could form the basis for the creation of a coalition for reform. Thus renegotiation could be pursued in isolation or as part of an attempt to redesign the format of the EU at a more fundamental level.

However, problems with the policy include its reliance upon the maintenance of bargaining strength to secure concessions within already agreed international treaties. Implicit to the renegotiation approach, made more difficult by enlargement and the resulting increased pressures on the EU budget, is the achievement of a compromise. It will inevitably entail that some costs are removed from British citizens to the detriment of enshrining others more deeply in any new arrangements.

Creation of an Associated European Area (AEA)

One proposal that Britain could pursue as part of a larger renegotiation of its relationship with the EU involves changing the EU's rules to facilitate the creation of an Associated European Area (AEA) (Cash, 2001). It would provide a distinctive choice for member states of the type of European supranational collaboration they desire, whether pursuit of ever-deeper integration via an inner core group of EU member states, or a looser, co-operative arrangement. The former could pursue their goal of creating a United States of Europe, complete with a single currency, one central bank and convergence of economic policy, together with other trappings of a nation state. Simultaneously, members of the AEA could continue their co-operation with member countries in trade and environmental areas, but retain national control over other areas of policy (i.e. macroeconomic, currency, social, labour market, foreign and security policy).

Furthermore, it would remove the requirement that each member of the EU has to accept in full the *acquis communautaire* upon membership. It would also restore authority to national parliaments, by removing the requirement of QMV from those areas of EU business where it currently applies. Such a strategy might prove feasible, because it would simultaneously release the impediments to a group of countries accelerating their integrationist agendas, whilst offering the looser arrangement that others prefer. Indeed, EU enlargement could facilitate this process.

However, in-so-far as the intention is to release Britain from most of the burdens by EU membership, whilst retaining membership of a trade-bloc through the SIM, it might be more easily achieved through membership of the already-existing European Free Trade Agreement (EFTA) and European Economic Area (EEA), rather than creating new institutional arrangements.

Membership of the Single Market Through the EEA

The UK would be eligible for membership of the EEA, which is an agreement made between EFTA (less Switzerland) to extend the internal market of the EU, creating the worlds largest and most comprehensive multinational trading area. Under the agreement, free movement of people, goods, services and capital exists across the entire area. Exceptions to coverage include agriculture and fisheries, whilst the EEA has no common external tariff and therefore requires the identification of the country of origin for all goods and services.

As a member of the EEA, the UK would possess full access to the SIM and retain some influence over the rules that affect trade with EU nations. Moreover, the EEA ensures free trade without the discrimination against external nations created by a customs union. The terms of the EEA stipulate that the UK business sector would operate under the same general conditions as its EU competitors, whilst ensuring that EEA member states negotiate relevant legislation jointly, without the EU imposing standards arbitrarily.

Furthermore, the EEA provides member states with the right to oppose and veto EU law if they feel that it operates against their national interest. Although a net transfer of income to the EU budget is part of the requirement for EEA membership, it would be significantly lower than the budgetary burden imposed by full EU participation. Membership of the EEA releases the UK from pressure to participate in the ERM and in eventual EMU.

A potential disadvantage of the EEA compared to full EU membership is the power imbalance between EU states and EEA members. However, this may be partly resolved if the UK reduced its membership to that of EEA status, as the UK and Norway would jointly provide a far more credible counter-balance to the EU in future negotiations.

An Independent, Global Britain

A common feature of the above alternatives is that some degree of formal linkage with the EU would remain. In contrast, a more profound option is the possibility of the UK's withdrawal from the EU and the development of a number of potential economic and political relationships it could thereby seek to foster.

Rather than withdrawal from the EU being the catastrophe that supporters of greater integration claim it to be, freedom from the restrictions imposed by over-concentration upon the EU could enable Britain to take an independent approach to political and economic issues confronting the nation.

Thereafter, the UK is free to operate any economic policy it wishes (Whyman, et al., 2000). The crucial point is that UK citizens would possess the power to decide how they are governed and how the economy is run, rather than exercising merely a token vote at British General Elections because important decisions concerning fiscal, monetary, exchange rate and trade policy are taken in Brussels and Frankfurt.

The potential arising from renewed economic independence is, not surprisingly, dismissed as illusory by supporters of EU economic integration. They argue that sterling would be prey to speculation, requiring higher interest rates to be maintained. Moreover, they believe that the only way in which the UK can exercise any power in world affairs is as part of the EU. Furthermore, withdrawal may endanger foreign investment in the UK and cause negative reactions from remaining EU members.

These arguments enjoy little factual basis and their predictions are unlikely to be fulfilled if the UK did withdraw from the EU. For instance, after the ERM debacle, it is disingenuous of the supporters of European integration to suggest that sterling would be damaged by floating its exchange rate.

Moreover, the argument that the UK can only exercise any influence on world events only from within the EU is questionable. The UK lost its former world position because of economic problems. If the UK is to regain influence, it must be based upon economic success, which is less likely to be secured within the EU straitjacket of deflationary European Central Bank and Stability and Growth Pact policies.

Indeed, a UK economy growing faster outside the EU with a permanently competitive exchange rate is more attractive to foreign-based companies. They locate productive facilities to enhance their profits through producing output they can sell in the British and European markets, together with utilising the skills and abilities of a well-educated and flexible labour force.

Nor is the idea that withdrawal from the EU would provoke retaliation from current EU 'partners' probable. Apart from EU Commission pressure attempting to persuade the UK to change its mind, most EU countries will not engage in a trade war because their surplus with the UK means that it would hurt them most.

Hence, if the UK could not secure fundamental reform of the EU, or alternatively renegotiate its current commitments bound by EU rules and international treaty, as Minford *et al.* (2005) state it would be in the UK's interest to withdraw from the EU and pursue a set of economic and social policies determined according to national priorities. However, withdrawal from the EU is only a first, necessary step. Once achieved, the UK can develop whatever trading relations with other nations it desires.

One option is a revitalised EFTA which would involve the UK formally withdrawing from the EU and re-joining the European Free Trade Association (EFTA) it helped to found four decades ago. Article 41 of the Convention establishing EFTA states that any country may accede, if it receives the approval of the EFTA Council. Alternatively the Council may negotiate bilateral agreements with individual states subject to the unanimous approval of all member states. The potential offered by EFTA is worth exploring, by establishing trade relationships supplementary to those with the EU member states.

A revitalised EFTA could provide an alternative to the EU as a looser form of co-operation between European nations. It might prove attractive to some political parties and segments of the electorate in the 2004 and 2007 accession countries where significant opposition to European integration was demonstrated in the 2004 elections to the European Parliament (Baimbridge, 2005). In addition to sizeable majorities occurred within Norway, Sweden, Denmark, Iceland and Switzerland who are broadly sceptical towards further European political and economic integration.

A second option is developing Commonwealth trade, whereby the greatest visible sign of economic weakness is the persistence of mass unemployment within EU nations, which is not matched by the North American, Asian 'Tiger' and Latin American areas. Indeed, it is interesting to note that many Commonwealth countries offer potentially faster growing markets than do other EU member states. Historic links with Commonwealth nations could give the UK a potential advantage in re-establishing trade links with these dynamic economies (West, 1995).

They include Singapore, India, Pakistan, Malaysia, New Zealand, Australia, Canada and South Africa. Moreover, the East Asian link is potentially also important as a bridgehead to closer trading links with China.

Estimates indicate that the areas of the world which grew most during the past two decades, namely South and East Asia, will continue to expand more rapidly in the next decade. Additionally, growth potential is expected to result in significantly higher rates amongst most developing/transitional, than amongst the developed, economies. Latin America, Africa and the Middle East join Asia in offering UK companies superior potential for increased export sales than does the EU single market.

However, the UK is distracted from taking advantage of such opportunities by the SIM and the EU's common external tariff. In particular, the latter is an impediment to free trade which encourages other nations to place tariffs upon EU nations' exports, thereby putting UK exporters at a competitive disadvantage against the rest of the world.

Another option for the British government following withdrawal is to seek its replacement with a bilateral trade agreement between the EU and UK. Since the UK is ill-served by participating in the CAP and the CFP, a restriction of free trade with EU nations to industrial and financial goods and services would prove more beneficial. The remaining EFTA countries negotiated such a free trade agreement with the EU in 1972, after the UK, Denmark and Ireland joined the EU.

Such a policy allows the UK to reorientate its economic policy to serve its own needs rather than those of competitor EU countries. The money saved by non-contribution to the EU budget could be used to increase incentives for productive investment within the UK, such as infrastructural and research-based projects that increase long-term competitiveness. This tactic closely resembles Switzerland's current position, which did not haemorrhage its economic vitality, but strengthened the Swiss economy, which has maintained relatively low levels of inflation, interest rates and unemployment, together with a significant balance of payments surplus.

A seemingly more radical option would be membership of the North American Free Trade Agreement (NAFTA) comprising the United States of American, Canada and Mexico. This would require the UK to leave the EU since the latter compels its member states to adopt a common external tariff and to subscribe to an EU-wide uniform external trade policy. There are, however, a number of compelling reasons why both the US and the UK should actively promote such a development (USITC, 2000; Baimbridge et al., 2004).

Firstly, the UK and USA economies are closely intertwined such that further trade liberalisation would result in immediate benefits, in terms of trade creation, for both. Over the last decade, for instance, UK net direct investment in North America was more than double its investment in the EU, whilst it would also be building upon success, because over the past 15 years the US and Canada have created 2 million more jobs than EU countries.

If Britain joins NAFTA, the larger group will help to protect both the US and the UK from whatever outcome emerges from the EU experiment in supranationalism. A more broadly-based NAFTA could counter the impact of either an imploding, or a successfully integrating, but by necessity largely inward-looking, EU, particularly given enlargement.

Moreover, the existing NAFTA countries are already negotiating with EFTA and Chile. If Britain participated in such a grouping, a revamped NAFTA could ultimately be transformed into a global free trade association, based solely upon a commitment to free trade. It would seek no control of member states' trade relations with non-members nor would it possess the motivation to pursue 'ever closer union' that renders the EU unpalatable.

Since its withdrawal from the ERM, the British economy has been convergent, both structurally and cyclically, with North America. Consequently, sterling tracks the US dollar not the euro, whilst its divergence from continental currencies has widened. Such oscillations determine the efficiency of interest rate harmonisation, leading to the conclusion that the American and British economies are more convergent with each other than either is with the eurozone.

In terms of the business cycle, the UK possessed traditionally a closer relationship with the USA than with EU member states (Bayoumi and Eichengreen, 1993). Furthermore, a noticeable change in both US and UK economies during the past decade has been the remarkable transition in their respective labour markets. The shift towards non-standard contracts, together with the deregulation of the labour market, has increased the ability of both economies to adapt flexibly to industrial restructuring. Moreover, productivity has been rising quickly in both nations, with US productivity growth outstripping average wage growth thereby dampening inflationary pressure from increasing oil prices and property market booms.

Finally, macroeconomic strategy is similar for both countries, with restrained fiscal policy permitting looser monetary policy to facilitate economic growth and increased levels of investment though lower real interest rates. Supply-side policy seeks to reduce taxation to encourage entrepreneurship, together with stimulation of investment in human capital. Consequently, both nations are ranked in the top ten most competitive nations in the world.

Conclusion

Britain's current relationship with the EU has imposed considerable costs upon the domestic economy. Consumers pay higher prices due to the interaction of agricultural subsidies and budgetary mismanagement, whilst businesses pay the cost of over-complicated regulation (Burkitt, *et al.*, 1996; Baimbridge, *et al.*, 2005). Future costs relate to a low growth environment via the deflationary economic policy infrastructure surrounding EMU, together with uncertain initiatives relating to the development of a social market, regulated labour relations and aspects facilitating political unification (such as defence, foreign policy and immigration controls).

One of the most fundamental problems that EU membership has imposed is that too greater a proportion of Britain's energies are dedicated towards facilitating convergence with European neighbour economies, rather than concentrating upon the national interest by developing markets for British goods and services amongst the fastest growing areas of the world.

In response to these problematic aspects of membership this chapter outlines a number of potential alternative approaches to the relationship between Britain and the EU. It has examined the case for the status quo (facilitating a multi-speed Europe), together with the renegotiation of Britain's membership terms and conditions with the EU (thereby potentially lowering future direct costs associated with membership).

Additionally, in response to these problematic aspects of membership this chapter has outlined a number of potential alternative approaches to the relationship between Britain and the EU following withdrawal. Each should be assessed on the basis of a cost-benefit analysis after an informed public debate.

Crucially, however, these alternatives explode forever the establishment claim that 'there is no alternative' to membership of an increasingly centralised, integrated EU. For the UK, a multiplicity of more attractive potential futures is possible, if the political will exists to pursue them.

Bibliography

Afonso, A. & Furceri, D. (2008) *Government size, composition, volatility and economic growth*, Working Paper no. 849, Frankfurt: European Central Bank.

Baimbridge (2005) EUphoria to apathy: EP turnout in the new member states; in Lodge, J. (ed.) *The 2004 elections to the European Parliament*, London: Palgrave Macmillan.

Baimbridge, M. and Whyman, P. (2008) *Britain, the euro and beyond*, Aldershot: Ashgate.

Baimbridge, M., Burkitt, B. and Whyman, P. (2005) *Britain and the European Union: alternative futures*, London: CIB.

Baimbridge, M., Harrop, J. and Philippidis, G. (2004) *Current economic issues in EU integration*, London: Palgrave Macmillan.

Bairoch, P. and Kozul-Wright, R. (1996) *Globalization Myths: Some Historical Reflections on Integration, Industrialization and Growth in the World Economy*. Paper presented at the WIDER Conference on Transnational Corporations and the Global Economy, Kings College Cambridge, September.

Bakan, J. (2005) *The Corporation: The Pathological Pursuit of Profit and Power*, London: Constable and Robinson.

Baldwin, T. (2007) *Blairs bridge between Europe & the US? Its falling down & he's left with nothing*, Times, 5th January.

Barratt Brown, M. (1991) *European Union: Fortress or Democracy? Towards a Democratic Market and a New Economic Order*, Nottingham: Spokesman

Bayoumi, T. and Eichengreen, B. (1993) Shocking aspects of European monetary integration; in Torres, F. and Giavazzi, F. (eds.) *Adjustment and growth in the European Monetary Union*, Cambridge University Press: Cambridge.

BBC (2008) Bid to link MPs pay to EU powers, http://news.bbc.co.uk/2/hi/uk_news/politics/7434075.stm

BBC News (2007) EU accounts failed for 13th year, http://news.bbc.co.uk/1/hi/world/europe/7092102.stm

Benn, T. and Hood, A. (1993) *Common Sense: A New Constitution for Britain*, London: Hutchinson.

Blackwell, N. (2008) *Why the Reform Treaty Matters*, London: Global Vision. [http://www.global-vision.net/files/downloads/download369.pdf]

Blum, W. (2000) *Rogue State: A Guide to the World's Only Superpower*, London: Zed Books.

Blum, W. (2003) *Killing Hope: US Military and CIA Interventions since World War II*, London: Zed Books.

Boyne, R. and Rattansi, A. (eds.) (1990) *Postmodernism and Society*, London: Macmillan

Bradford S. C. (2003) Paying the Price: Final Goods Protection in OECD Countries, *Review of Economics and Statistics,* 85(1) pp. 24-37.

Bradford. S. and R. Z. Lawrence (2004) *Has Globalization Gone Far Enough? The Costs of Fragmented Markets,* Institute for International Economics, Washington D. C.

Brady, R. (1943) *Business as a System of Power*, New York: Columbia University Press.

Broad, R. (2001) *Labours European Dilemmas: From Bevin to Blair*, Basingstoke: Palgrave.

Brown, G. (2005) *Global Europe: full-employment Europe*, London, HM Treasury.

Brown, G. (2008) *Speech at the Chamber of Commerce in Delhi*, http://www.number10.gov.uk/output/Page14323.asp

Burkitt, B., Baimbridge, M. and Whyman, P. (1996) *There is an alternative: Britain and its relationship with the EU,* Nelson and Pollard: Oxford.

Business Link (2008) *UK Trade Tariff,* http://www.businesslink.gov.uk/bdotg/action/tariff?r.s=a

Caesar, R. (2001) An EU Tax? – Not a Good Idea, *Intereconomics.*

Cameron, B. (2008) *Building the Transatlantic Bridge: the potential for Canada-UK trade*, London: Global Vision.

Cameron, D. (2008) *Speech to Business leaders in Davos*, http://www.conservatives.com/tile.do?def=news.story.page&obj_id=141851

Carswell, D. (2004) *Paying for Localism: How to revive local democracy by replacing VAT with a Local Sales Tax*, London: Adam Smith Institute.

Cash, W. (2001) *The Associated European Area: A constructive alternative to a single European state*, London: European Foundation.

Castle, S. (2004) Brown on collision course with EU over corporate tax, *Independent*

Castle, S. (2006) Austria wants EU-wide tax on flights to plug budget gap, *Independent*

Cecchini Report (1988) *The Cost of Non-Europe,* Brussels: European Commission.

Chakrabortty, A. (2008) Secret report: biofuel caused food crisis, *Guardian*

Chandler, D. (2007) Deconstructing sovereignty: constructing global civil society; in Bickerton, C., Cunliffe, P. and Gourevitch, A. (eds.) *Politics without Sovereignty*, London: UCL Press.

Chomsky, N. (1994) *World Orders, Old and New*, London: Pluto.

Chomsky, N. (2005) [Selected and edited by Barry Pateman] *Chomsky on Anarchism*, Edinburgh: AK Press.

Church, C. (ed.) *Switzerland and the European Union*, London: Routledge, 2007.

Congdon T. (2003) The Goal of a Single European Financial Market, in Booth P. M. and Currie D. A. (eds) *The Regulation of Financial Markets*, Readings 58, Institute of Economic Affairs, London, UK.

Congdon, T. (2008) *Northern Rock and the European Union*, London: Global Vision.

Craig, D. and Elliott, M. (2009) *The great European rip-off*, London: Random House Books.

Crockett A., Harris T., Mishkin F. S. and White E. N., (2003) *Conflicts of Interest in the Financial Services Industry: What Should We Do About Them*, London: Centre for Economic Policy Research.

Currid, N. (2009) The People who Matter, *These Tides*, 6 (1) May.

Curtis, M. (1995) *The Ambiguities of Power: British Foreign Policy since 1945*, London: Zed Books.

Curtis, M. (1998) *The Great Deception: Anglo-American Power and World Order*, London: Pluto.

Curtis, M. (2003) *Web of Deceit: Britain's Real Role in the World*, London: Vintage.

Curtis, M. (2004) *Unpeople: Britain's Secret Human Rights Abuses*, London: Vintage.

Davies H. (2002) *Rethinking the Listing Regime*, speech to the Annual Listing Rules Conference, London, UK.

Davis E. P. and Steil B. (2001) *Institutional Investors*, Cambridge MA: MIT Press.

Dean, M. and Sebastia-Barriel, M. (2004) *Why has world trade grown faster than world output?*, Bank of England Quarterly Bulletin, Autumn.

Deutsche Bundesbank (2004) *Effects of eastward enlargement of the EU on the German economy*, Monthly Report, May.

Deva, N. (2002) *Who really governs Britain?*, The June Press, Totnes.

EC Commission (2007) *The Single Market: Review of Achievements*, Brussels: EC Commission. http://ec.europa.eu/internal_market/benefits_en.htm

EFTA (2004) *EFTAs third country relations*, EFTA Fact Sheet.

Elliott, L. and Atkinson, D. (1998) *The Age of Insecurity*, London: Verso.

Elliott, L. and Atkinson, D. (2008) *The Gods That Failed: How Blind Faith in Markets Has Cost Us Our Future*, London: The Bodley Head.

Estevadeordal, A. and Suominem, K. (2003) *Measuring rules of origin in the world trading system and proposals for multilateral harmonisation*, paper presented at the APEC Capacity-Building Workshop on Quantitative Methods for Assessing NTMs and Trade Facilitation.

EU Commission (2004) *Financing the European Union*, Brussels: EU Commission.

EUR-Lex (2006) *Communication from the Commission to the Council, the European Parliament and the European Economic and Social Committee – Implementing the Community Lisbon Programme – Progress to date and next steps towards a Common Consolidated Tax Base (CCCTB), http://eur-lex.europa.eu/en/index.htm*

European Commission (2004) *A users handbook to the rules of preferential origin used in trade between the EC and other European countries*, Luxembourg: European Commission.

European Commission (2008) *How VAT works: General overview*, http://ec.europa.eu/taxation_customs/taxation/vat/how_vat_works/index_en.htm

European Court of Justice (2006) Cadbury Schweppes plc, Cadbury Schweppes Overseas Ltd vs. Commissioners of Inland Revenue, Judgement of the Court, *Case C-196/04*, Luxembourg: ECJ.

European Court of Justice (2008) Commission of the European Communities vs. Italian Republic, Judgement of the Court, *Case C-132/06*, Luxembourg: ECJ.

European Forecasting Network (2004) *The Euro Area and the Lisbon Strategy*, European University Institute: European Forecasting Network.

European Parliament (2008) *EU to maintain suspension of import duties on cereals*, Press release, Brussels: European Parliament.

Ferguson, N. (2003) *Empire: How Britain made the Modern World*, London: Allen Lane.

Feulner, E., Hulsman, J. and Schaefer, B. (2004) *Free Trade by Any Means: how the Global Free Trade AllianceEnhances Americasm Overall Trading Strategy*, Washington: Heritage Foundation.

Financial Times (2008) *Say goodbye to a flexible friend, Financial Times* 19 May.

Frankel, J.A. (2000) *Assessing the Efficiency Gains from Further Liberalization*, Faculty Research Working Papers Series, RWP01-030, Harvard University: John F. Kennedy School of Government.

FSA (2001) *The FSAs Approach to Regulation of Market Infrastructure*, Feedback Statement, London: Financial Services Authority.

FSA (2002) *Investment Research: Conflicts & Other Issues*, Discussion Paper 15, London: Financial Services Authority.

FSA (2005) *International Regulatory Outlook*, London: Financial Services Authority.

Giddens, A. (1998) *The Third Way and the Renewal of Social Democracy*, London: Polity, p 146.

Giscard dEstaing, V. (2008) *Britain & the EU: a special status?*, speech delivered at the conference What next for Britain and Europe? co-sponsored by *Global Vision* and *the Daily Telegraph* http://www.global-vision.net/files/downloads/download556.pdf

Global Britain (2002) *The Mexico-EU free trade agreement points the way*, Briefing Note No 19, London: Global Britain.

Global Britain (2004) *Cherry-picking: EFTA, EEA and the Swiss-EU trading Relationship, Briefing Note No 36*, London: Global Britain.

Global Britain (2005) *The Commonwealth: neglected colossus?*, Briefing Note no 38, London: Global Britain.

Green Party (2005) *Manifesto for a Sustainable Society*, London: Green Party.

Halimi, S., Michie, J. and Milne, S. (1994) The Mitterrand Experience; in Michie, J. and Grieve Smith, J. (eds.) *Unemployment in Europe*, London: Academic Press.

Hannan, D. (2004) *Voting on the European Constitution*, London: Politeia.

Helleiner, R. (1995) Explaining the Globalization of Financial Markets: Bringing States Back In, *Review of International Political Economy*, 2, 1-27.

Helmer, R. (2000) As an alternative to the EU, Britain should join NAFTA, *International Herald Tribune*, 19 January

Heywood, A. (1999) *Political Theory: An Introduction*, Basingstoke: Palgrave.

Hindley, B. and Howe, M. (1996) *Better-off out? The benefits or costs of EU Membership*, IEA Occasional paper 99, London: Institute of Economic Affairs.

Hindley, B. and Howe, M. (2001) *Better Off Out?*, London, Institute of Economic Affairs.

Hirst, P. and Thompson, G. (1999) *Globalization in Question*, Cambridge: Polity.

HM Revenue and Customs (2008) *Introduction to VAT*, http://www.hmrc.gov.uk/vat/vat-introduction.htm

HM Treasury and DTI (2007) *The Single Market: a vision for the 21st century*, London: HM Treasury and DTI.

HM Treasury, Bank of England and FSA, (2003) *The EU Financial Services Action Plan: a guide*, reprinted in Bank of England Quarterly Bulletin, 43 (3), 352-365.

Holland, S. (ed.) (1983) *Out of Crisis: A Project for European Recovery*, Nottingham: Spokesman.

Hutton, W. (2008) *Europe must not be derailed by lies and disinformation*, The Observer, 15 June.

IMF (2004) How will demographic change affect the global economy?, *World Economic Outlook*, September.

Jarvis, V. and Prais, S.J. (1989) Two nations of shopkeepers, *National Institute Economic Review*, 128, May, 58-74.

Kagan, R. (2003) *Paradise and power: America and Europe in the new world order*, London: Atlantic Books.

Kitson, M. and Michie, J. (1998) *Globalization, Unemployment and Government Policy*, Bath: Full Employment Forum.

KPMG (2007) *Corporate and Indirect Tax Rate Survey*, London: KPMG.

Labor Advisory Committee on the North American Free Trade Agreement (1992) *Preliminary Report submitted to the President and Congress*, Washington DC: US Government Printing Office

Lascelles, D. (2007) *The EU Reform Treaty and the City*, London: Global Vision.

Laughland, J. (2000) *The Tainted Source: the anti democratic origins of the European idea*, London: Little Brown & Company.

Laughland, J. (2002) *The EU and the Problems of Democracy: the potential consequences of the Nice Treaty, Prepisy Prednasek*, 22 January.

Lea, R. (2008a) *Europe's worsening demographics*, London: Global Vision.

Lea, R. (2008b) *A new trading relationship for Britain with the EU*, London: Global Vision.

Lea, R. (2008c) *UK-EU trade creates far fewer jobs in the UK than in the rest of the EU*, London: Global Vision.

Leach, R. (2004) *Europe: a concise encyclopaedia of the European Union*, London: Profile Books.

Leonard, M. (2005) *Europe's Transformative Power*, Centre for European Reform, Bulletin 40, February/March.

Libbenga, J. (2006) Europeans rail against SMS and email tax plan, *The Register*

Lightfoot W. (2003) Managing Financial Crises; in Booth P. M. and Currie D. A. (eds) *The Regulation of Financial Markets*, Readings 58, London: Institute of Economic Affairs.

Llewellyn D. (1999) *The Economic Rationale for Financial Regulation*, Occasional Paper 1, London: Financial Services Authority.

Lobell, S. (1999) Second Image Reversed Politics: Britain's Choice of Freer Trade or Imperial Preferences, 1903-1906, 1917-1923, 1930-1932, *International Studies Quarterly*, 43, 671-694.

London Stock Exchange (2006) *Understanding MiFID*, London: London Stock Exchange.

London Stock Exchange/Oxera (2006) *The Cost of Capital: An International Comparison*, London: London Stock Exchange.

Lundan, S.M. and Jones, G. (2001) The Commonwealth Effect and the Process of Internationalisation, in *The World Economy*, 24(1) 99-118.

MacArthur, J. (2000) *The Selling of Free Trade: NAFTA, Washington and the Subversion of American Democracy*, New York: Hill and Wang.

McCreevy, C. (2008) *A Value Added Treaty for Europe and its Citizens*, Speech to Navan Chamber of Commerce, Dublin. http://europa.eu/rapid/pressReleasesAction.do?reference=SPEECH/08/265&format=HTML&aged=0&language=EN&guiLanguage=en

Messerlin, P. (1990) Anti-dumping regulations or pro-cartel law? The EC Chemical cases, *The World Economy*, 13(4) 465-492.

Miliband, R. (1973) *The State in Capitalist Society: The Analysis of the Western System of Power*, London: Quartet.

Milne, I. (2004) *A cost too far? An analysis of the net economic costs and benefits for the UK of EU membership*, London: Civitas.

Minford, P., V. Mahambare and E. Nowell (2005) *Should Britain leave the EU? An Economic Analysis of a Troubled Relationship*, Edward Elgar, London.

Monbiot, G. (2000) Vote Tory for a federal superstate, *The Guardian*, 7 September.

Morrell, F. (1988) Beyond One-Nation Socialism: An Agenda for the European Left, *Political Quarterly*, 59(3) 300-310.

Mullen, A. (2007) *The British Lefts Great Debate on Europe*, London: Continuum.

Mullen, A. (2009) *Anti- and Pro-European Propaganda in Britain*, London: Continuum.

Mutén, L. (2001) The Case for an EU Tax Is Not Convincing, *Intereconomics*

Myddelton D. R. (2004) *Unshackling Accountants,* Hobart Paper 149, London: Institute of Economic Affairs.

National Security Council (1954) NSC-5432, US policy towards Latin America, *Foreign Relations, 1952-1954*, IV, 83.

National Security Council (1990) *National Security Strategy*, Washington DC: US Government Printing Office

Nicoletti, G. and S. Scarpetta (2001) *Interactions between Product and Labour Market Regulations: Do they Affect Employment? Evidence from OECD Countries*, Paper presented at the Banco de Portugal Conference on Labour Market Institutions and Economic Outcomes, 3-4 June, Cascais.

NIESR (2000) Continent Cut Off? The Macroeconomic Impact of British Withdrawal from the EU, *NIESR Quarterly Economic Review,* February.

O'Rourke, K. (2000) British trade policy in the 19th century: a review article, *European Journal of Political Economy*, 16, 829-842.

O'Sullivan, T. (2007)Business is blind to the risks of a shared tax system, *Financial Times*

OECD (2001) Fiscal Implications of Ageing: Projections of Age-related Spending, OECD Economics Department Working Papers No. 305, Paris: OECD.

OECD (2003) *Regionalism and the multilateral trading system*, Paris: OECD.

Office for National Statistics (2008) *Effects of taxes and benefits on household income tables*, London: ONS.

Office for National Statistics (2008) *Family Spending 2007*, Table A8, and Effects of taxes and benefits on household income tables 2006/07, Table A16, London: ONS.

Office of Technology Assessment [US congressional committee] (1992) *US-Mexico Trade: Pulling Together or Pulling Apart*, Washington DC: US Government Printing Office.

Open Europe (2006) *Getting a Grip: Reforming EU scrutiny at Westminster*, London: Open Europe.

Open Europe (2009) *Out of Control: Measuring a decade of regulation*, London: Open Europe.

Open Europe (2009) *Out of control? Measuring a decade of EU Regulation*, London, Open Europe.

Orwell, G. (1946) James Burnham and the Managerial Revolution, *New English Weekly*.

Pain, N. and Young, G. (2004) The macroeconomic impact of UK withdrawal from the EU, *Economic Modelling*, 21 (3) 387-408.

Pennant-Rea, R., Bean, C.R., Begg, D., Hardie, J., Lankester, T., Miles, D.K., Portes, R., Robinson, A. Seabright, P. and Wolf, M. (1997), *The Ostrich and the EMU - policy choices facing the UK*, Centre for Economic Policy Research, London.

Porter, M.E. (1990) *The competitive advantage of nations*, Macmillan, London.

Prais, S.J. and Wagner, K. (1988) Productivity and management: the training in foremen in Britain and Germany, *National Institute Economic Review*, 123, February, 34-47.

Pritchard A. (2003) Self-regulation and securities markets, *Regulation*, Spring, pp 32-39.

Public Citizen (2003) NAFTA at Ten Series [Available at http://www.citizen.org (Accessed on 29 July 2008)]

Radice, H. (1984) The National Economy: A Keynesian Myth? *Capital and Class*, 22, 111-140.

Radice, H. (1996) Globalization and the UK Economy; in Barratt Brown, M. and Radice, H. (eds.) *Democracy versus Capitalism*, Nottingham: Spokesman

Radice, H. (1999) Taking Globalization Seriously; in Panitch, L. and Leys, C. (eds.) *Socialist Register 1999*, London: Merlin Press.

Shafaeddin, M. (1998) *How Did Developed Countries Industrialize? The History of Trade and Industrial Policy: The Cases of Great Britain and the USA*. Paper presented at the Development Studies Association Conference, University of Reading, September.

Sovereign Group (2008) *France backtracks on CCCTB proposal*, http://www.sovereigngroup.com/offshore-news/sovereign-news/598/0/France+backtracks+on+CCCTB+proposal.html

State Department (1948) Executive Committee on Economic Foreign Policy, Statement of United States credit and investment policy, 11 August, *Foreign Relations of the United States*, I (2) 947.

Steedman, H. (1988) Vocational training in France and Britain, *National Institute Economic Review*, 126, November, 57-70.

Sternberg E. (2004) *Corporate Governance: Accountability in the Marketplace*, Hobart Paper 147, London: Institute of Economic Affairs.

Taylor, M. (1995) *A single currency – implications for the UK economy*, Institute of Directors, London.

Teather, D. (2008) Watching those havens, the Treasury, *The Guardian*

The British Chamber of Commerce (2008) *The Burdens Barometer,* http://www.britishchambers.org.uk/policy/pdf/Burdens_Barometer_2008.pdf

The Economist (1991) Japanese spoken here, *The Economist,* 14 September.

The Economist (1999) New Zealand's Advantage, *The Economist,*

The Economist (2006) Single market blues, *The Economist,* 10 November.

The Federation of Master Builders (2008) *The Case for a Reduction in VAT,* http://www.fmb.org.uk/cutthevat/(xnznv22ydnatb345ga5zkj55)/default.aspx?step=5

United States Department of Defense (2000) *Joint Vision 2020,* Washington DC: Department of Defense.

United States Department of Defense (2006) *Quadrennial Defense Review,* Washington DC: US Government Printing Office.

United States International Trade Commission (2000) *The impact on the US economy of including the United Kingdom in a free trade arrangement with the United States, Canada and Mexico,* Investigation No. 332-409, Publication 3339, August.

Weiss, L. (1998) *The Myth of the Powerless State: Governing the Economy in a Global Era,* London: Polity.

Weiss, L. (ed.) (2003) *States in the Global Economy: Bringing Domestic Institutions Back In,* Cambridge: Cambridge University Press.

West, K. (1995) *Economic Opportunities for Britain and the Commonwealth,* London: Royal Institute for International Affairs.

West, K. (1995), *Economic Opportunities for Britain and the Commonwealth,* London: Royal Institute for International Affairs.

Whyman, P., Burkitt, B. and Baimbridge, M. (2000) Economic policy outside EMU: strategies for a global Britain, *Political Quarterly,* 71 (4) 451-462.

Wight, M. (2007) quoted in Bickerton, C., Cunliffe, P. and Gourevitch, A. The unholy alliance against sovereignty; in Bickerton, C., Cunliffe, P. and Gourevitch, A. (eds.) *Politics without Sovereignty,* London: UCL Press, p.3.

WTO (2004) *Dictionary of trade policy terms,* Washington DC: WTO.

YouGov (2008) *YouGov Survey for The Economist and the Hoover Institution: Results,* March.